Educating the Disabled
Enabling Learners in Inclusive Settings

George R. Taylor
Frances T. Harrington

ScarecrowEducation
Lanham, Maryland, and Oxford
2003

Published in the United States of America
by ScarecrowEducation
An imprint of The Rowman & Littlefield Publishing Group, Inc.
4501 Forbes Boulevard, Suite 200, Lanham, Maryland 20706
www.scarecroweducation.com

PO Box 317
Oxford
OX2 9RU, UK

British Library Cataloguing in Publication Information Available

Library of Congress Cataloging-in-Publication Data
Taylor, George R.
  Educating the disabled : enabling learners in inclusive settings /
George R. Taylor, Frances T. Harrington.
      p. cm.
"A ScarecrowEducation book."
Includes bibliographical references and index.
  ISBN 0-8108-4614-4 (hard : alk. paper) — ISBN 0-8108-4616-0 (pbk. :
alk. paper)
  1. Children with disabilities—Education. 2. Inclusive education. I.
Harrington, Frances T. (Frances Taylor), 1946– II. Title.
LC4015 .T315 2003
371.9'046—dc21   2002013193

∞ ™ The paper used in this publication meets the minimum requirements of
American National Standard for Information Sciences—Permanence of
Paper for Printed Library Materials, ANSI/NISO Z39.48-1992.
Manufactured in the United States of America.

Contents

Illustrations

Figures

Tables

Preface

This book is designed for administrators who are responsible for educating individuals with disabilities. It is written for directors of special education, supervisors, consultants, superintendents, principals, coordinators of education, research directors, psychologists, counselors, social workers, site-based management teams, and teachers apiring to become school administrators. It may also be used as a textbook for courses in administering classes for individuals with disabilities, as well as providing information and strategies for schools in both the public and private sectors that serve individuals with disabilities.

The mainstream movement has confronted administrators for well over two decades. Many school districts are moving away from segregation to the integration of children with disabilities in the regular classroom. The mainstream movement has been spearheaded by PL 94-142 and its amendments and state laws and regulations, as well as national and local parental groups. Administrators have become responsible for implementing the inclusion of children with disabilities in the mainstream, but they cannot accomplish this formidable task alone. They need the combined assistance of all stakeholders in the community. School administrators must provide effective leadership. Issues such as understanding the meaning of integration, legal mandates and issues, instructional procedures, and related services must be discussed, understood, and supported by all stakeholders. Strategies for achieving this are discussed in detail throughout the text for administrators to implement.

Acknowledgments

We wish to acknowledge the contributions made by our professional development schools, Rosemont and John Edgar elementary schools, for providing valuable information reflected in this text.

The administrative strategies outlined here are a result of reading and analyzing much research as well as administering programs in special education. Compiling this textbook was not an individual endeavor. A deep sense of gratitude is extended to Dr. Thomas Terrell for reading and correcting the manuscript. We would also like to acknowledge our appreciation to Emma Crosby for typing the manuscript and Robernette Smith for providing valuable research and reference information.

CHAPTER 1

Administrative, Theory, Roles, and Leadership Characteristics

•• THEORETICAL CATEGORIES

Administration is commonly classified into four theoretical categories: (1) trait theory, (2) role theory, (3) system theory, and (4) process theory. These classifications are not inclusive; rather, they appear to represent the characteristics of school administrators, especially those who work with children with disabilities (Kahn & Rosenthal, 1964, Pfeffer & Salancik, 1978).

1. Trait theory implies that administration can be understood best through an understanding of personal characteristics. Leadership, friendliness, decisiveness, tact, courage, and self-confidence are often viewed as relevant traits in administrative decisions. Most research, however, suggests that administrators show no absolute traits. The traits appear to differ from study to study. More research is needed to validate trait theory.

2. Role theory views administration as a style of behavior. It implies that organizations are social systems made up of individuals who occupy various positions. Some of the roles that administrators play include mediator, supervisor, expediter, keeper of the process, and maintainer of the organization. The way that people behave in these positions depends on how the individual perceives his or her role. This theory appears very relevant for school administrators. School leaders must constantly serve as mediators to resolve disputes and conflicts. They must mediate between individuals and groups to resolve issues according to the best interests of all concerned. Administrative roles and functions are mandated by the board of education. In role theory, the administrator's roles and behaviors may change because of the board's directives (Yukl, 1981).

3. System theory presents a comprehensive view of a school system as a unified and dynamic whole with complex elements or forces mutually interacting.

These elements, which may include community structure, financial resources, board of education, administration, faculty, and student body, are examples of elements or forces whose accomplishments interact within the system. Each of the listed elements may be divided into subsystems. Systems are generally classified as open or closed. An open school system welcomes changes from its stakeholders; a closed system does not (Osborn & Hunt, 1975).

4. Process theory examines the processes of administration, planning, organizing, staffing, directing, coordinating, reporting, budgeting, communicating, decision making, influencing, and evaluating.

These theories help us understand how administrators can carry out their duties effectively using a variety of approaches depending on the circumstances and conditions they face (Bennis, 1984).

•• ROLES OF ADMINISTRATORS

Administrators have been defined as building managers, politicians, change agents, and instructional leaders. One of the administrator's most important duties is to develop a structure of relationships within the school so all children may profit from their educational experiences. Effective administrators appear to commit to established goals, understand school finances, create a positive climate with high expectations, provide a model for effective leadership, collaborate effectively with others, collect and use resources effectively, show skill in curriculum and instructional matters, and demonstrate ways for assessing and evaluating the effectiveness of educational programs.

Communication is an essential skill of effective administrators. A common vision must be articulated, shared, and supported by all stakeholders in small and large groups. Effective administrators employ communication skills as the basis for developing sound relationships with stakeholders that are consistent, objective, and fair. Administrators should demonstrate a sense of professionalism to teachers and stakeholders through leading discussions relevant to instruction and student achievement. They should know how to judge performance, evaluate classroom performance, make a commitment to professional growth for staff members, and encourage an appropriate level of preparation, scholarship, and advanced training (Smith & Andrews, 1989).

•• QUALIFICATIONS OF ADMINISTRATORS

There are no conclusive standards for judging competencies and leadership skills of administrators, or for judging their qualifications. These are the most commonly accepted qualifications:

Maturity. This quality relates to conceptual skills, having the ability to see a problem in its broad context and dealing effectively with ideas.

Dependability. Effective administrators earn the trust of stakeholders. They prove they have the ability to meet the demands of the position. Their decisions relative to operating their schools demonstrate a shared vision; consequently, stakeholders learn they can depend on administrators to make sound decisions.

Ability to work well with stakeholders. This qualification is related to human relations skills, which are key to leadership. Research has shown that successful administrators develop a set of skills that enables them to work successfully with stakeholders.

High intelligence. There appears to be a significant relationship between high intelligence and successful administrators. Social intelligence also becomes evident. These administrators have the ability to use superior intellect to accomplish goals and objectives.

Demonstration of leadership ability. Most successful administrators have had previous administrative experience in the school district as assistant principals, principals, and supervisors to name but a few possibilities. Some administrators have held professional positions in other agencies in both public and private domains.

Ability to communicate effectively. Effective administrators must be able to communicate ideas, goals, objectives, instructional strategies, attitudes, and values to stakeholders.

Sound health. The work of administrators is demanding and requires good health. Administrators must have an abundance of energy and stamina, necessary to keep up with the demands of the job (Smith & Andrews, 1989).

•• FACTORS INVOLVED IN SUCCESSFUL LEADERSHIP

Administrators must be well trained and knowledgeable about administrative functions. These functions have been classified as human relation skills, conceptual skills, technical skills, decision-making, planning, organizing, communicating, coordinating, and evaluation.

These competencies are important in leadership; however, successful leadership depends on the characteristics of the group with which administrators work. Additionally, the knowledge of the group can facilitate or retard the task of leadership, as well as the morale of the group concerning their beliefs is relevant to the situation under discussion.

Successful leadership must involve input from all stakeholders in the community. Competent administrators are acutely aware of this interrelationship. The success of their leadership ability depends greatly on how well they are able to reflect the culture of the school, assess a situation, determine relevant factors, and pose solutions to problems involving and considering the stakeholders' opinions and recommendations. These factors operate across all grade levels and organizational structures in the schools, including these serving children with disabilities. Another important responsibility is enforcing policies.

The principal role of an administrator is to execute policies of the school. These policies are frequently tied to laws with rules and regulations for executing same. An understanding of state and federal law pertaining to educating children with disabilities is vital, an issue addressed later in the text. The board of education, with advice from stakeholders, formulates the policies, and the administrators implement them. In order to implement and execute policies successfully, administrators must demonstrate the leadership traits of personality, purpose, knowledge base, and professional skills.

•• PERSONALITY TRAITS

Attempts to define the personality traits of administrators have not yielded universal traits that can be applied to all administrators. However, studies have confirmed that most administrators who maintain effective relations with stakeholders are friendly, socially attuned to others, lively, and cooperative. They are problem solvers who demonstrate a low degree of frustration and anxiety. Equally important are administrators who support parental and community involvement in the schools. Moreover, a certain degree of empathy, understanding, tolerance, and patience are needed for administrators who serve children with disabilities. Administration of programs for children with disabilities requires an especially high level of interpersonal communication and problem-solving skills.

•• INTERPERSONAL COMMUNICATION

The value of effective communication is key for school administrators. Communication underlies all aspects of collaboration and the performance of professional duties of administrators including curriculum development, intervention strategies, and collaboration with teachers, parents, and community members. Effective communication skills are essential for administrators to transmit information.

Gamble and Gamble (1996) state that communication is a process of exchanging information between the sender and the receiver. The information, or intent, of the communicative act is the message. Communication includes words, noises, facial expressions, and verbal and nonverbal messages conveyed by the sender to the receiver. Communication is incomplete if the receiver does not receive and interpret the communication (Okun, 1996; Peterson & Nisenholz, 1998).

All sensory mechanisms may be involved in sending and receiving information. Information may be transmitted through the visual, auditory, olfactory, and tactile channels. These channels must be intact in order to receive the information. Any deficits in any channel will impede the sender's message to the receiver. Role perception is also important in communication. Perception is designed to interpret sensory stimuli. It is a process of selecting, organizing, and making sense of information (Lustig & Koester, 1999).

•• INTERPERSONAL PROBLEM SOLVING

Administrators are challenged with professional tasks and activities that often require problem solving. They are constantly faced with choosing intervention techniques. However, solving school-related problems should not be the sole responsibility of the principal or the administrator. It should be shared with others. This process is referred to as interpersonal problem solving (Friend & Cook, 2000). Interpersonal problem solving in special education may be evident in identification, testing, placement, resources, related services, meeting individual needs, and service delivery models. These problems are usually solved through the team approach. Such an approach might be adapted by administrators through the use of proactive strategies.

Teams may use reactive and proactive strategies to solve problems. In reactive problem solving, administrators are faced with responding to a crisis. Reactive strategies are used too frequently in the schools to solve problems. In contrast, proactive strategies should supercede reactive strategies. In this process administrators have the opportunity to anticipate factors that might cause a problem before a crisis occurs.

Once a problem has been identified, the next step is to utilize techniques to solve it. Research conducted by Conoley and Conoley (1992), Johnson and Pugach (1996), Kratochwill and Bergan (1990), and Harris (1995) has provided us with steps for interpersonal problem solving. Although the steps are relatively easy to implement, according to the authors, their complexity lies in skillful implementation.

I. Identifying the problems

The process is difficult to accomplish and often made more so when the problem is not well defined or when the number of participants increases. The problem cannot be solved unless it is accurately delineated and defined (Jayanthi & Friend, 1992).

   A. State the problem clearly so the discrepancy between the current situation and the desired situation is apparent.
   B. Participants should share the perception that the problem exists.
   C. Participants should agree on the factors that indicate the discrepancy.
   D. Construct clear problem statements adequately describing the problem or behavior.
   E. Confirm problems with multiple sources of information, such as observations, records, interviews, and needs assessment data.
   F. Allow adequate time for problem identification.

II. Monitoring the problem-solving content (Friend & Cook, 2000)

III. Selecting and utilizing problem-solving techniques

Many of the techniques used for problem solving, according to Parnes (1992) and Salisbury, Evans, and Palombara, (1997), depend heavily upon the divergent thinking skills of brainstorming, brainwriting, and nominal group techniques.

   A. Brainstorming

   In brainstorming, participants offer solutions verbally to the problem as they think of them. Ideas are accepted without analyzing them. Participants are free to express any solutions with or without valid sources. Solutions generated are written down and grouped and classified to create additional ideas. It is recommended that a time limit be set for generating solutions to the problem. If conducted appropriately, brainstorming can be an effective technique for solving problems.

   B. Brainwriting

   Brainwriting works on the same principles of brainstorming except that the participants individually write their solutions to the problem. The solutions are placed in a pile and participants select someone else's list to stimulate discussions and to generate additional situations. The complete set of solutions is presented to the group, duplications are eliminated, and the group makes a decision.

   C. Nominal group techniques

   Nominal group technique is a strategy developed by Delbecg, Van de Ven, and Gustafson (1986). Participants individually write down as many solutions as they can to the problem. The solutions are shared with the group, one participant at a time. From the list, participants decide which ideas or solutions are the most important. The list is reduced and items are combined. Participants then rate the ideas on a scale from 1 to 5. After ratings are counted, ideas with the highest ratings are considered the solutions to the problem. Problems that are more severe require close collaboration between stakeholders.

IV. Difficult interactions

Difficult interactions pose special problems and thus sophisticated techniques to resolve. They manifest themselves in conflict and resistance and may impede or enhance collaboration efforts. Staff members are expected to work together. This close association may promote conflict, particularly in instances where tasks, roles, and responsibilities are not clearly delineated (Wood, 1998). Lee and Barnett (1994) explain that conflict exists in the schools as more needs of children with disabilities are expressed. Conflict is likely to emerge, since meeting some individual's needs can interfere with meeting the needs of others. Consequently, as professionals request smaller caseloads in order to implement innovative programs, conflict may occur. Lambert (1998) voiced his opinion about why conflict exists, stating that leadership approaches to managing the schools have changed from principals making decisions to participatory management. Increased state involvement in decision making is another influence that increases the chances for conflict. This factor, however, is neither good or bad in that participants determine whether conflicts have negative or positive outcomes. Several administrative styles may be used to solve conflicts and problems.

•• ADMINISTRATIVE STRUCTURAL STYLES

The conflicts that teachers experience may be attributed to the organization and administration of their schools. The principal's leadership style affects the level and style of conflict. For example, conflict may be promoted when the principal conveys different information to different staff members.

•• CONFLICT RESPONSE STYLES

Administrators can use many conflict response styles (e.g., competitive, avoidance, accommodative, compromising, leadership, and collaborative styles). No style is completely positive or negative, and the conflict will determine the style an administrator will use (Friend & Cook, 2000).

Competitive Style

This style is associated with overpowering others. The major thrust is to win regardless of negative reactions. An administrator may be justified in using this style when ethical issues are an issue or when the decision is the administrator's responsibility to make.

Avoidance Style

This style is characterized by administrators who employ avoidance techniques when dealing with conflict by turning away from it. The style may be used when the conflict is severe or emotionally charged. Temporary avoidance may enable teachers or participants to reconsider their positions.

Accommodative Style

One of the main characteristics of an accommodative style is that the administrator gives into the conflict. This style can be beneficial when the conflict issues are not important or when the condition cannot be altered. Accommodating usually bring the conflict to a rapid close.

Compromising Style

This style is commonly used in schools to resolve conflicts. When administrators use this style, they compromise their position and encourage others to do the same. The result is usually an outcome accepted by all. Compromising is often appropriate when a limited time is available to resolve a conflict or when the conflict issue is not problematic.

Leadership Style

A comprehensive study conducted by Day (2000) in the United Kingdom, consisting of twelve schools in different settings and demographic areas, revealed significant data on the leadership style of administrators. Principals' leadership skills as viewed by constituencies in the schools revealed that most school staff had favorable remarks concerning the administrators of their schools. Findings indicated that these administrators were values led, people centered, achievement oriented, inward and outward facing, and able to manage a number of ongoing tensions and dilemmas. Data suggested there were no catchall solutions that existed in all situations. However, when administrators employed collaborative and collective-making policies, rather than autocratic policies, all stakeholders profit, including the students (Sergiovanni, 1995; Stoll & Fink, 1996; Tampoe, 1998).

Effective leadership implies that an individual must have a broad knowledge base, a penetrating vision, a sense of humanity, sound values, and effective administrative and organizational skills (Elsbree, McNally, & Wynn, 1967).

According to Day (2000), effective leaders are educators who can balance a variety of pressures while never losing sight of their best values to inspire and serve the school community. An example of this trait is when an administrator can manage the boundaries of autocratic and democratic decision making. There should be no contest concerning what type of leadership skill is best (democratic); however, administrators must sometimes make decisions without input from stakeholders that may be autocratic. Sometimes conditions and situations do not lend themselves to democratic decision making.

Collaborative Style

The use of this style requires commitment to the characteristics of collaboration, and it may include developing new strategies to resolve the conflict. Collaboration may not be the style to use in many conflict situations because it is time consuming and requires that certain elements be in place. The process rests on individuals trusting each other. Without this trust, collaboration will not be effective. Administrators may favor one style but use a variety of styles as conditions dictate. Regardless of the style employed, administrators must use collaboration skills effectively to achieve their goals in the school.

•• COLLABORATION

Collaboration in education and special education is chiefly due to societal trends in social, political, and economic areas. Schools have been mandated to collaborate in order to improve educational opportunities for children, especially those with special needs or disabilities.

The impact of societal demands on the schools has led to many changes and reforms. These reforms historically have taken many forms, from departmentalizing the schools, to small classrooms, to innovations in school design, such as the open classroom, and innovative strategies in staff development. Today, societal trends are mandating that technology be infused in all aspects of the curriculum. Collaboration and teaming are essential if the schools are to meet these societal mandates successfully (Daniel & Stallion, 1996; Hilliard, 1997; Murphy, 1997; Sparks & Richardson, 1997). A significant number of authors have suggested strongly that the close working relationships among teachers, administrators and parents can have a significant impact on student learning (Kain, 1995; Slavin, 1995; Sparks & Richardson, 1997; Wohlsteter, 1995).

Friend and Cook (2000) describe collaboration as an interpersonal style that administrators may employ to improve interactions with teachers, parents, and others in the community. It can only exist voluntarily in situations in which individuals with parity have identified a mutual goal and have agreed to share resources and responsibilities to accomplish that goal (Idol, Nevin and Paolucci-Whitcomb, 1994).

Characteristics of Collaboration

Collaboration includes the following components. It (1) is voluntary, (2) requires parity among participants, (3) is based on mutual goals, (4) depends on shared responsibility for participation and decision making, (5) involves sharing resources, (6) involves sharing accountability for outcomes, (7) values interpersonal style, (8) involves trusting one another, and (9) involves a sense of community. These strategies and characteristics have been amply described elsewhere. Refer to Friend and Cook (1990) for specific strategies for implementation. According to Friend and Cook (1990), several characteristics of collaboration have multiple functions. They may serve as prerequisites or outcomes.

Collaboration Defined

Although many attempts have been made to define collaboration, none of the definitions appear adequate (Fishbaugh, 1997; Idol, Nervin, & Paolucci-Whitcomb, 1944; West, 1990). The definition advanced by Friend and Cook (2000) appears to be the most accepted. These researchers stated that collaboration includes working together in a supportive and mutually beneficial relationship, a style of interaction that cannot exist in isolation.

Collaborative Planning

Thompson's (1998) research clearly indicated that gaining public and professional support for the school involves developing strategies that incorporate widespread participation in the development of standards by stakeholders. Some of the strategies could be designed to assist teachers in drafting districtwide standards (Education Commission on the States, 1996).

Parental leadership skill workshops should be instituted to enable parents to become active participants in developing standards and educational decisions. Stakeholders who develop standards must share mutual commitments and responsibilities. Before enacting standards, the wider community should be informed and give its endorsement. The school must show concern and respect for all participants regardless of class, education, or diversity (Davies, 1996). This approach assures that democratic views and values are considered in educational planning.

Collaborative planning should be more than mere discussions and suggestions given by stakeholders. Rather, those involved should be engaged in developing strategies to bring about educational reforms and changes. Research findings tend to support that home to school collaboration is essential to the academic success of students. Collaborative arrangements increase parental decision making, and provide opportunities for school personnel to support parents in assisting their child to learn. Parents who have a conceptual understanding of the subject matter taught can better assist the child and augment the teacher's teaching strategies (Whiteford, 1998; Wolf, 1998).

A unique way for improving parent/teacher collaboration is to develop teams consisting of both parents and teachers. The following suggestions for improving parent/teacher teams are offered:

1. Be in touch long before the conference.

2. Be direct and personal in arranging the conference.

3. Be accommodating and try not to take no for an answer. Be flexible in setting meeting times around parents' schedules.

4. Be on time.

5. Be prepared with handouts and work sample.

6. Be specific about problems.

7. Be knowledgeable as a team about each student.

8. Be welcoming.

9. Be in charge.

10. Be supportive.

11. Consider student-led conferences, which can be very effective for positive home-school relations.

12. Follow up. Hold a team meeting to develop strategies for following up recommendations from the team and assigning duties and responsibilities.

Team interaction is an important essential for improving the education of children with disabilities. It can better assist the team in understanding the strengths and weaknesses of the child under study. The team may also act as an advocate for the child and assure that significant support is available to enable the disabled child to achieve his or her stated objectives.

Planning a Support Program

Collaboration involves planning, training, and identifying one's roles and responsibilities in achieving commonly developed goals and objectives. Several steps are advocated in order for collaborative activities to be successful. A first step should be to develop a detailed collaborative plan with time lines and general guidelines for the school year. The collaborative agreement will require a great deal of brainstorming and commitment of time and resources. A second step is implementing the agreement. A general meeting is recommended before implementation to refresh ideas and suggestions and allow for any additional relevant input. Further activities that lead to implementation for a meeting may include the following activities:

1. Discussion of a film, videotape, or cassette presentation

2. Guest speaker(s)

3. A program featuring student projects from the resource room and regular classroom

4. Appearances by former resource room students to discuss their experiences

5. A transition meeting for students and their parents

6. Meetings focusing on a particular theme

7. A panel of parents to share their experiences and field questions

8. A "Who's Who in Special Education" meeting to introduce parents to special education support staff

9. Role playing of home/school scenarios followed by discussions.

Collaboration Strategies

Administrators must explore and find other avenues and modes of human communication in solving school-related problems. They should recognize they are not the only mechanism for bringing about human exchange. An interactive collaborative model is needed. As administrators interact with others, they need to continue to show good interpersonal relationships, which is necessary for successful collaboration. According to Friend and Cook (2000), collaboration is crucial as educators move to integrate curriculum, create schedules, design site-based professional development plans, raise academic standards, and redefine school leadership committees. The authors also contend that collaboration is essential for many activities related to special education, such as intervention teams, assessment, IEP teams, parent conferences, mediation, and paraprofessional services.

Collaborative team approaches were used to instruct children with disabilities for several decades before the schools were mandated by federal laws to institute them (Elliott & Sheridan, 1992; Gallivan-Fenlon, 1994). PL 94-142 mandated that school districts use a team approach to assessment and decision making for individuals with disabilities. It is incumbent on administrators to choose team members with unique skills and perspectives who will interact directly to achieve the stated goals or objectives for delivering effective delivery and related services to individuals with disabilities (Downing, 1999, Johnson & Johnson, 1991; Thousand, Villa, & Nevin, 1994).

•• ROLE OF THE COMMUNITY AND PARENTS

It would be neglectful if we did not explore the role and dimensions of parents and the community in problem solving. A desirable relationship between school, home, and community is marked by a strong bond of understanding and cooperation between parents and school personnel. Parents should have a direct share in deciding what problem-solving techniques appear to serve their children best. Parents should feel comfortable to make suggestions, and administrators should welcome parental input provided for the guidance of their children. Through various channels, administrators can improve collaboration for children with disabilities through the cooperation of parents and the community.

An effective program cannot operate successfully for children with disabilities unless there is common understanding among various segments of the community and parents. All necessary information concerning the education of the child should be shared with the parent. Parents and the community should have direct input into the development of a program. For teachers and related school personnel, collaboration should involve the utilization of information from parents and the community to develop instructional programs (Floyd, 1998; Hatch, 1998; Lewis & Morris, 1998).

Researchers (Booth and Dunne, 1996; Cairney, Ruge, Buchanan, Lowe, & Munsie, 1995; Epstein, 1995) concur that effective collaboration implies more than simply establishing links with the home; rather, it requires a comprehensive and permanent program of partnership with families and communities. Marsh (1999) summarized some of the values of partnership or collaboration between the home, the community, and the school. Effective partnerships or collaboration can improve school climate and programs, family support services, parents' skills and leadership, family and community relationship, and teacher effectiveness.

•• COMMUNICATION SKILLS

Collaboration activities cannot be successful unless administrators have excellent communication skills that effectively relate their position on issues. Communication is a varied, multidimensional, complex process. It may involve the integration of listening, verbal, and nonverbal communication skills.

Listening

Listening is an interrelated process involving the use of several verbal and non-verbal skills. It is essential to effective communication skills and collaboration. Brammer and MacDonald (1998) wrote that listening involves attending to and comprehending accurately what is said and demonstrating an understanding of the message. Listening enables and provides assistance in establishing and building rapport (Helgesen, Brown, & Brown, 1994). An attentive listener communicates both concern and an intent to understand what the speaker is saying. Attention, willingness to learn, and a desire to understand are important elements in establishing rapport and promoting collaborative exchange.

Nonverbal Communication

Individuals who employ effective nonverbal communication skills are also considered effective communicators. Skillful use of this technique is essential in communicating attitudes needed for establishing and maintaining positive relationships and powerful in clarifying and emphasizing the meaning of verbal messages (Egan, 1997). The speaker may communicate nonverbal clues through body movements, facial expressions, eye contact, posture, gestures, quality of voice, flow of speech, and distance between participants. All of these factors can significantly influence communication between the speaker and participants (Hall, 1996). These communication skills will assist administrators in achieving their vision for the school.

•• SHARED VISION

The successful administrator must have a vision of how to reform and transform education practices. This vision should be explained and shared (refer to Chapter 2 for additional details). Louis and Miles (1990) logically summarized shared vision by stating,

> Visions are not generated solely by the principal or another individual in a leadership position, but, even where the principal is strong, are developed collectively through action and reflection, by all those who play active roles in the change effect. Visions become strong not because the faculty believe in the principals, but because they believe in themselves and their ability to really change the school for the better.

Brown and Moffett (1999) supported the concept of shared vision in schools by articulating that shared vision and investigation need to be the driving norms for learning organizations. Shared vision promotes collaboration between all stakeholders. When teachers, administrators, parents, board members, students, and the community collaborate, student achievement is improved throughout the school (Newmann & Wehlage, 1995; Rosenholtz, 1989). In this process, Louis and Miles (1990) wrote that the role of the administrator is to view each stakeholder as a leader and for those who do not have leadership abilities to provide activities to promote them. According to Katzen-Meyer and Moller (1996), this is especially true for teachers who have not demonstrated leadership abilities. The authors contend that empowering teachers brings an enormous resource to expanding the vision for school reform.

Saxl, Miles, and Lieberman (1990) have provided nine essential skills needed to bring about educational reform. These skills operate successfully across all organizations, including the schools. They are the ability to

1. Establish trust and rapport with all stakeholders.

2. Understand schools and districts as organizational systems.

3. Manage the process of collaboration.

4. Manage the process of conflict resolution.

5. Manage the process of problem solving.

6. Manage the process of decision making.

7. Identify and employ internal and external resources.

8. Deal with problems as they arise with a wide range of coping mechanisms.

9. Develop the capacity, skills, and confidence of others in the school community to be change facilitators themselves.

If administrators are to be effective change agents, they must collaborate, communicate, and have a vision shared by all stakeholders. Once these steps have been accomplished, administrators can plan and develop an instructional plan that will have the endorsement of all stakeholders.

•• INSTRUCTIONAL PLAN

A well-defined instructional plan with functional goals and objectives that specifically defines purposes and activities for achieving goals and objectives must be clearly outlined. Duties of all stakeholders must be clearly delineated with time lines for completion of tasks. Administrators who have not included the opinions of stakeholders in the formation of purposes have significantly minimized their abilities to lead the group effectively. The learning styles, abilities, and disabilities of children with disabilities must be an essential part of the purposes (goals and objectives) stated.

When responsibilities are delegated to stakeholders by administrators, teachers in these democratic schools engage in greater collaboration, both with their peers and other administrators, on curriculum instruction and non-academic tasks. These tasks may involve selecting teachers, providing assistance to new teachers, assisting in performance, evaluating the school's improvement plan, supervising instructional programs for children with disabilities, and providing in-service training for teachers.

Effective staff development should be directly related to the assessed needs of the staff, students, and stakeholders premised on collaborative leadership, designed to promote ownership and commitment to the process. In order for any collaboration arrangement to be effective, teachers and all stakeholders must be involved in decisions that link the goals and objectives of staff development with the development of the curriculum. Collaborative leadership must come from multiple sources simultaneously.

•• SUMMARY

Traditionally, schools were not constructed to foster collaboration. A significant part of the school's work was done in isolation from others (Goodlad, 1984; Sarason, 1982). In years past and often today as well, teachers were individually assigned to classrooms and little collaboration was done. Teachers simply closed their doors and taught their classes, creating a physical isolation that contrasts sharply with the concept of collaboration (Little, 1992).

Administrators of school programs for children require special leadership qualities. Individuals who manage children, especially those who administer programs for children with disabilities, must possess special leadership qualities. These qualities include administrators who understand instructional strategies, are values led, people centered, support collaborative efforts, demonstrate democratic values, and support orderly change and reforms in education (Oakes, Quartz, Ryan, & Lipton, 2000).

There appears to be a direct correlation between administrators' knowledge and their administrative styles. Stakeholders tend to place greater confidence in administrators who are knowledgeable about instructional and noninstructional problems associated with the schools, and this knowledge base influences stakeholders for more than their leadership behaviors and styles. Many administrators do not have specific knowledge relevant to the identification and treatment of children with disabilities. Mandatory workshops and seminars should be required for all administrators involved in the education of these children.

Administrators must manage the change process if the character of the school is to be developed to meet the needs of students effectively. For administrators not attending to the forces of change, their tenure may be short lived. In most school districts, change is tolerated and expected. Regardless of what administrators do, change will come. It is incumbent on administrators to direct changes rather than be driven by them.

•• REFERENCES

Bennis, W. (1984). The four competencies. *Leadership Training and Development Journal, 38*(8), 15–19.

Booth, A., & Dunne, J. (Eds.). (1996). *Family-school links: How do they affect education?* Hillsdale, NJ: Erlbaum.

Brammer, L. M., & MacDonald, G. (1998). *The helping relationship: Process and skills* (7th ed.). Boston: Allyn & Bacon.

Brown, J. L., & Moffett, C. A. (1999). *The hero's journey: How educators can transform schools and improve learning?* Alexandria, VA: Association for Supervision and Curriculum Development.

Cairney, T. H., Ruge, J., Buchanan, J., Lowe, K., & Munsie, L. (1995). *Developing partnership: The home, school, and community interface.* Canberra: Department of Employment, Education, and Training.

Conoley, J. C., & Conoley, C. W. (1992). *School consultation: Practice and training* (2nd ed.). Boston: Allyn & Bacon.

Daniel, P. L., & Stallion, B. K. (1996). Implementing school-based professional development in Kentucky. *Journal of Staff Development, 17*(4), 30–32.

Davies, D. (1996). Partnership for student success. *New Schools New Communities, 12*(13), 14–21.

Day, C. (2000). Beyond transformational leadership. *Educational Leadership, 57*(7), 56–59.

Delbecg, A. L., Van de Ven, A. H., & Gustafson, D. H. (1986). *Group techniques for program planning: A guide to nominal group and delphi processes.* Middletown, WI: Green Briar.

Downing, J. E. (1999). *Teaching communication skills to students with severe disabilities.* Baltimore, MD: Paul H. Brookes.

Education Commission on the States. (1996). *Listen, discuss, and aid.* Denver: ESC.

Egan, G. (1997). *The skilled helper: A systematic approach to effective helping* (6th ed.). Monterey, CA: Brooks/Cole.

Elliott, S. N., & Sheridan, S. M. (1992). Consultation and teaming: Problem solving among educators, parents, and support personnel. *Elementary School Journal, 92,* 315–338.

Elsbree, W. S., McNally, H. J., & Wynn, R. (1967). *Elementary school administration and supervision.* New York: Van Nostrand Reinhold.

Epstein, J. L. (1991). School, family, community partnerships: Caring for the children we share. *Phi Delta Kappan, 77*(9), 701–712.

Fishbaugh, M. S. E. (1997). *Model of collaboration.* Boston: Allyn & Bacon.

Floyd, L. (1998). Joining hands: A parental involvement program. Urban Education, 32, 123–135.

Friend, M., & Cook, L. (1990). Collaboration as a predictor for success in school reform. *Journal of Educational Psychology Consultation, 1,* 69–86.

Friend, M., & Cook, L. (2000). *Interactions: Collaboration skills for school professionals* (3rd ed.). New York: Longman.

Gallivan-Fenlon, A. (1994). Integrated transdisciplinary teams. *Teaching Exceptional Children, 26*(3), 16–20.

Gamble, T. K., & Gamble M. (1996). *Communication works* (5th ed.). New York: McGraw-Hill.

Goodlad, E. (1984). *A place called school.* New York: McGraw-Hill.

Hall, E. T. (1996). *The hidden dimension.* Garden City, NY: Doubleday.

Harris, K. C. (1995). School-based bilingual special education teacher teams. *Remedial and Special Education, 16,* 337–343.

Hatch, T. (1998). How community action contributes to achievement. *Educational Leadership, 55*(8), 16–19.

Helgesen, M., Brown, S., & Brown, S. (1994). *Active listening: Building skills for understanding.* Cambridge, MA: Cambridge University Press.

Hilliard, A. (1997). The structure of valid staff development. *Journal of Staff Development, 18*(2), 28–34.

Idol, L., Nevin, A., & Paolucci-Whitcomb, P. (1994). *Collaborative consultation* (2nd ed.). Austin, TX: Pro-Ed.

Jayanthi, M., & Friend, M. (1992). Interpersonal problem solving: A selected literature review to guide practice. *Journal of Educational and Psychological Consultation, 3,* 147–152.

Johnson, D. W., & Johnson, F. (1991). *Joining together* (4th ed.). Upper Saddle River, NJ: Prentice Hall.

Johnson, L. J., & Pugach, M. C. (1996). Role of collaborative dialogue in teachers' conceptions of appropriate practice for students at risk. *Journal of Educational and Psychological Consultation, 7,* 9–24.

Kahn, R. L., & Rosenthal, R. A. (1964). *Organizational stress: Studies in role conflict and ambiguity.* New York: Wiley.

Kain, D. L. (1995). Teaming with a purpose. *Schools in the Middle, 4*(4), 6–9.

Katzen-Meyer, M., & Moller, G. (1996). *Awakening the sleeping giant: Leadership development for teachers.* Thousand Oaks, CA: Corwin Press.

Kratochwill, T. R., & Bergan, J. R. (1990). *Behavioral consultation in applied settings: An individual guide.* New York: Plenum.

Lambert, L. (1998). How to build leadership capacity. *Educational Leadership, 55*(7), 17–19.

Lee, G. V., & Barnett, B. G. (1994). Using reflective questioning to promote collaborative dialogue. *Journal of Staff Development, 15*(1), 16–21.

Lewis, R., & Morris, J. (1998). Communities for children. *Educational Leadership, 55*(8), 34–36.

Little, J. W. (1992). Norms of collegiality and experimentation: Workplace conditions of school success. *American Educational Research Journal, 5,* 325–340.

Louis, K. S., & Miles, M. B. (1990). *Improving the urban high school: What works and why.* New York: Teachers College Press.

Lustig, M. W., & Koester, J. (1999). *Intercultural competence: Interpersonal communication across cultures* (3rd ed.). New York: Longman.

Marsh, D. (1999). *Yearbook: Preparing our schools for the 21st century.* Alexandria, VA: Association for Supervision and Curriculum Development.

Murphy, C. (1997). Finding time for faculties to study together. *Journal of Staff Development, 18*(3), 29–32.

Newmann, F., & Wehlage, G. (1995). *Successful school restructuring.* Madison, WI: Center on Organization and Restructuring of Schools.

Oakes, J., Quartz, J. H., Ryan, S., & Lipton, M. (2000). *The struggle for civic virtue in education reform.* San Francisco: Jossey-Bass.

Okun, B. (1996). *Effective helping: Interviewing and counseling techniques* (5th ed.). Pacific Grove, CA: Brooks/Cole.

Osborn, R. N., & Hunt, J. G. (1975). An adaptive-reactive theory of leadership: The role of macro variables in leadership research. In J. G. Hunt and L. L. Largon (Eds.), *Leadership Frontiers.* Kent, OH: Kent State University Press.

Parnes, S. J. (Ed.). (1992). *Sourcebook for creative problem-solving.* Buffalo, NY: Creative Education Foundation.

Peterson, J. V., & Nisenholz, B. (1998). *Orientation to counseling* (4th ed.). Newton, MA: Allyn & Bacon.

Pfeffer, J., & Salancik, G. R. (1978). *The external control of organizations: A resource dependence perspective*. New York: Harper and Row.

Rosenholtz, S. (1989). *Teachers' workplace: The social organization of schools*. New York: Longman.

Salisbury, C. L., Evans, I. M., & Palombara, M. M. (1997). Collaborative problem-solving to promote the inclusion of young children with significant disabilities in primary grades. *Exceptional Children, 63*, 195–209.

Sarason, S. B. (1982). *The culture of the school and the problem of change* (2nd ed.). Boston: Allyn & Bacon.

Saxl, E., Miles, M., & Lieberman, A. (1990). *Assisting change in education*. Alexandria, VA: Association for Supervision and Curriculum Development.

Sergiovanni, T. J. (1995). *The principalship: A reflective practice perspective*. Boston: Allyn & Bacon.

Slavin, R. E. (1995). *Cooperative learning: Theory, research, and practice* (2nd ed.). Boston: Allyn & Bacon.

Smith, W. F., & Andrews, R. L. (1989). *Instructional leadership: How principals make a difference?* Alexandria, VA: Association for Supervision and Curriculum Development.

Sparks, D., & Richardson, J. (1997). A primer on professional development. *Journal of Staff Development, 18*(4), 1–8.

Stoll, L., & Fink, D. (1996). *Changing our schools*. London: Open University Press.

Tampoe, M. (1998). *Liberating leadership*. London: The Industrial Society.

Thompson, S. (1998). Moving from publicity to engagement. *Educational Leadership, 55*(8), 54–57.

Thousand, J. S., Villa, R., & Nevin, A. (1994). *Creativity and collaborative learning*. Baltimore, MD: Paul H. Brookes.

West, J. F. (1990). Educational collaboration in restructuring of schools. *Journal of Educational and Psychological Consultation, 1*, 23–40.

Whiteford, T. (1998). Math for moms and dads. *Educational Leadership, 55*(3), 64–66.

Wohlsteter, P. (1995). Getting school-based management right: What works and what doesn't. *Phi Delta Kappan, 77*, 22–26.

Wolf, J. M. (1998). Just read. *Educational Leadership, 55*(8), 62–63.

Wood, M. (1998). Whose job is it anyway? Educational roles in inclusion. *Exceptional Children, 64*, 181–195.

Yukl, G. A. (1981). Leadership in organizations. Englewood Cliffs, NJ: Prentice Hall.

CHAPTER 2

Administering School Reforms

Many of the changes relevant to school reforms are defined in the concept of shared decision making, a concept that has spread rapidly throughout the country. School administrators must ensure that all stakeholders have an equal opportunity to participate in the decisions that are made (David, 1995, 1996; Holloway, 2000; Levey & Acker-Hocevar, 1998).

In a shared decision-making process, administrators refrain from giving directions and directives; rather, they develop teams and provide directions for the team to implement the goals and objectives of the schools and assist the team in developing communication and decision-making skills. A study conducted by McCloskey, Mikow-Porto, and Bingham (1998) revealed that many administrators and staff are not properly prepared to engage in shared decision making. Most of the stakeholders had received no training in implementing a school improvement plan, and several staff members did not understand their roles and responsibilities. Informed sessions should be provided by the central administration for stakeholders so they can be apprised of the school's objectives and strategies for achieving them. Stakeholders should include all individuals responsible for educating children including school administrators, teachers, parents, community groups, and, in some cases, the students themselves.

•• A REFORM MODEL

Parents and teachers should have an active role in planning school reforms. In schools where school-wide reforms have been implemented successfully, parents serve on site councils, planning teams, and accreditation committees (U.S. Department of Education, 1998). Effective comprehension school reform models should have the following characteristics:

1. Promote high standards for all children.

2. Address all academic subject areas and grade levels.

3. Be research-based and research tested.

4. Share a common focus on goals.

5. Include professional development.

6. Align all resources across grades and subject areas.

7. Facilitate parent and community involvement. (Education Commission on the States, 1998a, 1998b).

Additionally, research conducted by the Education Commission on the States confirmed that for any reform model to be implemented effectively, faculty, staff, parents, students, and communities must be involved and support the model. Once developed, benchmarks to measure progress should be evident and an evaluation system should be in place to determine how well the stated objectives have been met and how much the school and achievement of the students have improved (American Institutes for Research, 1999; Fege, 2000; Grasmick, 2000; McChesney & Hertling, 2000; Mofett, 2000; Olson, 1998; Viadero, 1989). School reforms have been termed site-based management, restructuring the schools, or performance-based education.

Several key factors must be in place before administrators can bring about reforms in the schools. The stakeholders must have genuine control over the budgets, personnel, and the curriculum. Stakeholders or team members must conduct schoolwide activities, disseminate information, and lead and delegate responsibilities (Holloway, 2000; Odden & Wohlstetter, 1995). Stakeholders must clearly understand that they share responsibility for the schools. They should have the authority for distributing appropriate human and physical resources equitably in concert with the goals and objectives reflected in the school plan. Reform movements should be centralized and employ expert resources within the school district, shared by and agreed to by all stakeholders, including school administrators (Van, 1995).

In the field of special education, many of the reforms and changes that have been made are based on federal and state laws. Thus administrators of programs for children with disabilities must be apprised of these laws. Much of the information may be gained through in-service workshops and courses at universities (see chapter 6).

•• THE CHANGE PROCESS

No reform can be successful until there is a uniform understanding of change. Fullan and Miles (1992) have attempted to provide administrators with a real understanding of change. They wrote,

After years of failed educational reform, educators are more and more in the habit of saying that "knowledge of the change process" is crucial. But few people really know what that means. The phrase is used superficially. Glibly, as if saying it over and over will lead to understanding and appropriate action. We do believe that knowing about the change process is crucial. But there are as many myths as there are truths associated with change, and it is time to deepen the way we think about the change. We need to assess our knowledge more critically and describe what we know. One needs a good deal of sophistication to grasp the fundamental of the change process and to use that knowledge wisely. (p. 745)

We also believe that serious educational reform will never be achieved until there is a significant increase in the number of people-leaders and other participants alike who have come to internalize and habitually act on basic knowledge of how successful change takes place. Reformers talk of the need for deeper, second-order changes in structures and cultures of schools, rather than superficial, first-order changes. But no change would be more fundamental than a dramatic expansion of the capacity of individuals and organizations to understand and deal with change. This generic capacity is worth more than a hundred individual success stories of implementing specific innovations. As we shall see, even individual success stories don't last long without an appreciation of how to keep change alive.

It is evident that change is a process involving all of the dimensions of human learning, including the cognitive, affective, and behavioral domains. Employing these dimensions may be the first process in achieving the kind of focuses administrators can use to bring about successful school reforms (Wohlsteter & Mohrman, 1994). Those leading or facilitating change need to gain skills in the art of observing behavior, feelings, and events associated with resisting change. Blumberg's (1986) remarks are still relevant for today's administrators. He stated, "[P]rincipals maybe the weak link in the quality improvement effort. This is not because principals are incompetent, but because principals have not been selected and trained on the basis of what a principal must do to make sweeping reform work. Few have been prepared to manage change, and managing change is essential for implementing current reforms" (p. 4).

One major reason people resist organizational change is they think they will lose something of value as a result. People also resist change when they do not understand its implications and perceive it might cost them much more than they will gain. Another reason is people perceive the situation differently from their managers/leaders.

One of the most common ways to overcome resistance to change is to educate people about the change before attempting to make it. If the initiators involve the potential resisters in some aspect of the design and implementation of the change, they can often forestall resistance. Another way is by being supportive of the resisters' point of view. Still another strategy to deal with resistance is to offer incentives to active or potential resisters. In some instances, managers/leaders resort to covert attempts to influence others. Finally, managers/leaders may often deal with resistance coercively.

In approaching an organizational change situation, managers/leaders explicitly or implicitly make strategic choices regarding the speed of the effort, the amount of preplanning, the involvement of others, and the relative emphasis they give to different approaches. Successful change efforts seem to be those in which the choices are internally consistent, fit some key situational variables, and operate across all organizational structures, including special education.

The norm in American school districts today is one of overload with the many promising innovations competing for attention and often partially implemented in a fragmented way. Becoming more aware of competing initiatives and engaging in dialogue about what real change involves may be a first step in achieving the kind of focus needed to bring about successful school reform.

There is value in stepping back from a change effort and analyzing what is happening now, what has gone on before, and what might lie ahead. It is especially useful for those leading or facilitating change to be skilled observers of the behaviors, feelings, and events going on in a change effort. Corey (1993) contended that change must take place with the involvement of those who will be affected by the change.

Management means keeping the current system operating through planning, budgeting, organizing, staffing, controlling, and problem solving. Management works through hierarchy and systems. It is harder and cooler. Leadership is the development of vision and strategies and the empowerment of individuals to make the vision happen, despite obstacles. Leadership works through people and culture. It is soft and hot. There is nothing more difficult to carry out, or more doubtful of success, or more dangerous to handle, than to initiate a new order to things.

Today, more and more administrators must deal with new government regulations, new products, growth, increased competition, technological developments, and a changing work force. In response, they must undertake moderate organizational changes at least once a year and major changes every four or five years. Many changes in special education are predicated on amendments and changes in federal and state laws governing educating children with disabilities.

Few organizational change efforts are complete failures, but few are entirely successful either. Most efforts encounter problems; they often take longer than expected and desired; they sometimes kill morale, and they cost a great deal in terms of managerial time or emotional upheaval. More than a few organizations have not tried to initiate needed changes because the managers involved were afraid they were simply incapable of implementing them successfully. Without risk of failure, nothing will change. Some type of model or structure is needed to regulate the change process. We display such a model in figure 1, which demonstrates the processes usually employed in bringing about successful change. Unsuccessful change would probably stop at step 5, but if step 5 is overcome, the process involved in successful change can resume.

Data in figure 1 summarizes typical factors associated with change. Change is a complex process and involves several cognitive and emotional factors as outlined previously in the text.

Figure 1: A Model for Implementing Change Successfully

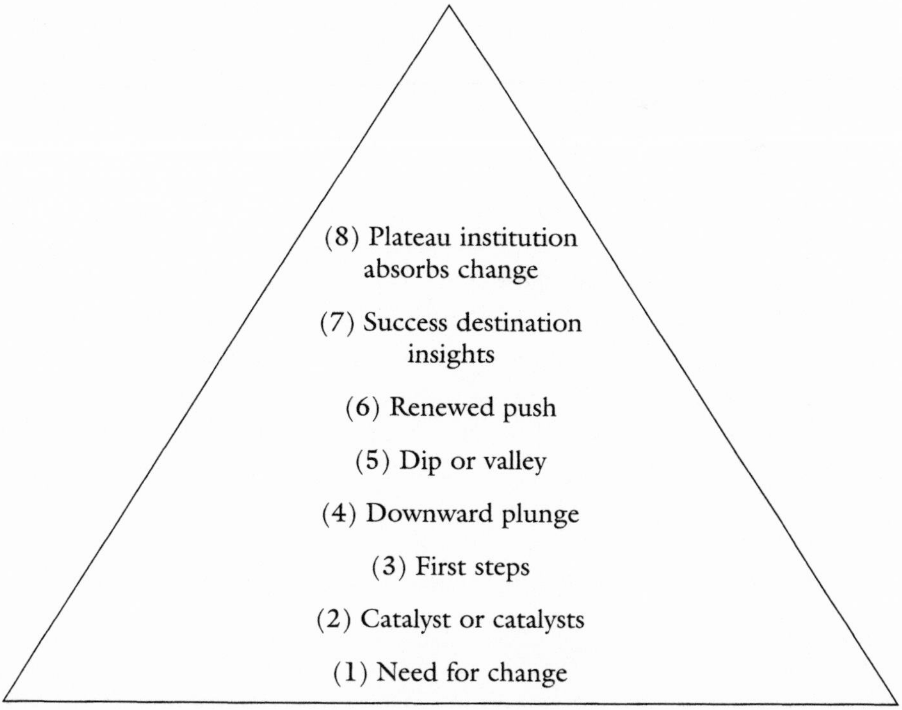

(8) Plateau institution
absorbs change

(7) Success destination
insights

(6) Renewed push

(5) Dip or valley

(4) Downward plunge

(3) First steps

(2) Catalyst or catalysts

(1) Need for change

Step 1. Change is imminent because of dissatisfaction with results, changes in available resources, and new leadership. It is accompanied by feelings of dissatisfaction, ambivalence about saying good-bye to the established ways, growing tension, or energetic anticipation about the future.

Stakeholders need:

- to feel included.
- the outside stimulus of an expert or a convert who has seen the innovations work.
- concrete examples.
- opportunities to examine new ideas with colleagues and program leadership.
- validation that their past contributions are significant and still valued.
- a climate in which questions are welcome.
- inspiration.

Step 2. A catalyst starts change with a whimper or a bang often depending on whether the change has been mandated and whether people feel a strong pressure or desire to change; in special education, both factors many operate. Feelings vary from being set free of old, tired paradigms to feeling set adrift, to feeling manipulated or controlled, to feeling energized by the possibilities of the journey ahead; beyond the inner group, suspicion often runs high.

Stakeholders need:

- information and inspiration.
- opportunities to examine new ideas with colleagues and leadership.
- to feel included and informed.

Step 3. First steps create some momentum, often depending on whether the change has been mandated and whether people feel a strong pressure or desire to change. Feelings of confusion or elation, high degree of concern about mistakes, frequent miscommunication, which can cause problems, and for some people, the exhilaration of a new beginning and adventure are characteristic.

Stakeholders need:

- frequent opportunities to talk about the distant vision and how this first step is part of the journey.
- open covenants, open doors, open communication.

- public and private recognition for initial efforts.
- opportunities to express concerns and ask questions.
- encouragement to risk change and make mistakes.
- opportunities to learn new skills and information.
- clear statements from the leadership regarding expectations, goals, outcomes, time lines, evaluation procedures, and new procedures.

Step 4. Downward plunge begins when people enter unknown territory often with new partners or collaborators, having incomplete knowledge and/or partially found skills; twists, turns, and surprise roadblocks appear from nowhere. Feeling of being unsure, incompetent, afraid of failure, or out of control in strange new environments with new partners, new norms, and/or partially formed skills are typical.

Stakeholders need:

- opportunities to try out new ideas.
- official support structures such as study groups, peer coaches, written step-by-step guides, and individual problem-solving consultation.
- constructive, corrective feedback.
- concrete examples.
- time to problem-solve with colleagues.
- clear statements of realistic interim goals and benchmarks from leaders.

Step 5. Dip or valley can occur when the going gets rough. Resources are often stretched as the journey takes longer and requires more effort than originally anticipated. The original vision now seems unrealistic, and some are ready to abandon the journey. Stakeholders experience feelings of despair, distrust, exhaustion, and abandonment as resources are depleted, leadership changes or commitment lags, and the less-than-stouthearted partners fall by the wayside.

Stakeholders need:

- emotional support from the leadership.
- time-out; a lull.
- celebration of achievements.
- recognition of successes.
- inspiration by leadership.
- on-site assistance in problem solving.
- collegial support.
- encouragement in looking at long-term goal, not at the problems.

Step 6. Renewed momentum pushes onward coupled with a revised, somewhat more focused vision of the destination and often reconstituted inner core of advocates on board. Feelings of renewed vigor, competence, and bonding are enjoyed among the inner core of advocates, and there is a sense of guarded ownership and having survived a shared ordeal.

Stakeholders need:
- opportunities to sort out and share their "lessons learned."
- celebration of successes.
- encouragement in documenting processes used.
- continued official support for their efforts (e.g., policy changes, etc.).
- encouragement in making adjustments and refinements.

Step 7. Some success occurs; the journey's end is in sight. With some modifications and/or new spin-offs emerging as the work ends, stakeholders experience feelings of elation, increased capacity, competence, relief, and/or pride of ownership.

Stakeholders need:
- time to document their efforts to aid in institutionalization.
- opportunities to plan the institutionalization.

Step 8. A plateau of institutionlization of the innovation, routinization, and incorporation of the change into everyday life occurs. After some negotiation among the project's architects about what is essential in the project and what is peripheral, the realization comes that the innovation is still not fully routinized and could disappear without policies and other strategies to protect its future and prolong its life span. There are feelings of accomplishment, exhaustion, comfortable familiarity, relief, and disappointment as the spotlight fades and the committee or team disbands; pride of ownership expands, and the difficult times and conflicts fade somewhat.

Stakeholders need:
- opportunities to refine, fine-tune, or revise change to make improvements.
- policies and other official support to ensure the future of the innovation.

We support the views advocated by Lounsbury (1991) concerning reforms in education. He has reminded us that reforms in education must address the moral fiber in our society.

He stated,

> I believe further that unless Americans can be brought to a deeper appreciation of the place of values, attitudes, and the effective domain in public education, reform efforts will fall short of the success so desperately needed in this last decade of the 20th century. Unfortunately, people continue to talk about training, performance on tests, mastery of discrete subjects, and grades as if these were the beginning and end of education. (p. 5)

•• MAJOR CURRICULUM REFORMS

Curriculum changes and reforms are directly associated with the social, political, and historical factors in society. Anderson (1996) pointed out that these factors may advance or inhibit curriculum development and reform. Existing social, political, or historical conditions may have a significant impact on curriculum development. An example of the influence of these conditions on curriculum may be seen in the Soviet launching of Sputnik. Brandt (2000) wrote that federal funds were made available immediately to develop demanding curriculum that emphasized in-depth knowledge of the disciplines. The impact of World War II, the civil rights movement, computerized curriculums, total quality education curriculum, outcome-based education curriculums, constructivist curriculums, and standard-based conditions have each had an urgent visible impact on curricula development in the United States.

All of these curriculum reforms were initiated based on societal conditions. Generally, they tend to have short life spans. The major purposes of curricula reforms are to improve the quality of education and to bring it up to the prevailing standards of the times. It is not our intent here to repeat the history of curriculum reforms in the United States, but rather to expose you to the many types and kinds of reforms. For a comprehensive view of the many curriculum reforms, see Ronald S. Brandt's *Education in a New Era* (2000).

General Principles

All of the curriculums just listed were directed to solving or reacting to a single problem. Most research on curriculum reforms indicates that they must be global and focus on issues such as these:

1. Reflect greater depth and less superficial coverage (Knapp et al., 1991).

2. Focus on problem solving that requires using learning strategies (Brandt, 2000).

3. Emphasize both skills and knowledge of the subjects (Brooks & Brooks, 1993).

4. Provide for students' individual differences (Anderson, 1996).

5. Offer a common core to all students (Hill, Foster, & Gendler, 1990).

6. Coordinate related subject closely (McDonnell, 1989).

Several researchers have advocated that an effective curriculum must be integrated in order to improve achievement and be personally relevant to the students (Glatthorn, 1998; Roth, 1994; Vars, 1991). Curriculums should have both unity and diversity, make connections, reflect human values, and emphasize responsibility.

Grandmont (1995) offered the following suggestions for implementing curriculum revision:

• Avoid changing curriculum without justification and support.

• Gain knowledge about proposed changes by reviewing current articles and attending seminars and workshops.

• Use scheduled meetings to get district approval for curriculum revision plans.

• Conduct meetings to convince teachers and staff that curriculum revisions are necessary.

• Provide teachers with supportive information such as journal articles and other professional publications.

• Use in-service days to train staff regarding revision plans and implementation.

• Create newsletters and presentations to inform parents of proposed changes.

• Select enthusiastic teachers who are willing to pilot the curriculum revision.

• Implement the revision by providing continuous training and support and by monitoring classrooms through formal and information observations.

In addition to the strategies listed for school reforms, the concept of placing children in educational settings and educating them must be carefully considered by administrators when making school reforms. The issues of inclusion, natural goals and objectives, and site-based decision-making policies are equally important in reforming schools for children with disabilities.

Many stakeholders are calling for reforms in education. Special education has not been eliminated from this outcry. The most common type of school reform initiatives include inclusion, site-based decision making, and national education goals. These initiatives have been designed to make school systems accountable for the education of all children with special emphasis on reforming education and services for these children. Administrators have been charged with directing and implementing reform initiatives.

Inclusion

The inclusion movement in the United States has a long history. In the 1970s, recommendations were advanced for mainstreaming children with disabilities in the regular classroom. In the 1980s, the concept of the regular education initiative (REI) was debated, especially the efficacy of special education programs. By the 1990s, full inclusion was advocated for children with disabilities (Hollis & Gallegos, 1993) (see Chapter 10).

Inclusive education has been defined in as many ways as there are attitudes toward this educational concept. For instance, Roach (1995) defined the term as serving students with a full range of abilities and disabilities in the general education classroom, with appropriate in-class support. For others, (Brown et al., 1991), inclusion is a way to implement the least restricted environment (LRE), however not necessarily in the regular classroom. According to Bennett, Deluca, and Burns (1997) and Scruggs and Mostropieri (1996), inclusion means integrating students with disabilities into a heterogeneous classroom for the entire school day. This inclusive model is typically referred to as the regular education initiative (REI).

It is the attitudes of administrators of special education programs involved in, or affected by, inclusive models that define and determine the impact of this practice on the students who will be placed in this setting. For example, Berger (1995) asserted that the process of including individuals with special needs into the mainstream classroom has become a pressing issue among those in administration responsible for their education.

A preponderance of literature indicates to administrators that most children with disabilities should be placed in inclusive classrooms. This position has created some controversy regarding inclusive versus special class placement (see Baker, Wang, & Walberg, 1995; Borthwick-Duffy, Palmer, & Lane, 1996; Fuchs & Fuchs, 1994, 1995; Rogers, 1993; Waldron and McLeskey, 1998; Zigmond et al., 1995). The common consensus of these researchers indicated that the concept of inclusion is an excellent idea; however, it may not work for all children at all times.

Most administrators are acutely aware that teaching students with disabilities in inclusive settings is a multifaceted task that cannot be accomplished by one person. Inclusive education happens when a team of mutually supportive players pledge to provide the best practices for a student with disabilities. Inclusive education must focus on a combination of best practices in education, including cooperative learning, peer tutoring, and community building in classrooms and schools. Teaching strategies for inclusive settings are synonymous with effective teaching strategies used in any area of education (Aefsy, 1995). Depending on the disability and the level of student need, a team with unique but complementary skills should be consulted to guide, advocate for, and implement this student's educational program. More than any other element, the need for a team effort to manage, deliver, and support a student's inclusive education is a drastic change for regular educators. Administrators must develop a plan to integrate the lifelong goals and specific needs of students with disabilities within the context of the regular curriculum (Taylor, 2000).

Administrators of programs for children with disabilities should be informed of the controversies surrounding inclusion. For example, advocates for full inclusion of children with disabilities claim it is the democratic right of the disabled to be educated with their peers and that integration of children with disabilities with nondisabled children enhances interpersonal skills. Other studies indicate that curricula in inclusive schools should be appropriate for different levels of disabilities and sensory acuity because there is no separate knowledge base for teaching students with disabilities. Teachers must be innovative and employ creative teaching strategies, such as learning centers, cooperative learning, concept teaching, directed teaching, and team teaching. Many adaptations and modifications will be needed in the instructional process, depending on the amount and degree of disabling conditions present. To the extent possible, students with disabilities should be included in the learning process with their peers (Barry, 1995; Baker, Wang, & Walberg, 1995; Johnston, Proctor, & Carey, 1995; Staub, & Peck, 1995; Wang, & Walberg, 1995).

Opponents of full inclusion believe a one-size-fits-all approach will be disastrous for children with disabilities, and this approach moreover is not only unrealistic but also unjust. According to Shanker (1995), to correct such an injustice, public laws addressing inclusion need to be rewritten to determine the cost of inclusion. Adequate training for all teachers should be provided, equal weight to requests from parents and referrals from teachers should be given, teachers must be totally involved in writing the IEP, and alternative arrangements should be made to place in secure settings children with disabilities who are violent or disruptive. The National Association of State Boards of Education voiced that many special education programs are superior to regular classrooms for some types of children with disabilities (Baker & Zigmond, 1990), and some reported (Fuchs, Fuchs, & Bishop, 1992; Fuchs & Fuchs, 1995) that individualizing strategies employed in special classes are superior to the one-size-fits-all approach observed in many regular classrooms. They supported the view that separate is better for some children with disabilities, and to abolish special education placement in the name of full inclusion is to deprive many children with disabilities of an appropriate education.

Administrative views toward inclusion should consider the research cited here in planning inclusion programs. Additionally, before inclusion can be effective, the following questions must be considered:

1. Have goals and objectives been well defined?

2. Have the personality and attitudes of teachers and staff members toward disability been considered?

3. Are the adequate supportive and related services, technical support, technology, and resources present for serving various disabilities?

4. Are competent personnel available?

5. Are staff members aware of the many innovative instructional packages, strategies, and delivery models for serving these children presently in use?

6. Is parental and community support present?

Site-Based Decision Making

According to Podemski, Marsh, Smith, Tom, & Price (1995), site-based decision making is an emerging school organizational structure associated with decentralized decision making. The concept derives from Japanese manufacturing, and can be located in the sociological literature on the advantages of participative management. This organizational structure involves decentralizing decision making through collaborating with stakeholders.

Administrators using site-based decision-making strategies are given greater autonomy to make decisions, which usually results in a more dynamic and responsive school for educating children with disabilities. Decisions made about operating the school are likely to work because local administrators who have been involved in making the decisions are committed to seeing the decisions implemented (Podemski et al., 1995). For other types of organizational structures for special education programs, see chapter 4.

National Education Goals

The National Education Goals Panel (1992), Young (1993), and Riley (1993) concurred that the National Goals do not address specific concerns for students with disabilities, but administrators should be aware of their implications for these children, as follows:

1. All American children will start school ready to learn. Due to development delays of many children with disabilities, if they are to achieve significant experiences from schools, they must be admitted at an earlier age than their nondisabled peers. This will permit personnel to develop strategies to minimize, eradicate, or reduce the disabling conditions, which if not corrected will impeded school progress.

2. At least 90 percent of our students will graduate from high school. Podemski et al. (1995) provided the following implication for children with disabilities: "If this goal is not equating the traditional high school diploma as the standard of graduation, this could be a powerful goal for special population students. In reality, there is controversy over special diplomas and boards of education making a variety of decisions related to graduate requirements and processes. Unfortunately, some of these decisions exclude students with disabilities and primary language other than English." (p. 115)

3. Our students will demonstrate competency in challenging subject matter and will learn to use their minds well, so they may be prepared for responsible citizenship, further learning, and productive employment. School experiences for children with disabilities must provide academic, social, and vocational skills to equip them for the world of work and productive citizenship.

4. American students will be first in the world in science and mathematic achievement. Children with disabilities have a need for science and mathematic skills in order to prepare them for employment in the 21st century. Many of the jobs in this century will require skills in high technology. Children with disabilities will need all possible science and mathematical skills to compete for employment.

5. Every adult will be literate and have the knowledge and skills necessary to compete in the a world economy and exercise their rights and responsibilities

of citizenship. It is the democratic right of all children with disabilities to profit sufficiently from educational experiences that will equip them for competitive employment as adults.

6. Every school will be safe and drug free and offer a disciplined environment. Children with disabilities must be provided with appropriate intervention, conducted by competent personnel, for reducing and treating behavior and drug-related behavior associated with antisocial behaviors. The policy of "zero tolerance" must be reviewed in light of drug-induced behaviors of children with disabilities.

•• SUMMARY

Reforms in education greatly depend on teachers reconsidering their roles. Administrators and teachers will have to make several changes if transitions are to be significant. McLaughlin and Talbert (1993) state that teachers should move from individualism to professional community by substituting individual work for joint and team work. This approach will permit a strong school element to develop based on trust, collegiality, and openness.

Newmann and Wehlage (1995) state that teachers should change their focus from teaching at the center to learning at the center. When teachers deemphasize the technology of teaching and emphasize the construction of learning, they instruct children differently (Schaefer, 1995). Teachers who employ this approach design individual programs based on the assessed needs of children, and they relate school learning to the world of work.

Teachers in reformed schools must be accountable for the performances of children with disabilities under their supervision. High teacher expectations should be established in classes as well as the total school. Expectations of children must expand beyond the boundaries of the classroom and encompass the total school. Effective teacher involvement can contribute significantly to the school's management plan. Strategies for improving teacher leadership require teachers to become equal partners in the decision-making process; such an arrangement can augment the principal's leadership ability in the schools.

Administrators must consider educational reforms for children with disabilities carefully. Historically, they have ignored reforms in special education. Many have not been sensitive to the needs of these children in reforming practices and policies. Administrators must examine reform issues closely and take initiative in areas that promote the treatment and education of these children.

•• REFERENCES

Aefsy, F. (1995). *Inclusion confusion: A guide to educating students with exceptional needs.* Thousand Oaks, CA: Corwin Press.

American Institutes for Research. (1999). *An educator's guide to school-wide reform.* Arlington, VA: Educational Research Service.

Anderson, R. D. (1996). *Study of curriculum reform* (ORAD-96-1309). Washington, DC: U.S. Department of Education.

Baker, E. T., Wang, M. & Walberg, H. G. (1995). The effects of inclusion on learning. *Educational Leadership, 59*(4), 33–35.

Baker, J., & Zigmond, N. (1990). *Full-time mainstreaming: Are learning disabled students integrated into the instructional program?* Paper presented at the Annual Meeting of the American Education Research Association, Boston, MA: ERIC Document Reproduction Service, No. PD 320 373.

Barry, A. L. (1995). Easing into inclusion classrooms. *Educational Leadership, 52*(4), 406.

Bennett, R., Deluca, D., & Burns, D. (1997). Putting inclusion into practice. *Exceptional Children, 64*(1), 115–131.

Berger, S. (1995). Incluson: A legal mandate—An educational dream. *Updating School Board Politics, 26*(4), 104.

Blumberg, A. (1986). *Effective school principals.* Report of the Southern Regional Education Board. Atlanta, GA: ERIC Document Reproduction Service No. Ed. 376 740, U.S. Department of Education.

Borthwick-Duffy, S. A., Palmer, D. S., & Lane, K. L. (1996). One size doesn't fit all: Full inclusion and individual differences. *Journal of Behavioral Education, 6*, 311–329.

Brandt, R. S. (2000). *Education in a new era.* Alexandria, VA: Association for Supervision and Curriculum Development.

Brooks, J. G., & Brooks, M. G. (1993). *In search of understanding: The case of constructivist classrooms.* Alexandria, VA: Association for Supervision and Curriculum Development.

Brown, L. P., Schwartz, A., Unvari-Solner, E. F., Kampshroer, F., Johnson, J., Jorgensen, J., & Greenwald, L. (1991). How much time should students with severe disabilities spend in regular classrooms and elsewhere? *Journal of the Association for Persons with Severe Disabilities, 16*, 39–47.

Corey, S. (1993). *Helping other people change.* Columbus, OH: State University Press.

David, J. (1995, 1996). The who, what, and why of site-based management. *Educational Leadership, 53*, 4–9.

Education Commission on the States. (1998a). *Comprehensive school reform: Allocating federal funds.* Denver, CO: Author.

Education Commission on the States. (1998b). *Comprehensive school reform: Allocating federal funds.* Denver, CO: Author.

Fege, A. F. (2000). From fund raising to hell raising: New roles for parents. *Educational Leadership, 57*(7), 39–43.

Fuchs, D., & Fuchs, L. (1994). Inclusive schools movement and the radicalization of special education reform. *Exceptional Children, 60,* 294–309.

Fuchs, D., & Fuchs, L. (1995). Sometimes separate is better. *Educational Leadership, 50*(4), 22–26.

Fuchs, D., Fuchs, L., & Bishop, N. (1992). Teacher planning for students with learning disabilities: Differences between general and special education. *Learning Disabilities Research and Practice, 7,* 120–128.

Fullan, M., & Miles, M. B. C. (1992). Getting reform right: What works and what doesn't? *Phi Delta Kappan, 73,* 744–752.

Glatthorn, A. A. (1998). *Performance assessment and standard-based curriculums.* Larchmont, NY: Eye on Education.

Grandmont, R. P. (1995, March). Curriculum revision: A step-by-step approach. *Principal, 80*(569), 46–47.

Grasmick, N. S. (2000). How Maryland communicates change? *Educational Leadership, 57*(7), 44–47.

Hill, P. T., Foster, D. E., & Gendler, T. (1990). *High schools with character.* Santa Monica, CA: Rand.

Hollis, J., & Gallegos, E. (1993). Inclusion: What is the extent of a school district's duty to accommodate students with disabilities in the regular classroom? *Texas School Administrator's Legal Digest, 9*(9), 4–7.

Holloway, J. H. (2000). The promise and pitfalls of site-based management. *Educational Leadership, 57*(7), 81–82.

Johnston, D., Proctor, W., & Carey, S. (1995). Not a way out: A way in. *Educational Leadership, 50*(4), 46–49.

Knapp, M. S., Adelman, N. E., Needels, M. C., Zucker, A.A., McCollum, H., Turnbull, B. L., Marder, C., & Shields, P. M. (1991). *What is taught and how to teach children of poverty* (LC 88054001). Washington, DC: U.S. Department of Education.

Levey, J., & Acker-Hocevar, M. (1998). *Site-based management: Retrospective understanding and future directions* (ERIC Document Reproductive Service No. ED 428 439).

Lounsbury, J. H. (1991). A fresh start for the middle school curriculum. *Middle School Journal, 23*(2), 3–7.

McChesney, J., & Hertling, E. (2000). The path to comprehensive school reform. *Educational Leadership, 57*(7), 10–15.

McCloskey, W., Mikow-Porto, V., & Bingham, S. (1998). *Reflecting on progress: Site-based management and school improvement in North Carolina.* U.S. Department of Education, ERIC Document Reproduction Service No. 421 766.

McDonnell, L. (1989). *Restructuring American schools: The promise and the pitfalls* (Conference paper No. 10). New York: Institute on Education and the Economy, Teachers College, Columbia University.

McLaughlin, M. W., & Talbert, J. (1993). *Contexts that matter for teaching and learning.* Stanford, CA: Stanford University, Context Center on Secondary School Teaching.

Mofett, C. A. (2000). Sustaining change: The answers are blowing in the wind. *Educational Leadership, 57*(7), 35–38.

National Educational Goals Panel. (1992). *World class standards for American education.* Washington, DC: U.S. Department of Education.

Newmann, F., & Wehlage, G. (1995). *Successful school restructuring.* Board of Regents, University of Wisconsin.

Odden, E., & Wohlstetter, P. (1995). Making school-based management work. *Educational Leadership, 52*, 32–36.

Olson, L. (1998). Study: School-wide reform not easy. *Education Week, 22*, 3.

Podemski, R. S., Marsh II, G. E., Smith, D., & Price, J. B. (1995). *Comprehensive administration of special education.* Englewood Cliffs, NJ: Prentice Hall.

Roach, V. (1995). Beyond the rhetoric. *Phi Delta Kappan, 77*, 295–299.

Riley, R. (1993). A conversation with the U.S. Secretary of Education. *National Forum, 73*(4), 5–7.

Rogers, J. (1993). The inclusion revolution. *Research Bulletin, 1*(11), 106.

Roth, K. L. (1994). Second thoughts about interdisciplinary studies. *American Educator, 19*(1), 44–48.

Schaefer, C. M. (1995). Technology can extend your school's art program. *The Executive Educator, 22*(1), 37–38.

Scruggs, T. E., & Mostropierei, M. A. (1996). Teachers perceptions mainstreaming/inclusion: A research synthesis. *Exceptional Children, 63*(1), 59–74.

Shanker, A. (1995). Full inclusion is neither force nor appropriate. *Educational Leadership, 50*(4), 18–21.

Staub, D., & Peck, C. (1995). What are the outcomes for non-disabled students? *Educational Leadership, 50*(4), 36–39.

Taylor, G. R. (2000). *Parental involvement: A practical guide for collaboration and team work for students with disabilities.* Springfield, IL: Charles C Thomas.

U.S. Department of Education. (1998). *Profiles of successful school-wide programs.* Washington, DC: Author.

Vann, A. S. (1995). Give us a say on school budgets. *The Executive Educator,* *22*(1), 41.

Vars, G. (1991). Integrated curriculum in historical perspective. *Educational Leadership, 49*(2), 14–15.

Viadero, D. (June 1989). Who's in, who's out. *Education Week,* pp. 1–12.

Waldron, N. L., & McLeskey, J. (1998). The effects of an inclusive school program on students with mild and severe learning disabilities. *Exceptional Children, 64*(3), 395–405.

Wang, M. C., Reynold, M. C., & Walberg, H. J. (1995). Serving students at the margins. *Educational Leadership, 50*(4), 12–17.

Wohlstetter, P., & Mohrman, S. A. (1994). School-based management: Promise and process. *Consortium for Policy Research in Education,* 1–8.

Young, M. W. (1993). Countdown: The goals 2000 Educate American Act. *National Forum, 73*(4), 3–4.

Zigmond, N., Jenkins, J., Fuchs, L., Fuchs, D., Baker, J., Jenkins, L., & Couthino, M. (1995). Special education in restricted schools: Finds from three multi-year students. *Phi Delta Kappan, 76*, 531–540.

CHAPTER 3

Incidences
of Disability

During the past two decades, tremendous progress has been made in the field of special education. One of the major outgrowths of this thrust has been directed toward making special education a part, rather than a separate entity, of regular education.

Traditionally, special education programs were not initiated in response to the needs of disabled individuals, but rather as expedient measures to resist a perceived threat to the existing goals for normal children. The anticipated purpose of such classes was to develop within the student basic attitudes, habits, and skills that would enable his or her satisfactory adjustment to life in an increasingly complex society. Basic to the achievement of this goal was the ability of the pupils to use these attitudes, habits, and skills in securing and holding a job. Much controversy exists because many specialists agree that special education has not provided disabled individuals with a viable education.

Today, many organizational structures are being developed to maintain disabled individuals in the mainstream of education. However, these structures do not appear to eliminate categorical labels that have plagued special education since its inception. Another type of classification system is needed that focuses on educational variables rather than etiology. This chapter reviews incidences of disability and provides an overview of the classification system used by some school districts (Taylor, 1999).

•• HISTORICAL OVERVIEW

Prior to the early part of the nineteenth century, disabled individuals were at the mercy of the societies in which they lived. Notions regarding handicapping conditions were closely linked with spirits and mysticism. Since there was no universal understanding of individual differences, some exceptional individuals were avoided or placed in institutions and ignored. Inhuman treatment was rather pronounced for many of the mentally and physically handicapped. The gifted individual was usually exploited and his or her abilities were used to promote selfish interests within society. Research concerning the exceptional individual was practically unheard of prior to the eighteenth century.

The early history of the United States was closely linked with a strong religious philosophy. Imperfect individuals were believed to be bedeviled. Consequently, disabled individuals were considered outside the realm of religion. Since religion played a dominant role in the politics of the United States during this time, realistic planning and treatment for the disabled individual was severely hampered.

During the early nineteenth century, improved attitudes toward disabled individuals were championed by such leaders as Horace Mann, Samuel Gridley Howe, Dorothea Dix, and Thomas Gallaudet. Mann and Howe spoke out on behalf of the retarded; Dix pleaded for the socially maladjusted; and Gallaudet was instrumental in promoting programs for the deaf. These leaders gave impetus to the movement establishing residential schools for the disabled. It was proven that appropriate teaching procedures could be successful in helping disabled individuals became useful citizens. Societal pressure, including numerous protests from the parents of disabled children, led to the change from residential schools to day schools.

Classification of disabled children was accelerated by Goddard. He brought the Binet-Simon Intelligence Test to the United States in 1914, which Lewis Terman standardized for American children by Lewis Terman in 1916. This began the era of mental testing in the United States. Mental testing revealed that distinct differences exist between individuals. Practices and attitudes began to change from concepts of custodial care and treatment to creating programs of education and rehabilitation for disabled individuals. The influence of the world wars had far-reaching effects on the education of disabled individuals. Many servicemen, including professionals and businessmen, frequently returned from combat with a disability, thus focusing public attention on disabilities. People were forced to think about previous familial attitudes and religious positions regarding disabilities. Combined, these factors caused public agencies, especially the schools, to give increasing attention to individuals who had exceptional differences (Taylor, 2001).

•• PRESENT-DAY TRENDS

The role of U.S. public schools parallels the social and historical movements in our culture. Education was viewed as such an important function that the constitution of each state provides for a system designed to provide educational opportunities for all children. Children who deviated in mental, physical, social, or emotional traits to a degree that they could not reach their optimum growth in regular classes were not covered in most state constitutions until the beginning of the nineteenth century. Today, most states provide educational opportunities for all disabled individuals.

Interest in special education has greatly increased because of the events of recent years. The influence of parent movement groups shows their deep concern for the future welfare of disabled individuals. A significant factor is the social change in attitude toward the disabled individual, instilled into the minds of the general public by parents. Changes in attitude with regard to the education of the disabled have led to their inclusion in the public school system. Scientific advances have enabled many individuals with disabilities to enter the mainstream of education. A case in point is the development of electronic devices that have made it more practical to maintain the hard of hearing in the schools. Another advance was the launching of the Russian Sputnik that spurred technology, renewing interest in education of the gifted.

As a result of these developments, administrators had to institute many reforms in educating children with disabilities. John F. Kennedy was the first president to introduce a national plan to combat mental retardation. Since then, federal, local, and state governments support programs for disabled individuals financially through several agencies. Therefore, administrators of special education programs are being presented with a new thrust that stresses continuity and appropriateness of educational programs and also emphasizes effectiveness in delivering services to disabled individuals (Taylor, 1999, 2001). Advancements have been made in knowledge, program development, remedial techniques, behavior modification, evaluation, and a variety of individualized techniques unparalleled in the history of special education. Significant advances have also been made during the past decade toward the economic and social integration of disabled individuals into society, rectifying some of the ills resulting from segregating disabled individuals. Unfortunately, modifications in instructional strategies are still sometimes based on outdated psychological or medical models as well as conventional classification systems.

•• CONVENTIONAL DEFINITIONS AND CLASSIFICATIONS OF DISABLED CHILDREN

The conventional term *disabled children* denotes many different degrees of disability. According to numerous authorities, the term is difficult to define because disability represents a variety of medical and psychological categories.

The consensus, therefore, is that a general definition for a disabled child is one who deviates mentally, physically, socially, or emotionally so markedly from what is considered normal growth and development that the child cannot receive maximum benefit from a regular school program unless modifications are made in the instructional program or special instruction and ancillary services are provided to enable the child to achieve at a level commensurate with the child's respective abilities (Blackhurst & Berdine, 1993; Gallagher & Ansastasiow, 1933; Hardman, Drew, Egan, & Wolf, 1993; Heyward & Orlansky, 1992; Kaplan, 1996; Taylor, 1998, 1999, 2001).

These authors generally agreed that many operational definitions of exceptionality are statistical and quantitative. The mentally retarded can be defined as the intellectually lowest 2 or 3 percent of the population as indicated by intelligence tests, whereas the intellectually gifted can be defined in terms of test scores at the upper 1 or 2 percent of the general population. The hard of hearing and the deaf can be identified in terms of hearing loss as measured in decibels by a standard audiometer. Blindness is typically defined legally as a visual acuity of 20/200 or less in the better eye after maximum correction or as a possession of a visual field limited to 20 degrees or less. There are no conventional qualitative indexes of most other types of individuals, such as the orthopedically handicapped, the socially maladjusted, the emotionally disturbed, the epileptic, and the individuals with speech defects. In most of these conditions, the diagnostic judgment of trained specialists replaces quantitative measurement. Administrators of special education programs should be apprised that all of the definitions here appear to operate from medical or psychological terminology and have little relevancy for educational intervention.

Disabled individuals are generally grouped on the basis of their major deviation or handicapped and may be classified as follows: (1) mentally handicapped, (2) learning disabled (3) emotionally unstable, (4) traumatic brain injury and socially maladjusted health impairments (those with special or language defects) (6) blind and hard of seeing, (7) deaf and hard of hearing, (8) orthopedic impairments, (9) those with special health impairments, and (10) multiple handicapped.

Various authorities have advanced different categories for areas of disabilities in the following areas: (1) communication disorders, (2) mental deviations, including the gifted and the mentally retarded, (3) sensory handicaps, including individuals with auditory and visual handicaps, (4) neuralgic, orthopedic, and other health impairments, and (5) behavior disorders, including the socially maladjusted and the emotionally disturbed (Blackhurst & Berdine, 1993; Heyward & Orlansky, 1992; Kaplan, 1996; Meyen, 1990; Norris, Haring, &

Haring, 1994; Taylor, 1998, 1999, 2001; Ysseldyke, Alozzine, & Thurlow, 1992). Similarly, Cruickshank (1963) divided the areas of deviations into the following categories: (1) the intellectually exceptional individual, including the gifted and the mentally retarded, and (2) the physically handicapped, including visual and auditory handicaps, speech handicaps, and orthopedic and neurological impairments. The classification systems discussed here are based on the authors just cited.

Mental Retardation

Mental retarded pupils demonstrate significantly subaverage intellectual functioning existing concurrently with deficits in adaptive behavior, manifested during the developmental period, that adversely affects a child's educational performance. Students eventually labeled "mentally retarded" are often referred because of generalized slowness. They lag behind their age-mates in most areas of academic achievements, social and emotional development, language ability, and perhaps physical development. This slowness must be demonstrated on an individually administered test of intelligence that is appropriate for the student being assessed. Thus the test must be appropriate not only for the age of the student but also for the pupil's acculturation and physical and sensory abilities. However, a test of intelligence is not enough. The pupil must also demonstrate slowness in adaptive behavior. An assessment for mental retardation should always contain an assessment of achievement, intelligence, and adaptive behavior.

Learning Disability

Learning disabled pupils are those who demonstrate a disorder in one or more of the basic psychological processes involved in understanding or in using language, spoken or written, that may manifest itself in the imperfect ability to listen, think, read, write, spell, or do mathematical calculations. The term learning disabilities includes such conditions as perceptual handicaps, brain injury, minimal brain dysfunction, dyslexia, and development aphasia. The term does not apply to children who have learning problems that are primarily the result of visual or hearing deficits or environmental, cultural, or economic disadvantages. Students eventually labeled "learned disabled" are often referred because of inconsistent performance; they are likely to have pronounced patterns of academic and cognitive strengths and weaknesses. For example, Joe is unable to learn to read, no matter what his teacher tries; Joyce may be reading at grade level, be a good speller, have highly developed language skills, but not be able to master addition and subtraction facts.

Criteria for eligibility for services for the learning disabled vary considerably from state to state. Generally, a pupil must demonstrate normal (or at least non-retarded) general intellectual development on an individually administered test of intelligence. The student must also demonstrate, on an individually administered test of achievement, some areas within the normal range while demonstrating significantly delayed development in other areas of achievement and demonstrating (correct) hearing and vision within normal limits. Eligible pupils do not have significant emotional problems or cultural disadvantages. Finally, the basic process disorder that causes the learning disability may or may not have to be tested, depending on the particular state's education code. If it is assessed, measures of visual and auditory perception, as well as measures of linguistic and psycholinguistic abilities, could be administered.

Emotional Disturbed and Socially Maladjusted

Emotionally disturbed and socially maladjusted pupils exhibit one or more of the following characteristics over a long period of time and to a marked degree that adversely affects educational performance: (1) an inability to learn that cannot be explained by intellectual, sensory, or health factors; (2) an inability to build or maintain satisfactory interpersonal relationships with peers and teachers; (3) inappropriate types of behavior or feelings under normal circumstances; (4) a general pervasive mood of unhappiness or depression; or (5) a tendency to develop physical symptoms or fears associated with personal or school problems. Students eventually labeled "emotionally disturbed" are often referred for problems in interpersonal relations (for example, fighting or extreme noncompliance) or unusual behavior (for example, unexplained noncompliance or unexplained episodes of crying or extreme mood swings). Requirements for establishing a pupil's eligibility for special education services for the emotionally disturbed vary markedly among the states. Some or all of the following sources of information may be used in determining eligibility: observational data, behavioral rating scales, psychological evaluations, and examination by a board-certified psychiatrist or psychologist.

Traumatic Brain Injury

Students with traumatic brain injury have an acquired injury to the brain caused by an external physical force, resulting in total or partial functional disability or psychology impairment, or both, that adversely affects a child's educational performance. The term applies to open or closed head injuries resulting in impairments in one or more areas, such as cognition, language, memory, attention, reasoning, abstract thinking, judgment, problem solving, sensory, perceptual, and motor abilities, psychosocial behavior, physical functions, information processing, and speech. The term does not apply to brain injuries that are congenital or degenerative or brain injuries induced by birth trauma. Students with traumatic brain injury have normal development until they sustain a severe head injury. As a result of injury, they are disabled. Most head injuries are the result of an accident (frequently, automobile accidents) but may also occur as a result of physical abuse or intentional harm (for example, being shot). Traumatic brain injury is diagnosed by a physician, who is usually a specialist (a neurologist), and educators identify the school-based deficits.

Speech or Language Impairment

A student with a speech or language impairment has a communication disorder such as stuttering, impaired articulation, a language impairment, or a voice impairment that adversely affects his or her educational performance. Many children experience some developmental problems in their speech and language. For example, children frequently have difficulty with the "r" sound and say "wabbit" instead of "rabbit." Similarly, many children use incorrect grammar, especially with internal plurals; for example, children may say, "My dog has four foots." Such difficulties are so common they are considered a part of normal speech development. However, when such speech and language errors continue to occur beyond the age when most children have developed correct speech or language, there is cause for concern. School personnel identify the educational disability, and speech and language specialists use a variety of assessment procedures, norm-referenced tests, systematic observation, and criterion-referenced tests to identify the speech and language disability.

Visual Impairment

A student with a visual impairment has impairment in vision that, even with correction, adversely affects the child's educational development. Visual impairment includes both partial sight and blindness. Students with severe visual impairments are usually identified before entering school, although some partially sighted students may not be identified until school age, when visual demands increase. Assessments of previously undiagnosed visually impaired students may indicate gross- and fine-motor problems or variable visual performance (that is, performance that varies with the size of print, amount of light, and fatigue, for example). Visual acuity and visual field are usually assessed by an ophthalmologist. A specialist assesses functional vision through systemic observation of a student's responses to various types of paper, print sizes, lighting conditions, and so forth.

Deafness and Hearing Impairment

Deafness is impairment in hearing so severe that the child is impaired in processing linguistic information through hearing, with or without amplification, and the deficit adversely affects the child's educational performance. A student with a hearing impairment has impairment in hearing, whether permanent or fluctuating, that adversely affects a child's educational performance, but this is not included under the definition of deafness. Even severe hearing impairments may be difficult to identify in the first years of life, and students with milder hearing impairments may not be identified until school age. Referrals for undiagnosed hearing-impaired students may indicate both expressive and receptive language problems, variable hearing performance, problems in attending to aural tasks, and perhaps problems in peer relationships. Diagnosis of hearing impairment is usually made by audiologists, who identify the auditory disability, in conjunction with school personnel, who identify the educational disability.

Orthopedic Impairments

An orthopedic impairment adversely affects a child's education performance. The terms includes impairments caused by congenital anomaly (e.g., clubfoot, absence of some member, etc.), impairments caused by disease (e.g., poliomyelitis, bone tuberculosis, etc.), and impairments from other causes (e.g., cerebral palsy, amputations, and fractures or burns that cause contractors). Pupils with physical disabilities are generally identified prior to entering school. However, accidents and disease may impair a previously normal student. Medical diagnosis establishes the presence of the condition. The severity of the condition may be established in part by medical opinion and in part by systematic observation of the particular student.

Other Health Impairments

Other health impairments are conditions that limit strength, vitality, or alertness and chronic or acute health problems such as a heart condition, tuberculosis, rheumatic fever, nephritis, asthma, sickle-cell anemia, hemophilia, epilepsy, lead poisoning, leukemia, or diabetes that adversely affect a child's educational performance. Diagnosis of health impairments is usually made by physicians, who identify health problems, and school personnel, who identify the educational disability.

Multiple Disabilities

Individuals with multiple disabilities comprise a small percentage of the population. Estimates range from 0.1 to 1.0 percent. Approximately 4 out of every 1,000 individuals are multiple disabled when the primary symptom is mental retardation. Multiple disabilities are the results of many causes, including birth defects, genetic disorders, chromosomal abnormalities, phenylketonuria, poor maternal health, drugs, poor nutrition, and infectious diseases. These children are generally recognized easily at birth due to many physical abnormalities. Additionally, they may have a combination of the disabilities listed here.

•• INCIDENCES OF DISABLED CHILDREN

Disabled children constitute approximately 7 to 12 percent of the general population. Part of the difficulty in determining the number of disabled children is due to various definitions used by different disciplines in identifying the disabled individual and the lack of consensus concerning the classification and selection criteria. States differ in their classification systems, and to compound the problem, local school districts in various states also differ (Taylor, 2001).

The number of children identified as retarded reflects certain political connotations. In the United States, the number of retarded individuals is generally accepted as approximately 3 percent of the total population. In some countries, such as the former Soviet Union, there is a generally accepted figure of 1 percent. The difference in the Soviet figures reflects two basic concepts: first, mental retardation is a condition caused by heredity or some central nervous system condition (approximately 1 percent); second, the 2 percent additionally identified in the United States, according to Soviet authorities, is the direct result of social inadequacies reflecting the evils of capitalism and exploitation. Growing numbers of scientists in the United States are beginning to recognize there are large numbers of individuals who function as though they are retarded because of factors in society such as social class, race, inappropriate use of tests, inadequate environments, attitude, health, diet, and quality of education, which modify performance as measured by intelligence tests. How many of these factors are the result of capitalism and exploitation, as suggested by the Russians, is difficult to assess. However, unquestionably changes in social policies and attitudes may alter the number of children classified as retarded.

A different way of evaluating incidence is to identify the severity of the handicap. This often occurs when administrators must provide school programs and services. The severely to profoundly handicapped, the totally deaf, the multiple handicapped, the blind, the severely retarded, and the psychotic are a comparatively small number (less than 1 percent of the population) and usually identified long before they come to school. Most children with severe disabilities are currently served outside of the regular public school, and they require the efforts of many public and private programs.

U.S. Office of Education statistics appear to provide the best data on the number of exceptional children in schools. The Office of Education has provided estimates since 1922. In 1964 Congress created the Bureau of Education for the Handicapped within the Office of Education. In order to provide more reliable data from the states, federal regulation in 1967 required all state departments of education to submit reports on the number of exceptional children that schools were serving. The office, presently housed in the U.S. Department of Education, is called the Office of Special Education Programs (OSEP). It is presently engaged in providing updated, precise data for future use. The data in Table 1 are based on estimated 1994 to 1996 population statistics as reported by the Office of Special Education Programs.

•• THE PROCESS OF DETERMINING DISABILITY

In practice, deciding whether a student is disabled can be complex. Multidisciplinary team (MDT) evaluations frequently, and correctly, go beyond the information required by the entitlement criteria. MDTs collect information to rule out other possible disabling conditions. Sometimes the condition that initiates the referral is not the disabling condition. Administrators responsible for classifying pupils must adopt a point of view that is, in part, disconfirmatory, a point of view that looks to disprove the working hypothesis. Administrators must collect information that would allow them to reject the classification if a pupil proves either to be not disabled or suffer from a different disability (Ysseldyke & Alozzine, 1990).

An analysis of definitions, criteria, and diagnostic procedures in the classification of disabled individuals must be based on an understanding of the interrelationships among the various disabling conditions. Others avoid categorical definitions, describing disability individuals. The classification system used by the various states are designed to facilitate identification, evaluation, placement, and programming for disabled individuals.

Most states provide a written description of characteristics based on the IDEA for each categorical type for whom they provide an education. Most states have added two additional categories not found in PL 94-142: (1) multiple disabled and (2) homebound and hospitalized.

•• COMMONALITY AMONG DISABLED INDIVIDUALS

Characteristics attributed to most disabled individuals seem to overlap. Regardless of how disabled individuals are classified, they cannot really be described in neatly self-contained compartments without some overlapping. For example, impaired communication is recognized as a common element in

Table 1: Number of Students Served under IDEA, Part B, by Age Group, 1994–1996

Age Group	1994–1995	Percentage of Total	1995–1996	Percentage of Total	Change Number	Change Percentage
3–5	522,710	9.63	548,441	9.76	25.731	4.9
6–11	2,515,487	46.32	2,581,061	45.93	65,574	2.6
12–17	2,153,448	39.66	2,237,124	39.81	83,676	3.9
18–21	238,578	4.39	252,473	4.49	13,895	5.8
6–17	4,668,935	85.98	4,818,185	85.75	149,250	3.2
6–21	4,907,513	90.37	5,070,658	90.24	163,145	3.3
3–21	5,430,223	100.00	5,619,099	100.00	188,876	3.5

Source: U.S. Department of Education, Office of Special Education Programs. Data Analysis Systems (DANS).

the assessment and remediation of learning disabilities, emotional disturbance, and mental retardation.

Perceptual disorders are identified as important characteristics frequently attributed to individuals with learning disorders. The same characteristics of perceptual disorders are also seen among some individuals with cerebral palsy, mental retardation, hearing handicaps, and others. It thus seems reasonable to state that with few major exceptions, most disabled children have in common many similar characteristics.

Characteristics that differentiate disabled individuals from each other are directly related to categorical classifications that should be of interest to administrators. They should know that retardates have problems chiefly in the area of cognitive development; the crippled in motor development; the blind and deaf in sensory deficiencies. The majority of disabled individuals not only have primary disabilities but also associated secondary disabilities that may contribute significantly to their disabling conditions (Taylor, 2001).

•• HANDICAPS VERSUS DISABILITIES

Disabled individuals may have disabilities in several areas of functioning, such as hearing and speech. Most authorities agree that the impairment of structure or function is a disability. It is incumbent on administrators to distinguish the difference between a disability and a handicap. A disability does not necessarily denote a handicap. A handicap is a social phenomenon. Handicaps arise when standards instituted by society make a person stand out or draw attention to his or her disability.

Special education exists mainly because society chooses to treat disabled individuals differently. Special classes, treatment, labeling, and attitudes displayed by society combine to single out individuals as disabled. These factors operate to remove disabled individuals further from the mainstream of society and pinpoint their disabilities. Minimal adaptations are often enough to help disabled individuals overcome the negative effects of their disabilities.

A handicap should be defined in terms of the situation or condition. A disabled individual who is crippled should not be classified as disabled if he or she can perform a task that does not require excessive movement or locomotion. Blindness should not constitute a disability if vision is not required to perform the task. These examples may be generalized to most areas of disabilities. If disabled individuals can perform as normal under certain conditions, their disabilities should not be classified as disabling conditions. In essence, for example, simply because Joe is blind, his disability should not be equated with a global disability. Joyce might be able to operate within normal ranges on certain tasks if society provides the opportunities for her to demonstrate her skills (Taylor, 2001).

Note that within each disability category, conditions might exist in mild, moderate, and severe forms. The mild to moderate levels are those pupils who have more contact with regular education programs. Pupils who have severe disabling conditions are most often educated in more restrictive settings with fewer interactions with the regular education program. All disabled children should be educated with their normal peers to the extent their disabilities permit.

•• SUMMARY

The history of educating children with disabilities does not reflect equality of education opportunities. Since the early nineteenth century, some progress has been made. Recognition of the educational rights of children with disabilities was not completed in isolation. A variety of forces, such as parental groups, national associations representing the various exceptionalities, and federal and state laws, have been instrumental in bringing about change. Changes have been slow, but continual. Today, all children with disabilities have the right to a free and appropriate education.

In spite of the various federal laws, school districts throughout the country have not done a satisfactory job in providing quality education for children with disabilities. In order for the schools to come into compliance with the law, administrators must use the available research and resources and experiment with radical intervention models that address the needs of children with disabilities as reflected throughout this text.

As a practical guide to understanding and helping disabled individuals, the following suggestions are made for administrators of special education programs to consider:

1. Individuals with disabilities, with rare exceptions, are basically more like other individuals than they are different, and areas of similarity and strengths should not be neglected.

2. Acceptance is of paramount concern to disabled individuals. When acceptance is clearly communicated, disabled individuals see themselves as important, unique, and useful.

3. Disabled individuals are likely to have more difficulties than their normal peers. Thus extra effort must be devoted to provide strategies, materials, adaptations, and assistance in helping them overcome their difficulties.

4. Individuals, regardless of their disabilities, have highly individual learning and personality patterns. No two individuals learn at exactly the same way or at the same speed. Therefore, lockstep methods are usually not desirable and are often ineffectual for disabled individuals. The strengths and weaknesses of individuals, learning styles and modalities, task analyses, and other factors need to be considered in planning learning activities and individualized instruction.

5. Some individuals considered as severely disabled seem to require specific instruction in highly structured settings.

6. Academic skills are part of what disabled individuals need to acquire. Developing adequate self-concept, a sense of worth, coping with skills, and appropriate attitude are also essential for many disabled individuals.

7. Research findings have consistently showed that categorical labels have little significance for educational intervention.

8. Special education should focus on providing services for individuals who have special needs, in most instances through innovating programs in the regular classroom.

•• REFERENCES

Blackhurst, A. E., & Berdine, W. H. (1993). *An introduction to special education* (3rd ed.). Lexington, MA: HarperCollins.

Cruickshank, W. A. (1963). *Psychology of exceptional children and youth.* Englewood Cliffs, NJ: Prentice Hall.

Gallagher, K., & Ansastasiow, N. (1993). *Educating exceptional children.* Boston: Houghton Mifflin.

Goddard, H. H. (1913). *The Kallikak family.* New York: The Macmillan Company.

Hardman, M. L., Drew, C. J., Egan, M. W., & Wolf, B. (1993). *Human exceptionality: Society, school, and family.* Needham Heights, MA: Allyn & Bacon.

Heyward, W., & Orlansky, D. (1992). *Exceptional children* (4th ed.). New York: Merrill.

Kaplan, P. (1996). *Pathways for exceptional children.* Minneapolis: West.

Meyen, E. (1990). *Exceptional children in today's schools.* Denver: Love.

Norris, G., Haring, L., & Haring, T. (1994). *Exceptional children and youth* (6th ed.). New York: Macmillan.

Taylor, G. R. (1998). *Curriculum strategies for teaching social skills to the disabled.* Springfield, IL: Charles C Thomas.

Taylor, G. R. (1999). *Curriculum models and strategies for educating individuals with disabilities in inclusive classrooms.* Springfield, IL: Charles C Thomas.

Taylor, G. R. (2001). *Educational interventions and services for children with exceptionalities: Strategies and perspectives.* Springfield, IL: Charles C Thomas.

Ysseldyke, J., & Alozzine, B. (1990). *Introduction to special education.* Boston: Houghton Mifflin.

Ysseldyke, J., Alozzine, B., & Thurlow, M. (1992). *Critical issues in special education.* Dallas: Houghton Mifflin.

CHAPTER 4

Organizing School Programs for Individuals with Disabilities

•• OVERVIEW

Administrators responsible for administering school programs for individuals with disabilities have similar problems. Some of the challenges include assessment, identification, treatment, transportation, placement, curriculum development, in-service training for teachers, and collaborating with parents and community agencies. This chapter provides guidelines and strategies to help administrators address these problems.

The responsibilities of administrators of special education programs have increased significantly during the last several decades. Much of this increase may be attributed to the passing of recent federal and state laws concerning educating children with disabilities. See chapter 6 for a detailed analysis of legal requirements and rights of individuals with disabilities (Podemski, Marsh, Smith, Tom, & Price, 1995).

It is generally accepted today by our society that all children are entitled to equality of educational opportunities. We recognize that the perpetuation and improvement of the democratic way of life depends on an educated citizenry. Millions of dollars are spent on public education so all individuals with disabilities may have the opportunity for learning cooperatively and successfully in a democratic society (Taylor, 1999).

For many children with disabilities, unfortunately, public school attendance does not guarantee equality of educational opportunity. This is evident when we look at assessment, treatment, services, resources, and placement of children with disabilities. These areas are fully explored later in the text, and we outline strategies for the school to follow in improving opportunities for these individuals (Jackson & Taylor, 1973).

Although the school does not and should not assume full responsibility for the absence of improved educational opportunities for these children, the school must share responsibility with the community when the educational needs of children with disabilities are not met. A major function of the public school is to recognize each pupil as a unique personality and to assist each one to develop his or her abilities to the fullest in a socially acceptable and desirable way. To achieve this global goal, administrators and educators must carefully take into account the individual differences among individuals with disabilities; all should not be expected to have the same purposes, to progress at the similar rate, or to achieve identical ends (Taylor, 2000).

Additionally, the school environment that administrators help create can encourage or discourage, release or stifle, the development of ideas, the adoption of innovations, and the promotion of cooperative working arrangements for effective education. Administrators can facilitate or retard the degree of success of the school in meeting the needs of individuals with disabilities. Administrators have a major responsibility for providing the conditions and services that will contribute to effective education of individuals with disabilities. Pupil grouping and placement, promotion, management of supplies and equipment, identification of needed resources, assessment and testing programs, and selection and assignment of teachers are among the aspects of school organization and administration that affect the education of the disabled (Podemski et al., 1995).

•• WHAT IS THE SCHOOLS' RESPONSIBILITY IN EDUCATING INDIVIDUALS WITH DISABILITIES?

Children who do deviate greatly and for whom a differentiated school curriculum is needed are commonly called children with disabilities. These children require a generous share of most educators' time, thoughts, and actions. The public school thus faces a special challenge in providing a suitable education for many of these children who may deviate directly in their development. The school usually attempts to provide adequately for children with disabilities, but its efforts are often far from successful. Nevertheless, the administrator's responsibility still remains to provide equal educational opportunities for children with disabilities who now fail to receive them. Providing equal educational opportunities for these children is intricate, expensive, and complex. The administrator must learn to draw on the services of community agencies and groups to meet their diverse needs. Coordinating community services will assist the individual with disabilities with his or her maximum growth and development in socially desirable directions. Pressure from various sources is demanding that the schools provide quality education for all children with disabilities (Jackson & Taylor, 1973).

Interest in special education is increasingly greatly because of the events of recent years. The influence of parent movement groups is showing they have a deep concern for the future and the welfare of children with disabilities.

•• WHAT IS THE SCHOOL'S RESPONSIBILITY?

Federal, local, and state governments are financially supporting programs for children with disabilities through various agencies. The services rendered to these children are improving considerably. Agencies and the schools are seeking new ways to help children with disabilities, some of whom were once excluded from school. These interests have led to increased research in the fields of bio-chemistry, medicine, psychology, sociology, education, and other allied disci-plines. This surge of interest has increased greatly our understanding of dis-abilities.

Due chiefly to these trends, educational opportunities are available to more children with disabilities in more parts of the United States and in greater variety than ever before, despite a large gap between the number of those in need and those being serviced. The challenge of providing educational oppor-tunities for children with disabilities is being met by local, public, and private schools and by public and private residential schools. Most children with dis-abilities are being educated in public day school programs, commonly called inclusive schools.

Since most children with disabilities are educated in public schools, adminis-trators must assume the direct responsibility for improving educational pro-visions for them and providing an environment that is conducive for their learning.

•• ADMINISTRATIVE RESPONSIBILITIES

As stated, teachers are the ones most directly concerned with the education of children with disabilities, but their effectiveness depends in large measure on the influence of administrators. Teachers must have the support and guidance of able administrators. A modern program of supervision based on sound edu-cational principles enables teachers to gain a deeper understanding of the factors and principles underlying and influencing their practices. Supervision by com-petent, adequately prepared administrators will improve the total teaching and learning process for children with disabilities.

Administrators thus have a major responsibility for providing the conditions and services that will contribute to effective education of these children. Pupil grouping and placement, promotion, management of supplies and equipment, the testing program, and selection and assignment of teachers are among the aspects of school organization and administration that affect the education of all children. How effectively these services contribute to the education of children with disabilities will determine the degree to which equal educational opportunities are provided for them (Castetter, 1981).

•• GOALS OF SPECIAL EDUCATION

The goals of special education are similar to those of the education for all children: to develop and utilize one's physical and mental aptitudes in a socially desirable way. Special education is committed to educating children with disabilities by seeing that each child contributes to his or her own maintenance and becomes a personally and socially adequate person to the extent of his or her abilities.

The National Education Goals listed for all children are appropriate for children with disabilities as well. These goals are addressed in greater detail later and only summarized here:

1. All American children will start school ready to learn.

2. At least 90 percent of our students will graduate.

3. Our students will demonstrate competency in challenging subject matter and will learn to use their minds well, so that they may be prepared for responsible citizenship, further learning, and productive employment.

4. American children will be first in the world in science and mathematic achievements.

5. Every adult will be literate and have the knowledge and skills necessary to compete in a world economy and exercise the rights and responsibilities of citizenship.

6. Every school will be safe and drug-free and offer a disciplined environment conducive to learning. (National Education Goals Panel, 1992)

It is both legally and morally just for administrators of special education programs to provide directions for school personnel to assist children with disabilities in achieving these stated goals.

•• EDUCATIONAL PROVISIONS

The fundamental purposes of special education are the same as those of regular education: to promote the optimal development of the individual as a skillful, free, and purposeful person, able to plan and manage his or her own life and to reach his or her highest potential as an individual and as a member of society. Indeed, special education developed as a set of highly specialized areas of education in order to provide children with disabilities with the same opportunities as other children for a meaningful, purposeful, and fulfilling life (Jackson & Taylor, 1973).

Perhaps the most important concept that has been developed in special education as the result of experiences with these children is that of the fundamental individualism of every child. The aspiration of administrators is to see every child as a unique composite of potentials, abilities, and learning needs for whom an educational program must be designed to meet his or her particular needs. From its beginnings, special education has championed the cause of children with disabilities. Professionals and administrators dedicated to the optimal education of children with disabilities reject the misconception of schooling that is nothing but custodial care.

Special education for children with disabilities was recognized historically as the best service for them to adapt to the traditional educational system. Today, special education may not be the best vehicle to serve the needs of children with disabilities. Therefore, administrators should not perceive special education placement as the sole organizational school structure, but as one part of the total educational process. Children may receive services in inclusive classrooms within the public school. Special instruction and methods for children with disabilities requires that provisions be made for their unique needs in inclusive settings and that school personnel be able to monitor and instruct in a personalized manner (Council for Exceptional Children, 1993; Fuchs & Fuchs, 1994; National Association of State Board of Education, 1992; Waldron & McLeskey, 1998).

A centrally coordinated approach is needed to improve the educational program for children with disabilities. Many school districts do not have adequate services for comprehensive psychological, social, medical, and educational evaluation of children with disabilities; conversely, techniques used for educational diagnosis and evaluation are frequently inadequate. (Refer to chapter 7 for specific details on assessment.)

•• LEGAL PRINCIPLES

Recently, public schools have increasingly assumed responsibility for educating children with disabilities in our society. This surge of interest cannot be significantly equated with the basic principle of free education for all children. The courts and mandates from local, state, and federal governments have insisted that all children in our society have a right to free public education. The result has been the enactment of laws in most states to provide educational opportunities for children with disabilities of all ages (Rabe & Peterson, 1988).

Concomitantly, many school districts have been sued, with the charge that they have not provided educational opportunities for children with disabilities. In the event that disabled children are excused or excluded from school, for illness or medical treatment, they should be readmitted as soon as the reasons for their exclusion have been determined or treated. Exclusion should be temporary and as specifically as possible outline specific procedures governing the child's reentry to school. Administrators should examine the legal issue of suspension carefully before recommending a plan, as outlined under legal requirements in Chapter 6. All possible techniques and resources should be examined before a decision is made. If at all feasible, modification should be made in the program to keep the child in school by providing supportive and specialized services.

•• GUIDANCE

The purpose of guidance is to help the individual achieve personal and social adjustment through a better understanding and use of his or her abilities. In order for guidance to be effective, it must be a continuous process that starts when the child first enters school and available for as long a period of time as necessary. The administrator and teaching personnel should play formal or informal roles in the system of continuous guidance. Hence all will be important to the total concept. Although a special education program in essence is a guidance program, one of the basic techniques of special education is personal guidance or individualization of instruction. Personal guidance can be equated with recognizing the unique problems of each individual and the formulation of techniques for assisting children with disabilities in solving his or her problems.

Vocational or occupational guidance is very important for children with disabilities. Administrators responsible for training programs should consider and plan for the ultimate goal of placement for the disabled. They must be aware of the reported causes of vocational failures and design programs to emphasize desirable behavior patterns. Through accurate appraisal of the disabled's vocational potential, suitable training programs, and selective placement and improved understanding of the relevant factors in the community, the available benefits of training and placement program can be maximized.

The guidance techniques used in special education should be similar to those employed in the regular school program with some adjustment made to meet the special needs of the disabled and the family. Administrators should realize that planning may be intensified due to the many problems inherited with disability. Nevertheless, guidance and counseling for the disabled should be designated to aid the child's adjustment to school from the time of his or her entrance as well as to address the many problems inherited with the disability. Guidance activities should begin with initial contacts to acquaint parents and community with the school's educational program and be extended directly to the child as his or her needs dictate. Guidance services should also seek to provide school personnel with important data useful in planning and adjusting the school program to each child's needs.

•• GROUPING

Grouping for instruction requires the teacher to demonstrate clinical awareness of each child's pattern of strengths and weaknesses by frequently surveying the performance of students in important dimensions. Since many children with disabilities employ certain techniques of learning, irrespective of the one preferred by teachers, the teacher should be aware of these patterns and groups assumed in the classroom. Activities should be sequenced so realistic goals and objectives can be achieved. They must be feasible for these children and relate to the roles they may play in society. Administrators should make modifications in the instructional program as new societal trends and information dictate. School personnel should not be restricted from experimenting with a variety of activities in search for a program adapted to the needs, interests, and ability of children with disabilities.

The attainment of goals for children with disabilities basically is not different from other children, as long as realistic behavioral objectives are developed, based on needs, characteristics, interests, and ability of the child in question. Equally important is the assessment of areas in which the disabled child can achieve some level of success and to sequence methodically his or her educational experiences toward stated objectives. Program content must be individualized and modified to meet the unique needs of each child. No one instructional procedure can serve the needs of any group of disabled children. Moreover, the type of curriculum or instructional procedure used will greatly depend on the observed traits of each child.

During the course of a school year, administrators may need to request the consultative services of specialists in various disciplines. The integrated approach to learning, which is so necessary for the disabled, requires that the services of specialists be coordinated and integrated with the work of the school. Joint participation of school and allied disciplines enables research and current findings in the field of disability to become a part of daily classroom teaching.

If the schools are going to commit to providing universal education for disabled children, special services must be provided so they might have equal educational opportunities. Many disabled children deviate so greatly in physical, mental, emotional, and cultural needs that special services and modification in the instructional program must be made if they are to attend school or to profit from its instruction. The schools have not been very effective in serving many of the needs of disabled children. The educational system has consistently ignored pleas for change to make school experiences more relevant to children who may not be neither highly motivated nor achievement oriented or who come from culturally different backgrounds. The schools can more effectively serve the disabled child if a thorough assessment of his or her abilities or disabilities is made, and the disabled has the right to be placed in an inclusive environment or one that supports his or her needs. Providing special services to the disabled should not be misconstrued by the schools as a social service, but rather understood as fulfilling the educational rights of disabled children as mandated under local, state, and federal laws.

•• FINANCIAL PROBLEMS

The cost of an adequate educational program for children with disabilities requires special allocations in the school budget (Berne, 1998; Hartman, 1988). An adequate enriched program for the disabled requires a financial outlay that is proportionately greater than that for normal children. The materials and equipment needed for the practical experiences of these children are expensive when provided in sufficient quantity and variety. Proper education for the disabled requires higher per capita expenditure than for the nondisabled. Federal, state, and local governments are mandated by law to provide financial support to improve the educational opportunities of disabled children.

It is doubtful that local school systems can design comprehensive programs for the disabled without the aid of external financial support. Through federal and state support and grants, school districts are motivated to improve and develop new programs. The high cost of educating children with disabilities can be justified when we consider the consequences to the community of not providing a suitable education for them. A community that neglects children with disabilities is likely to pay a higher price later for unemployment, welfare, relief, and delinquency that stem largely from lack of proper education. In the long run, effective school programs for these children does not nearly equal the price of neglect.

Administrators should be cognizant of other provisions that require financial support, over and beyond that required for nondisabled children, such as transportation, instructional programs, and supportive services and personnel. If democratic principles of education are to be adhered to for educating children with disabilities, financial considerations must be given without additional financial burden placed on parents or guardians.

One of the most expensive expenditures in providing quality education for disabled children and youth is that of securing teaching and supportive personnel. The success of any administrative organization depends greatly on the abilities of the personnel on all levels. Administrators should work with facilities that train personnel who are qualified for diagnosing and teaching children with disabilities.

•• SUMMARY

The functions and responsibilities of administrators in providing services to children with disabilities are complex. They must be willing to adapt to the realities of the times and cooperate with other agencies in the community in order to affect present as well as future changes brought about as a result of our complex society, innovation in the field, and improved technology. Quality education for these mandates requires administrators to work cooperatively with other agencies for better ways and methods of identifying individuals with disabilities at an early age. A first step should be to assess needs of the children and from the assessed needs develop relevant instructional procedures. Equally important is using proper resources and facilities, coordinating activities in the community, and evaluating the success of the program based on realistic objectives by administrators of special education programs. In a democratic society, the schools should assume the responsibility for educating disabled children. The school must guarantee that the human rights of the disabled are not abridged by failing to offer services and provisions commensurate with their abilities.

•• REFERENCES

Berne, R. (1988). Equity issues in school finance. *Journal of Education Finance,* *14*(2), 159–180.

Castetter, W. B. (1981). *The personnel function in educational administration* (3rd ed.). New York: Macmillan.

Council for Exceptional Children. (1993). *Council for Exceptional Children (CEC) policy on inclusive schools and community setting.* Reston, VA: Author.

Fuchs, D., & Fuchs, L. (1994). Inclusive schools movement and the radicalization of special education reform. *Exceptional Children, 60,* 294–309.

Hartman, W. (1988). *School district budgeting.* Englewood Cliffs, NJ: Prentice Hall.

Jackson, S., & Taylor, G. R. (1973). *School organization for the mentally retarded.* Springfield, IL: Charles C Thomas.

National Association of State Board of Education. (1992). *Winners all: A call for inclusive schools.* Alexandria, VA: Author.

National Education Goals Panel. (1992). *World class standards for American education.* Washington, DC: U.S. Department of Education.

Podemski, R. S., Marsh, G. E., Smith, D., Tom, E. C., & Price, J. P. (1995). *Comprehensive administration of special education.* Englewood Cliffs, NJ: Merrill.

Rabe, B. G., & Peterson, P. E. (1988). The evolution of a new cooperative federalism. In N. J. Boyan (Ed.), *Handbook on research on education administration.* New York: Longman.

Taylor, G. R. (1999). *Curriculum models and strategies for educating children with disabilities in inclusive classrooms.* Springfield, IL: Charles C Thomas.

Taylor, G. R. (2000). *Parental involvement: A practical guide for collaboration and teamwork for students with disabilities.* Springfield, IL: Charles C Thomas.

Waldron, N. L., & McLeskey, J. (1998). The effects of an inclusive school program on students with mild and severe learning disabilities. *Exceptional Children, 64*(3), 395–405.

CHAPTER 5

Staff Development

Staff development is a necessary component in administration. Most effective administrators are well aware of this factor in improving changes learning and instruction in the schools. Several studies have suggested that to be effective, staff development should be local, focused, carefully planned, implemented, and monitored, with input from teachers and stakeholders (Joyce & Showers, 1995; Little, 1992; Sparks & Hirsh, 1997).

The value of staff development in the field of special education is of the utmost importance. Collaboration and team teaching are needed for regular and special teachers to meet the diverse needs of individuals with disabilities. Staff development activities help special teachers improve competencies in subject matter fields and regular teachers understand the needs, characteristics, and intervention strategies employed with individuals with disabilities. Collaborative strategies are essential in providing quality services and education for disabled individuals (Taylor, 1999, 2000, 2001).

•• STAFF DEVELOPMENT MODELS

Administrators must set the tone in their buildings in order for staff activities to be successful. According to Sparks and Loucks-Horsley (1998), there are five commonly used models for delivering staff development.: individually guided, observation/assessment, involvement in the development/improvement process, training, and inquiry. The five models have been succinctly described by Sparks and Loucks-Horsley (1989) and are only summarized here (see figure 2).

Administrators should pick the model they believe best suits their staff's needs. There is no one best model. Conditions such as resources, time, needs, cost, and personnel are factors to consider when choosing a model to implement for children with disabilities.

Figure 2: Models of Staff Development for Teachers

Model	Key Characteristics	Assumptions	Theory Research
Individually Guided Staff Development	• Teachers set own goals • Learning activities designed by teachers.	• Teachers are best judges of own needs. • Teachers are capable of self-directed learning.	• Adult learning theorists and stage theory: individuals have different needs.
Observation/ Assessment	• Regular observation and feedback on teaching.	• Observation data stimulate reflection and analysis and promote professional growth.	• Teaching can be objectively observed and analyzed. • Improvement can result from feedback.
Development/ Improvement Process	• Teachers involved in developing or adapting curriculum or other activities to improve instruction.	• Demands of problem solving drive teacher learning. • Teachers know best how to improve their performance.	• Encouragement in curriculum development/ school improvement sharpens teachers' thinking.
Training	• Workshop-type activity conducted by expert. High participant to trainer ratio.	• There are behaviors or techniques worthy of replication by teachers.	• Critical training elements are exploration of theory, demonstration of modeling, practice, feedback, and classroom coaching.
Inquiry	• Teachers formulate questions about their practice and search for answers.	• Teachers are intelligent and have legitimate expertise and experience • Teachers tend to search for data and reflect to find new solutions. • New understanding results from formulating and answering self-generated questions.	• Action research and self-monitoring develop teachers' thought.

Source: Adapted from Sparks and Loucks-Horsley (1989).

•• THREE PERSPECTIVES FOR STAFF DEVELOPMENT

Administrators of school programs, based on research conducted by Fullan (1990), may use three perspectives to develop strategies for conducting staff development sessions. The first principle in staff development is selecting a strategy. This principle is based on the idea of getting teachers to adopt and use innovations developed and advanced by individuals not related to the school. Fullan (1990) further articulated that this approach to staff development was based on the concept that teachers were "empty vessels" that experts should fill with appropriate knowledge and into whose hands foolproof curriculum should be placed. Without teacher support and involvement, no type of staff development will be successful. Teachers are most likely to modify their behaviors and instructional practices if they are actively involved in their own learning.

The second principle is concerned with innovation, which implies the focus is on new strategies and structures for school improvement through teacher growth (Friend & Cook, 2000). All stakeholders are involved in this process. Innovative practices such as mentoring and peer coaching are introduced as structures for delivering staff development. These structures must be tied to the instructional program and employed to increase the achievement of students (Friend & Cook, 2000). This is especially true for children with disabilities.

The third principle is associated with institutional development, which is a strategy for building an institution's capacity for continuous improvement and growth. This principle recognizes the importance of the school culture and the school as a workplace. The philosophy of collegiality and collaboration underlies all staff development. Schools that project this philosophy involve teachers at all stages. Fullan (1990) claims that staff development will never achieve its full potential until it is reconceptualized to emphasize teachers as individuals with vital personal and professional lives who exist within the culture of the school.

•• ELEMENTS IN STAFF DEVELOPMENT

According to Elsbree, McNally, and Wynn (1967), there are several essential phases in staff development: The first is determining the number and kinds of positions needed. In serving children with disabilities, many types of positions are needed depending on the disabling conditions of the children. For those children with multidisabling conditions, staffing becomes more critical. Staff will be needed to cover all deficit areas. The second phase is finding and persuading talented and well-prepared individuals to accept appointments. Administrators must select staff members with competencies in selected fields, including assistants, teacher aides, secretaries, custodians, special and resource teachers, and noninstructional staff. Additionally, administrators should develop specifications for teaching and other cited positions on the school staff and provide job descriptions relevant to educating children with disabilities. In the last phase, the orientation of new teachers, administrators should apprise them of their responsibilities, requirements, regulations, instructional packages, related services, parental involvement, community resources, and other issues relevant to educating children with disabilities (Taylor, 1999, 2000).

•• SELECTION CRITERIA

Administrators have several selection criteria they may employ, such as the interview, observations, and knowledge of the school system. The interview may be used to validate recommendations and determine the training and competencies needed. This interview should be well structured and information recorded for future references. Observation of staff members on the job can also be an effective way to select competent candidates. During this process strengths and weaknesses can be noted. Candidates should have a knowledge of the school system including school policies, salary, retirement plans, tenure, promotion procedures, in-service education, and the basic philosophy of the school.

•• DESIGNING STAFF DEVELOPMENT ACTIVITIES

In designing staff development activities, Friend and Cook (2000) recommend adhering to the following principles: (1) conducting need assessment, (2) incorporating principles of adult learning, and (3) addressing appropriate instructional principles in designing and delivering staff development. Additionally, when planning staff activities for teachers of children with disabilities, specific characteristics, learning styles, and instrumental strategies must be considered.

Although teachers vary significantly in age, training, experiences, background, ethnicity, and other traits, the issue of individual differences should be considered before planning staff development activities. Conducting a need assessment of teachers will provide essential information that may be incorporated into the staff development activity. Collecting need assessment data may be accomplished by administering a questionnaire, a survey, face-to-face interviews, telephone interviews, content analysis of written records, and through observations. The data sources may then be grouped to give a composite picture of the groups needs. Remember that interview and observational techniques may require trained individuals to administer them.

Teachers bring a rich source of information to the learning environment when their competencies are recognized. When administrators ignore or do not use the competencies of teachers, learning and achievement of children are at risk and teachers may become resistant to administration. Involving them in collaborative planning will assure a balance between theory and practice. Administrative and teachers' roles and expectations are clarified, and the content is presented in a timely manner (Garmston & Wellman, 1992; Joyce & Showers, 1995).

•• PLANNING AND CONDUCTING STAFF DEVELOPMENT

Much of the information in this chapter can be used to plan and conduct staff development activities. Assessment data, using sound educational principles, parental and community input, and collaborative strategies may to used to decide on the content to be addressed. The desired outcomes to be accomplished must be based on the state objectives, and the activities and strategies developed must be aimed at achieving expected objectives and outcomes stated for children with disabilities.

Friend and Cook (2000) found that conducting a staff development activity is a time-consuming and complex process that requires collaboration from stakeholders and includes practice and feedback. They recommend that administrators/presenters be aware of their voice quality and tone, positioning (so everyone can see), and a need to present a summary of the major points covered. In addition, a knowledge of the field of special education, learning styles of children with disabilities, curriculum innovations, assessment techniques, assisted technology devices, and current research findings in the field are to name but a few factors that should be considered in staff development (Taylor, 1999).

Administrators should seek out community resources to aid in conducting staff development activities. Local college and universities, central school administrators, specialists in various fields, parental groups, and community agencies can provide valuable information regarding resource individuals or presenters.

Today, most administrators are acutely aware of the purposes and meanings of staff development. The major purposes of staff development are to assist teachers in extending, building, and enriching their knowledge and skills related to effective student learning. Magestro and Stanford-Blair (2000) have provided administrators with a template for staff development. They list the following steps:

1. Identify the purpose and the objectives of the meeting.

   • What are participants expected to learn and be able to do as a result of the activity?

2. Select the resources used as a basis for the activity (e.g., journal articles, books, videos, flip charts, overhead transparencies, etc.).

3. Prepare an agenda that fits the time frame available. Each agenda should include:

   • An activity to elicit prior knowledge, beliefs, or attitudes.

   • Information drawn from the resources identified in number 2 and delivered using multiple modalities.

   • Opportunities for participants to reflect on and respond to information.

   • Personal commitments to follow up with a new strategy.

4. Revisit or follow-up activities with emphasis on support strategies for teachers.

Administrators may use the template as a mechanism for planning effective staff development for teachers. In so doing professional growth of teachers will remain exciting and productive. This template provides a tool for administrators to provide effective, high-challenging, low-threat, and hands-on activities to teachers under their supervision. As mentioned earlier, administrators may use selected community resources and individuals to augment the staff training needs for teachers of children with disabilities.

•• STAFF DEVELOPMENT AS EMPOWERMENT FOR TEACHERS

Staff development can be delivered in many forms. However, two ways are used most often. The first commonly used method is through short courses and ongoing in-service initiatives. Many in-service courses do not lead to a formal degree. Rather, these courses provide practical strategies that can be incorporated into one's teaching style. The second approach is through enrolling in formal courses at institutions of higher learning that may lead to certification and the awarding of degrees. Both types of staff development may be defined as a deliberate learning activity that focuses on empowering teachers to improve their instructional skills, attitudes, and understandings that will inevitably create better outcomes for all children, especially those with disabilities.

Think of empowerment as a mediating variable between staff development and the development of policies and programs and the use of better and more appropriate teaching techniques. When teachers are empowered, students' attitudes and achievement improves. Additionally, when teachers are empowered, administrators recognize that staff have the necessary skills and competencies to affect change and promote better outcomes. Today, it is commonly recognized that teachers have tremendous learning capacities that have been largely untapped. Four guidelines have been developed for administrators to encourage the competencies of teachers in creating productive school environments (Taylor, 2001).

Guideline 1: Treat the Teacher as a Whole Person, with Competencies in Selective Subject Areas

Administrators may provide challenges for teachers by making realistic classroom assignments, assisting with classroom management skills and instructional techniques, and recognizing the ability and competencies of teachers in expanding their instructional repertories. Teachers should be involved in the planning and execution of staff development activities. They should serve as resources in areas where they are competent to instruct children with disabilities.

Guideline 2: Establish a School Culture Based on Collaboration and Professional Inquiry

Administrative strategies are most likely to succeed within a school when teachers are encouraged and rewarded to reflect consciously on their own practices, to share ideas about their instructional strategies, and to experiment with innovative techniques in a collaborative manner with stakeholders in the school and community. Information received from collaboration can be used by the teacher to strengthen his or her instructional program for children with disabilities.

Guideline 3: Assess and Diagnose the Need for Staff Development

Successful staff development programs are built on well-designed assessment instruments to evaluate the perceptions of teachers relevant to needs. Once these needs have been diagnosed, realistic and functional staff development plans can be constructed, implemented, and evaluated. Administrators may use results from the evaluation to revise strategies, introduce new strategies, and assign priorities to future staff development activities based on the perception of teachers.

Guideline 4: Infuse Administrative Activities into Teacher Development Strategies

Effective administrators create a school climate in which teachers are involved with the administration of their schools. The more administrators involve teachers in day-to-day administrative decisions, the more effective they are in fostering and developing teacher development. Teachers develop competencies about budget, discipline, reporting, and staff, which will aid them in making realistic decisions relevant to these areas. Teacher groups like a teacher council, for example, can serve as an advisory board to the administration. This council can represent the views of the teachers to the administration.

•• EVALUATION AND STAFF DEVELOPMENT

Most staff development programs do not have a built-in evaluation design to determine how well or to what extent the stated objectives have been achieved. Evaluation of staff development should focus chiefly on behavioral changes of participants. Administrators may use the stated objectives to evaluate the effectiveness of the school's programs. Teachers and noninstructional staff members should be fully apprised of the evaluation system used; adequate time should be given to evaluation; and the instrument used should provide a comprehensive overview of the staff member's strengths and weaknesses. Many school districts have developed and field-tested their own instruments. Administrators who desire a standardized instrument may consult the latest Buros Mental Measurement Yearbook.

•• A TOTAL APPROACH

Administrative personnel can ensure continuous progress for children with disabilities by providing a systematic program with assessment and reassessment of each child's abilities for his or her total school experience. The schools are not equipped to provide this service alone, but will need the combined support of many agencies and disciplines. Realistic goals and objectives must be stated concisely. Educational tasks must be sequenced to permit the child to receive some measure of success in his or her academic pursuits. Tasks should be sequenced to serve the child's immediate as well as his or her long-range needs. To achieve this end, administrators should incorporate the educational program with comprehensive community services and related agencies dealing with training and certification of administrators and teaching personnel.

Institutions responsible for the preparation of teaching personnel, college professors, state departments of education, the public schools, and other groups are too fragmented and appear to be working in opposite directions. In order to ensure continuous progress for the disabled, acceptable standards of competencies are needed for all teaching personnel, combined with professional education legislated at the state level that addresses such standards. These standards should be administered by educators representing all personnel concerned with educating disabled children.

A major function of the school is to recognize each pupil as a unique individual and to help each one develop his or her abilities to the fullest. The educational program must therefore take carefully into account the individual differences among pupils. Administrators and school personnel, adequately trained, can assist the school in reaching this basic goal. Programming for disabled children involves the commitment of the total school and community, as well as supportive services and programs to meet their many needs.

•• SUMMARY

Administrators have a major responsibility for providing the conditions and services that contribute to the effective education of individuals with disabilities. Pupil grouping and placement, promotion, management of supplies and equipment, the testing program, and selection and assignment of teachers are among the aspects of school organization and administration that affect the education of all children.

The effectiveness of these services to individuals with disabilities will determine the degree to which equal educational opportunities are provided for them. To ensure individuals with disabilities an equal educational opportunity, a first step is to define objectives in light of the needs, abilities, and interests of the children, and to sequence tasks that will lead to desired behavior. Equally important is that activities and materials match the objectives of the program. By making use of specificity and objectivity in instruction, administrators will better ensure equal education opportunities for the disabled. Administrators should insist on well-defined objectives that are observable and measurable, as well as learning activities and materials that will allow the objectives to be met.

The absence of necessary modifications in school organization and unsuitable administration of the educational program for individuals with disabilities can result in undesirable consequences. Many individuals with disabilities may experience several years of failure before being identified and receiving special services. These children may be placed with teachers who are unprepared, do not understand their problems, or do not know how to select the influences that will best advance their growth.

The values and attitudes of teachers and their effects on pupils' self-perceptions and performances cannot be minimized. In addition, discovering the pupil characteristics that a given teacher will accept or reject becomes a critical administrative question. The competencies of teachers and administrators are more than a collection of objectives or instructional skills. They should consist of internal philosophies that emerge and support our democratic value of education for all children.

•• REFERENCES

Elsbree, W. S., McNally, H. J., & Wynn, R. (1967). *Elementary administration and supervision* (3rd ed.). New York: Van Nostrand Reinhold.

Friend, M., & Cook, L. (2000). *Interactions: Collaboration skills for school professions* (3rd ed.). White Plains, NY: Longman.

Fullan, M.G. (1990). Staff development innovation and institutional development. In B. Joyce (Ed.), *Changing school culture through staff development: 1990 Yearbook of the Association for Supervision and Curriculum Development*. Alexandria, VA: Association for Supervision and Curriculum Development.

Garmston, R. L., & Wellman, B. M. (1992). *How to make presentations that teach and transform*. Alexandria, VA: Association for Supervision and Curriculum Development.

Joyce, B., & Showers, B. (1995). *Student achievement: Fundamental of school renewal* (2nd ed.). White Plains, NY: Longman.

Little, J. W. (1992). Teacher's professional development in a climate of educational reform. *Education Evaluation and Policy Analysis, 15,* 129–151.

Magestro, P. V., & Stanford-Blair, N. (2000). A tool for meaningful staff development. *Educational Leadership, 57*(8), 34–35.

Sparks, D., & Hirsh, S. (1997). *A new vision for staff development*. Alexandria, VA: Association for Supervision and Curriculum Development.

Sparks, D., & Loucks-Horsley, S. (1989). Five models for staff development for teachers. *Journal of Staff Development, 10*(4), 40–57.

Taylor, G. R. (1999). *Curriculum models and strategies for educating children with disabilities in inclusive classrooms*. Springfield, IL: Charles C Thomas.

Taylor, G. R. (2000). *Parental involvement: Team work and collaboration for children with disabilities*. Springfield, IL: Charles C Thomas.

Taylor, G. R. (2001). *Educational interventions and services for children with exceptionalities: Strategies and perspectives*. Springfield, IL: Charles C Thomas.

CHAPTER 6

Legal
Responsibilities

Administrators of school programs serving children with disabilities are bound by legal responsibilities and restrictions. School programs and services must comply with state and federal regulations and mandates. Therefore, knowledge of school law of your state is essential for serving children with disabilities. In a study conducted by Hirth and Valesky (1990) concerning principals' knowledge of special education, the following was revealed:

1. A majority of principals needed to learn more about due process, parental notification procedures, student suspension and expulsion, the relationship between the concept of mainstreaming and the legal term *least restrictive environment*.

2. Most principals believed all students in special education must receive special education instruction and related services.

3. Several principals were not aware of the extended-year services or special services for students.

These findings support our view that many administrators lack the necessary training to administer programs effectively for children with disabilities. There is an urgent need for universities and state departments of education to collaborate and develop effective programs to train administrators of special education programs. Administrators need to be made aware of the legislation and litigation affecting special education in order of the more recent court cases to as far back as those of the early nineteenth century (Taylor, 1999, 2000, 2001).

Administrators should know current and updated information relevant to providing equal access and appropriate education to the disabled. Additionally, they should be knowledgeable about court cases and congressional actions, often taken in response to litigation, as well as encouragement from parents, professionals, and advocacy groups. Prior to the 1970s, efforts to meet the needs of the disabled within the public schools varied widely in form and intent. The landmark decision in *Brown v. Board of Education* (1954) established the right of children to an equal educational opportunity. The sentiment of the following language contained in the Supreme Court's opinion is common to litigation and legislation of the past four decades seeking equal educational access and opportunity for the disabled.

Today, education is perhaps the most important function of state and local governments.

Compulsory school attendance laws and the great expenditures for education . . . demonstrate our recognition of the importance of education to our democratic society. It is required in the performance of our basic public responsibilities, even service in the armed forces. It is the very foundation of good citizenship. Today, it is a principal instrument in awakening the child to cultural values, in preparing him or her for later professional training, and in helping him or her to adjust normally to his or her environment. In these days, it is doubtful that any child may reasonably be expected to succeed in life if he or she is denied the opportunity of an education. Such an opportunity, where the state has undertaken to provide it, is a right which must be made available to all on equal terms.

Although Congress (through the adoption of the Education of Handicapped Act of 1970) attempted to overcome the historical inadequacy of educational services to the disabled, it was two court cases decided in 1971–1972 that helped established the right of access of the disabled to a free appropriate public education and outlined the protection that such students could be afforded.

•• IMPACT OF COURT DECREES

In *Pennsylvania Association for Retarded Children [PARC] v. Commonwealth* (1972), the court was asked to examine policies that permitted Pennsylvania to deny access and a free appropriate education to mentally retarded children.

A consent decree, approved by the district court, enjoined the state from denying education to mentally retarded children and required that retarded children be provided a free, public program of education and training appropriate to the child's capacity, within the context of the general education policy that, among the alternative programs of education and training required by statute to be available, placement in a regular public school class is preferable to placement in a special public school class [i.e., a class for "handicapped" children] and placement in a special public school class is preferable to placement in any other type of program of education and training.

The consent decree further required that retarded children be provided procedural due process and periodic reevaluation. *Mills v. Board of Education of the District of Columbia* (1972), also approved by consent decree, greatly expanded the *PARC* decision to include all disabled children and incorporated an extensive plan created by the District of Columbia Board of Education to provide (1) a free appropriate education, (2) an individualized education plan, and (3) due process procedures. The language of the final order provided significant guidance for litigants in cases in other states as well as for the development of appropriate state and federal legislative responses to provide equal educational access and opportunity for the disabled. *Board of Education of Hendrick Hudson School District v. Rowley* (1982), attempted to minimize confusion by establishing a standard to determine compliance. The Court indicated that a child's education program would be appropriate if it meet the following criteria: "First, has the state complied with the procedures set forth in the Act? And second, is the individualized education program developed through the Act's procedures reasonably calculated to enable the child to receive educational benefits?"

Further, the courts did not agree that an appropriate education was one that assisted a child in reaching his or her maximum potential; rather, "the intent of the Act was more to open the door of public education to children with disabilities on appropriate terms than to guarantee any particular level of education once inside." Special education programs were to provide "a basic floor of educational opportunities."

An examination of the case law following *Rowley* indicates that judges are unwilling to overturn the decisions of education professionals as to what constitutes an appropriate education as long as the procedures, services, and rights afforded by the act are provided. However, the courts appear to be moving away from such procedural evaluations to substantive evaluations of proposed education programs as the movement toward full inclusion continues. One substantive issue impacting curriculum decisions or strategies employed could be the need to respond to the act's "related services" requirements (*Seventeenth Annual Report to Congress*, 1997).

As greater efforts are made to provide instruction to the disabled in inclusive settings, the possibility exists to misinterpret or misapply the concept of "maximum extent possible." The U.S. Court of Appeals (Sixth Circuit) in *Ronker v. Walter* identified three exceptions to inclusive placement that may be helpful to remember. Such placements may be precluded if there exists (1) no benefit to the child, (2) greater benefits in segregated settings even after the feasibility standard is applied, and (3) the potential for disruption to a nonsegregated setting (*Ronker v. Walker*, 1983). These are important considerations when creating the child's individualized education program. Federal legislation was introduced following the *PARC* and *Mills* decisions to eliminate discrimination against the disabled.

•• IMPACT OF FEDERAL LEGISLATION

In addition to the court cases cited, administrators should have knowledge of past federal legislative acts and their intent for special education programming:

1. PL 85-926 (1958) provided funds for the training of college instructors who would prepare teachers of students with mental retardation.

2. PL 88-164 (1963), the Mental Retardation Facilities and Mental Health Construction Centers Act, amended PL 85-926, included training in other major disability areas, not just mental retardation. In addition to expanding teacher training, the act provided funding for the establishment of research and demonstration projects for educating children with disabilities. Although not included in the legislation but as a result of it, President Kennedy created the Division of Handicapped Children and Youth to administer all programs dealing with children and youth with disabilities.

3. PL 89-110 (1965), the Elementary and Secondary Education Act (ESEA), was the first truly broad-scale aid to education enacted by the U.S. Congress. Although the primary focus of this act was not on children with disabilities, minimal gains received by children who were disabled and from low-income families resulted from its passage. One negative effect was the reorganization of the U.S. Office of Education and the disbandment of the Division of Disabled Children and Youth.

4. PL 89-313 (1965) provided support for children with disabilities in hospitals, institutions, and other state-administered programs. This act did a great deal to improve appropriate services to children with disabilities. PL 94-142, approved ten years later created some obstacles. Administrators were confronted with a dilemma, in that they could use PL 89-313 funds for some programs but had to utilize PL 94-142 monies for others.

5. PL 89-750 (1966) (1) created the Bureau of Education for the Handicapped, (2) provided for preschool programs for children with disabilities, and (3) established a National Advisory Committee on the Handicapped to advise the U.S. Commissioner of Education. The establishment of the

Bureau of Education for the Handicapped reflected a commitment at the federal level for the education of children with disabilities and indicated the growing trend in society that children with disabilities should be provided more services. Many excellent model programs were established under this act that demonstrated the potential of shared responsibility for children with disabilities among federal, state, and local agencies.

6. PL 90-480 (1968) focused on eliminating architectural barriers for people with disabilities.

7. PL 90-538, the Handicapped Children's Early Assistance Act of 1968, focused on children with educational disabilities by establishing experimental demonstration centers.

8. PL 92-230 (1969) (1) consolidated all legislation dealing with children with disabilities, (2) recognized learning disabilities as a new category of disability, (3) included provisions for research, model programs, and teacher training, and (4) authorized certain actions dealing with children who are gifted.

9. PL 92-424, known as the Economic Opportunity Act Amendments of 1974, was considered the first major legislation protecting the civil rights of disabled persons. This act provided that no otherwise qualified handicapped individual in the United States . . . shall, solely by reason of his or her handicap, be excluded from participation in, be denied the benefits of, or be subjected to discrimination under any program or activity receiving federal financial assistance.

   A principal concern of Section 504 is discrimination in employment and the provision of health, welfare, and other social services. However, the legislation does recognize the educational needs of disabled children and requires five issues be considered in meeting those needs: (1) location and notification, (2) free appropriate public education, (3) educational settings, (4) evaluation and placement, and (5) procedural safeguards. Failure to comply with these requirements could result in the withdrawal of federal funding.

10. PL 93-380 (1973) mandated that in order for schools to remain eligible for federal funds, they would have to comply with certain requirements related to the education of children with disabilities. The act addressed the following areas of compliance: (1) least restrictive environment, (2) due process procedures, and (3) right to education for all children with disabilities.

11. PL 94-142, known as The All Handicapped Children's Act of 1975, is considered the most significant piece of legislation. This law was intended to make certain that disabled children receive equal educational access and provided extensive rules and regulations to guide state and local school actions in proving an appropriate education. The basic educational rights of the EAHCA (see 20 U.S.C.§1401 [16-91]) have been described by Turnbull and Turnbull (1993) in six primary principles:

   a. Zero reject: every disabled child (regardless of the severity of his or her disability) must be provided a free, appropriate, publicly supported education. No child may be excluded.

   b. Nondiscriminatory assessment: each child must be provided a multi-factored evaluation (free of race, cultural, or native language bias) to determine the presence of a disability and guide special education program development.

   c. Appropriate education: an individualized education (IEP) is to be developed and implemented to meet the child's unique needs and to ensure a meaningful educational experience.

   d. Least restrictive environment (LRE): each disabled child is to be educated with nondisabled peers to the maximum extent practicable, favoring inclusion as a means of supporting the child's right to nor-malization.

   e. Due process: procedures to protect the rights of disabled children and their parents must be provided, safeguarding the right to protest program planning and placement decisions or records and confiden-tiality issues by providing an impartial hearing and appeals process to resolve disputes.

   f. Parent participation: parents have the right to participate in planning their child's educational program. Mutual benefits can be realized through collaboration in program development.

   g. PL 99-457, the Education of the Handicapped Amendments of 1986, provided that the multidisciplinary team develop an individualized family service plan (IFSP).

The development of an individualized program or IFSP, and the provision of that program utilizing the continuum of services associated with the least restrictive environment, are fundamental to providing an appropriate education.

As defined in the Individuals with Disabilities Education Act (PL 101-476), the term *free appropriate public education* means special education and related services that

• have been provided at public expense, under public supervision and direction, and without charge.

• meet the standards of the state educational agency.

• include an appropriate preschool, elementary, or secondary school education in the state involved.

• are provided in conformity with the individualized education program under section 1414 (a) (5) of this title.

The Education Handicapped Act (EHA) was amended in 1990. Although the basic provisions established in PL 94-142 were retained, several modifications were made. In PL 101-476, the title of EHA was changed to the Individual with Disabilities Education Act, better known today by its acronym IDEA. The same title change was made applicable to all laws making reference to the original Education of the Handicapped Act. In addition, the term *handicap* was replaced with *disability* (e.g., "handicapped children" became "children with disabilities"). Such modifications made the language consistent with the American with Disabilities Act (PL 101-336) enacted earlier in the year. Other modifications made are as follows:

1. Autism and traumatic brain injury were added to the list of distinct disabilities.

2. Monies were made available to establish centers to organize, synthesize, and disseminate current knowledge relating to children with attention deficit disorders.

3. Students' IEPs are to include transition services as may be required by individual need. Transition services are defined as "a coordinated set of activities for a student, designed within an outcome-oriented process which promotes movement from school to post-school activities."

4. Support services were included, specifically of "assistive technology device" and "assistive technology service" as they appeared in the Technology-Related Assistance for Individuals with Disabilities Act of 1988.

5. Rehabilitation counseling was added to the definition of related services.

Administrators of special education programs serving disabled children, whether in fully inclusion or self-contained classrooms, must have a basic under-standing of the key provisions of current law. Three such provisions—least restrictive environment, individualized education program, and appropriate education—can have a significant impact on the curriculum strategies that may be employed in the teaching of social skills to the disabled.

The Individuals with Disabilities Education Act requires:

to the maximum extent appropriate, children with disabilities, including children in public or private institutions or other care facilities, are educated with children who are not disabled and that special classes, separate schooling, or other removal of children with disabilities from the regular educational environment occurs only when the nature or severity of the disability is such that education in regular classes with the use of supplementary aids and services cannot be achieved satisfactorily.

Unfortunately, neither the statutory law nor the following language of the reg-ulations clearly prescribe how school districts are to determine what the least restrictive environment is:

(a) Each public agency shall ensure that a continuum of alternative placements is available to meet the needs of children with disabilities for special education and related services.

(b) The continuum required under paragraph (a) of this section must

(1) Include the alternative placements listed in the definition of special education under §300.17 (instruction in regular classes, special classes, special schools, home instruction, and instruction in hospitals and institutions); and

(2) Make provision for supplementary services (such as resource room or itinerant instruction) to be provided in conjunction with regular class placement. (*Sixteenth Annual Report to Congress*, 1995)

An essential element of free appropriate education is the development of an individualized education program. The IDEA defines individualized education program as:

a written statement for each child with a disability developed in any meeting by a representative of the local educational agency or an inter-mediate educational unit who shall be qualified to provide, or supervise the provision of, specially designed instruction to meet the unique needs of children with disabilities, the teacher, the parents or guardian of such child, and whenever appropriate, such child, which statement shall include:

(A) a statement of the present levels of educational performance of such child,

(B) a statement of annual goals, including short-term instructional objectives,

(C) a statement of the specific educational services to be provided to such child, and the extent to which such child will be able to participate in regular educational programs;

(D) a statement of the needed transition services for students beginning no later than age 16 and annually thereafter (and, when determined appropriate for the individual, beginning at age 14 or younger), including when appropriate, a statement of the interagency responsibilities or linkages (or both) before the student leaves the school settings,

(E) the project date for initiation and anticipated duration of such services, and

(F) appropriate objective criteria and evaluation procedures and schedules for determining, on at least an annual basis, whether instructional objectives are being achieved. (Individuals with Disabilities Act, 1997)

The EHA was amended in 1997. Although the basic provisions established in IDEA 1990 were retained, several modifications were made as follows:

1. Participation of children and youth with disabilities in state and districtwide assessment (testing) programs.

2. Development and review of the individualized education program (IEP), including increased emphasis on participation of children and youth with disabilities in the general education classroom and the general curriculum with appropriate aids and services.

3. Parent participation in eligibility and placement decisions.

4. The way in which reevaluations are conducted.

5. The addition of transition planning.

6. Voluntary mediation as a means of resolving parent-school controversies.

7. Discipline and behavior issues of children and youth with disabilities (IDEA Reauthorization Special Report, 1997; Underwood & Mead, 1985).

The lengthy comprehensive extension of IDEA cannot be totally covered in this chapter. You may obtain a copy of the new law by contacting the following sources:

• Your senator or representative (refer to S.717/H.R.5).

• Office of Special Education and Rehabilitative Services (OSERS) (*www. ed.gov/offices/OSERS/IDEA*).

• Education Administration Online (*www.rp.com/ed*).

• Internet Web sites (see appendix C).

PL 105-17 (IDEA) has several areas of change that influence the manner in which educators, psychologists, and researchers conduct their professional responsibilities within the context of the classroom. One change promoted in PL 105-17 involves changes in the IEP process. These changes make the IEP document and process a better tool for instruction, accountability/assessment, and involvement of parents. Another change involves promoting discipline procedures that provide safety for all. In particular, this change is challenging in that discipline procedures must be developed and implemented to meet the needs of children and at the same time not mean giving up on any student. A third change includes exploring inclusive classrooms and collaborative general/special education teaching. Efforts in this area have been under way for several years now. Interestingly, little attention is given to the fact that the reauthorization of IDEA ensures a continuum of services model that meets the needs and strengths of all children and is a collaboration between early intervention and preschool programs. Underscoring this change is the need for looking at early screening and early preventative measures/interventions for all students who may be at risk for academic, discipline, physical, and mental health issues (*The New IDEA Reauthorization Law*, 1998).

The changes cited here are only a few that must be addressed through the new IDEA Reauthorization. Another aspect of the IDEA reauthorization is that it may be interpreted as invitations to engage in research. One such invitation is extended to researchers interested in exploring the large number of issues related to children who may be at risk for failure in school due to diverse ethnic backgrounds, environmental/home situations, physical, academic, and emotional disabilities, and social/emotional situations.

•• AN INVITATION TO EXPLORE THE IEP/ASSESSMENT PROCESS

Development of research questions in the area of the IEP and assessment process may begin with researchers asking questions concerning the involvement of parents, especially parents who represent different cultures and who are non-English speakers. Some questions may include how professionals involve parents so they are respected, their needs are met, and their participation is valued.

The assessment process will continue to ask research questions concerning the appropriateness of tests as well as whether an overrepresentation of students from diverse backgrounds are receiving special education services. Additionally, greater expectations are being placed on students to improve test scores. Questions concerning whether testing procedures accommodate students with disabilities must be addressed (see chapter 11). The assessment issue expands when the variables of ethnicity, culture, and language are factored into a research agenda.

•• AN INVITATION TO EXPLORE DISCIPLINE PROCEDURES

The issue of discipline in the schools is of great interest to administrators when considering the new IDEA regulations. Some invitations for research in this area may include the following:

1. Are discipline measures effective in inclusive classrooms?

2. Is the use of expulsion avoided because of alternative disciplinary actions being exercised?

3. Are the number of student dropouts decreasing due to the changes in school disciplinary policies?

•• AN INVITATION TO EXPLORE SERVICES THAT MEET THE NEEDS AND STRENGTHS OF ALL CHILDREN

Because the IDEA emphasizes the importance of meeting the needs of all children, regardless of age, administrators must ask questions that encourage the development of effective teaching procedures for all children in a variety of settings. Determining whether these interventions work for children in certain settings is a primary concern. Currently, administrators are finding that the majority of students from different ethnic backgrounds who are disabled can benefit from specific instruction in an inclusive classroom. These encouraging results demand the exploration of why some children experienced success and others did not. What factors contributed to the successes? Do the success variables exist within the disability, the student, or in the home or learning environment? Finally, what is being done to eliminate failure in this group of disabled children and youth?

•• RELATED SERVICES

Related services means transportation and such developmental, corrective, and other support services as required to assist a child with a disability to benefit from special education. Speech pathology and audiology, psychological services, physical and occupational therapy, recreation (including therapeutic recreation), early identification and assessment of disabilities, counseling services, (including rehabilitation counseling), medical services for diagnostic or evaluation purposes, school health services, social work services in the schools, and parent counseling and training are included in related services. Subsequent sections of the regulation, taken collectively, demonstrate a recognition of the importance of having diverse services available to support the development of appropriate social skills.

Counseling services means services provided by qualified social workers, psychologists, guidance counselors, or other qualified personnel.

Parent counseling and training refers to assisting parents in understanding the special needs of their child and providing parents with information about child development.

Psychological services means
- Administering psychological and other assessment procedures.
- Interpreting assessment results.
- Obtaining, integrating, and interpreting information about child behavior and conditions relating to learning.
- Consulting with other staff members in planning school programs to meet the special needs of children as indicated by psychological tests, interviews, and behavioral evaluations.
- Planning and managing a program of services, including psychological counseling, for children and parents.

Social work services in schools include
- Preparing a social or developmental history on a child with a disability.
- Group and individual counseling with child and family.
- Working with those problems in a child's living situation (home, school, community) that affect the child's adjustment in school.
- Mobilizing school and community resources to enable the child to learn as effectively as possible in his or her education program.

Underwood and Mead (1985) suggested three questions that must be considered to determine whether a child will be eligible for related services:

1. Is the service necessary for the student to gain access to or remain in the special programs?

2. Is the service necessary to resolve other needs for the student before educational efforts will be successful?

3. Is the service necessary for the student to make meaningful progress on the identified goals?

•• DUE PROCESS

If for any reason parents or guardians feel their child is not being provided a free, appropriate public education, or if there is any disagreement between the parent and the local education agency regarding identification, evaluation, or educational placement, the parents or guardians have the right to a due process hearing.

Due process, simply stated, means fair procedure. Under the law, schools must use fair procedures in all matters regarding parents and students. Due process is one of the most important constitutional rights of parents and students (see due process checklist in appendix A).

The rights specified will assist parents in staying informed of every decision about their children. Although a due process hearing is a parental right, it can be exhausting. Before proceeding to a hearing, parents should have tried to resolve differences through every other avenue, by being as well prepared and persuasive as possible with teachers, specialists, and administrators. If conflicting points of view cannot be resolved except by way of a due process hearing, parents should prepare their cases as thoroughly as possible. Parents may wish to seek advice or other assistance from any one of a number of sources, including the State Department of Education, recognized associations representing disabled people, established advocacy groups, or they may consider legal consultation. The school system is obligated to advise parents of sources of free or low-cost legal aid.

The following points ensure the implementation of due process procedures for everyone:

1. The law states that local hearings are to begin and be completed as soon as possible, and in most states the interpretation means no later than 45 days after receipt of a written request for a hearing.

2. Parents have the right to be notified in writing about the decision as a result of the local hearing. This written decision must be rendered within

5 days of the hearing, and written notification of this decision must be made to the parents within 5 days. If parents are dissatisfied with the decision, they may appeal the decision within 30 days to the State Department of Education, for a hearing before a three-member board of independent hearing officers, which will conduct an impartial review (within 30 days of receipt of a written appeal) and render a decision.

3. Should the decision by the State Hearing Review Board not be agreeable to the parents, they have the right to take civil action in the State or U.S. District Court, or any one of the three common Law Courts of the Supreme Bench.

4. The hearing shall be impartial. That is, it must be conducted by someone not employed by the agency responsible for the child's education or care. For example, any local education agency employee may not serve or be considered an impartial hearing officer.

5. Parents or guardians have the right to legal advice or counsel and to be accompanied by counsel at this hearing. Parents may also be accompanied by individuals who have special knowledge or training related to the problems of their child.

6. Parents, either themselves or through their counsel, have the right to present evidence and to question witnesses. They also have the right to compel the attendance of any witnesses with special knowledge or training related to their child.

7. Both parties at the hearing have the right to prohibit the introduction of any evidence that has not been disclosed to them at least five days prior to the hearing.

8. When it seems appropriate, the child himself or herself has the right to be present.

9. When the parents or guardians wish, the hearing may be open to the public.

10. Parents have a right to a written or electronic verbatim record of the hearing at reasonable cost.

One question often raised is "What happens to the children while these decisions are pending?" According to the law, the children have the right to remain in the educational program in which they were originally placed before any action began. If the parents or guardians of the children are applying for initial admission to a public school program, the children may be placed in that program until all the proceedings have been completed. The parents or guardians must agree, however, to that placement. During any of these proceedings, the educational program agreed on must be provided at no cost to the parents or guardians. (See appendix B for strategies that administrators can employ when a child's behavior is a manifestation of his or her disability.)

If the parent is dissatisfied with the school district's plans or the related services being provided, the parent may request an impartial due process hearing. At such a hearing, the parents and school officials may be represented by legal counsel. When a request for a due process hearing is made, an impartial hearing officer is appointed by the state education agency, and a formal hearing is held at which time both sides present evidence and a verbatim transcript of the proceedings is kept. The impartial hearing officer evaluates the evidence and issues a ruling. If the parties do not wish to abide by the ruling, a state-level hearing may be requested. The impartial hearing officer makes a recommendation to the chief state school officer, who issues a ruling that is binding to all parties involved. The only recourse available to a parent or a school district beyond the state-level hearing is to take the matter to court. The process outlined here is accurate with minor variations for nearly all of the fifty states.

The due process procedure makes no presumptions of who is right or wrong in a conflict. The impartial hearing officer's role is to hear both sides and render a decision. Although the major purpose of the due process is to protect the rights of children and their parents, frequently judgments and decisions are made that do not support the parental position. The impartial process is imperfect for the following reasons:

1. An assumption exists that the impartial hearing officer is trained and competent in special education matters and understands the process.

2. Many parents are not familiar with the process and are not aware of the procedural safeguards that have been mandated by law.

3. Many parents do not want to get involved in the long time-consuming process required to prepare for a hearing.

4. Parents who receive a favorable ruling feel they have created negative feelings in the school district in having their cases supported.

The impartial hearing process is not a panacea, but it is an important first step in the due process for parents. One major contribution of due process hearings is that they have reduced the number of special education cases going to court.

•• NEW SAFEGUARD PROCEDURES

The new law (IDEA) added specific requirements regarding minimal safeguard procedures for parents. A copy of the procedural safeguards available is given to the parents of a child with a disability:

1. upon initial evaluation;
2. upon each notification of an individualized education program meeting and upon re-evaluation of the child;
3. upon registration of a complaint under subsection (b) (6);
4. contents—The procedural safeguards notice shall include a full explanation of the procedural safeguards, written in the native language of the parents, unless it clearly is not feasible to do so, and written in an easily, understandable manner, available under this section and under regulations promulgated by the Secretary relating to:
   a. independent educational evaluation;
   b. prior written notice;
   c. access to educational records;
   d. opportunity to present complaints;
   e. the child's placement during due process procedures;
   f. procedures for students who are subject to placement in an alternative educational setting;
   g. requirements for unilateral placement by parents of children in private schools at public expenses;
   h. mediation;
   i. due process hearing, including requirements for disclosure of evaluation results and recommendation;
   j. state-level appeals (if applicable in that state);
   k. civil action; and
   l. attorney's fees.

•• SUMMARY

Congressional investigations clearly showed that the needs of individuals with disabilities were not being met. These investigations were chiefly prompted by demands from parents, professional groups, court cases, and advocacy groups for disabled individuals. The result was the reenactment of several federal laws that were passed to provide equal educational opportunities for all disabled individuals in inclusive settings as much as possible. The most recent federal legislation (PL 105-17) has mandated increased involvement of parents in the planning and implementation of individualized education programs. Administrators must make sure that procedural safeguards for parents are fully explained, and they must improve collaborative efforts between school personnel and parents as well.

•• REFERENCES

Brown v Board of Education of Topeka. 347 U.S. 483, 74 S. Ct. 689 (1954).

Hirth, M. A., & Valesky, T. C. (1990). Principal's knowledge of special education. *National Forum of Educational Administration and Supervision Journal,* 6(3), 131-141.

Pennsylvania Association for Retarded Children (PARC). Commonwealth of Pennsylvania, 343 F. Supp. 279. (E.D. Pa. 1972).

Ronker v. Walter, 700 F21058, 1063 (6th Cir. 1983).

Rowley v. Board of Education of Hendrick Hudson School District. 458 U.S., 176 (1982).

Sixteenth Annual Report to Congress. (1995). U.S. Department of Education. Washington, DC: U.S. Government Printing Office.

Taylor, G. R. (1999). *Curriculum models and strategies for educating individuals with disabilities in inclusive classrooms.* Springfield, IL: Charles C Thomas.

Taylor, G. R. (2000). *Parental involvement: A practical guide for collaboration and teamwork for students with disabilities.* Springfield, IL: Charles C Thomas.

Taylor, G. R. (2001). *Educational services and strategies for educating exceptional individuals.* Springfield, IL: Charles C Thomas.

The New IDEA Reauthorization Law. (1998). U.S. Department of Education. Washington, DC: U.S. Government Printing Office.

Turnbull, H., R. (1993). *Free appropriate public education: The law and children with disabilities* (4th ed.). Reston, VA: Love.

U.S. Department of Education. (1997). *Individuals with Disabilities Education Act Amendments of 1995.* Washington, DC: U.S. Government Printing Office.

Underwood, J., & Mead, J. (1985). *Legal aspects of special education and pupil services.* Needham Heights, MA: Allyn & Bacon.

CHAPTER 7

Including Students with Disabilities in Statewide Assessments

Educational reforms provide unique opportunities for administrators of special education programs to provide students with disabilities an opportunity to participate more fully in the educational system. State and local educational agencies are exploring ways to improve the gains of education for all students, including those with disabilities. In particular, these agencies are setting high student performance standards that necessitat implementing innovative instructional methodologies (including new technologies) to help students reach those high standards. Further, developing assessments designed to measure the extent to which students are reaching the high standards have been initiated (*Nineteenth Annual Report to Congress*, 1997).

According to Kearns, Kleinert, and Kennedy (1999), IDEA 1997 mandates that all states must include students with disabilities in statewide and districtwide educational assessments (Section 612 [a] [17] [A]). This law applies unless states have developed alternate assessment plans to accommodate individuals with disabilities by July 1, 2000 (Bond, Braskamp, & Roeber, 1996). Data from the National Center on Education Outcomes reported that a large number of students with disabilities are excluded from state assessment and accountability systems based on disability categories, the child's reading level, or the destructiveness of the child's placement. Most students with disabilities should participate in statewide assessments. If they are excluded from testing, there is no mechanism to determine whether they have received the benefits of educational reforms. Additionally, schools will have less incentive to improve education for students whose scores do not count, as well as not considering children with disabilities in important educational policy decision making.

•• TYPES OF LARGE-SCALE ASSESSMENTS

Statewide large-scale assessments are usually standardized paper-and-pencil tests (Elliott, Thurlow, & Ysseldyke, 1996). Other forms may include multiple-choice questions, performance-based assessment, and portfolio assessment (see Chapter 8). Assessment results provide data relevant to individual student achievement as well as gauging the success of schools.

Several authorities in the field suggest that large numbers of disabled students could participate in state and national assessments if accommodations were provided (Erickson, Thurlow, & Thor, 1995; McGrew, Thurlow, Shriner, & Spiegel, 1992; Ysseldyke, Thurlow, McGrew, & Vanderwood, 1994a). A set of guidelines should be made available to assist administrators in making decisions about participation, accommodation, alternative assessment, and reporting. Additional information on these strategies may be found in Chapter 8. States and school districts must become accountable for the education of all children with disabilities.

Data from statewide assessments are not only used to measure what students are learning but also to help make decisions about state-level educational reform. In addition, data from statewide assessments are being used as indicators of the level of performance of school boards, school administrators, and school staff, who increasingly are being held accountable for the performance of students on the statewide assessments.

•• BENEFITS OF DISABLED CHILDREN PARTICIPATING

As a result of these actions to improve educational results for all students, larger number of students with disabilities are participating in statewide assessment systems. Students with disabilities benefit in several ways:

1. By ensuring that students with disabilities participate in statewide assessments, the educational system commits itself to the notion that all educators are accountable for the learning of all students, including students with disabilities.

2. The expectations for students with disabilities are raised. Often these higher expectations lead to changes in curriculum or educational strategies or increased use of accommodations or adaptations to assist these students in reaching higher standards.

3. When policy and other decisions are made on the basis of statewide assessment results, the performance of students with disabilities is considered.

In addition, administrators should realize that most parents favor assessment because they realize their children need to know how to do well in assessment situations, which continue throughout life, particularly in employment (*Nineteenth Annual Report to Congress*, 1997).

•• STANDARDS FOR PARTICIPATING

Most school districts have developed standards in the major academic subjects for students achievement. Administrators enjoying the greatest success have standards that are well defined, clearly articulated goals and objectives, appropriate resources, assessment instruments, and curriculum sequences, and consider the interests of all stakeholders (Doyle, 1992; Rosenholtz, 1991; Schmidt, McKnight, & Raizen, 1996; Schmoker & Marzano, 1999). In order for standards to be achieved successfully, teachers should have knowledge of essential skills to be covered in each content area and teach to achieve the same standards employing a standard curriculum.

Administrators and related school personnel should employ proven methods and instructional techniques aligned with appropriate standards. Assessment techniques may be used to assess student's progress toward achieving the stated standards. Patterns of strengths and weaknesses should be identified and appropriate intervention strategies implemented to reduce the identified weakness (Colby, 1999). As much as possible students should be involved in the assessment and be apprised of the standards they are to achieve. Many administrators are struggling with keeping assessment tests up to date while ensuring that all students are meeting state standards.

In 1995 (the most recent year in which data were published), 45 to 50 states administered a statewide assessment to measure the performance of students; and another three states were developing their statewide assessments (Bond et al., 1996). Statewide assessments vary widely in terms of the number of assessment components, the content area and grade levels assessed, the types of assessments used, their purposes, and how the results affect students with disabilities. Assessments emerged as an issue in the early 1990s, when it became clear that disabled students were being excluded from assessments in which they could have participated (McGrew et al., 1992; Ysseldyke & Thurlow, 1994). Students were being excluded for many different reasons, ranging from concerns about their test scores lowering overall scores when aggregated with those of students without disabilities to concerns about the effect of assessments on the self-esteem or emotional health of students with disabilities.

•• EXCLUDING STUDENTS WITH DISABILITIES

The reasons for excluding students with disabilities from statewide assessments generally have been unfounded. Participation by students with disabilities does not appear to lower significantly the average performance level of students in a state because the number of students with disabilities who participate in relation to the total number of students who participate in the assessments is not large enough to change the overall average. As far as assessments affecting the emotional health of students with disabilities, many already participate in assessments and seem to benefit from the experience.

In fact, national and state assessment personnel (Ysseldyke, Thurlow, McGrew, & Shriner, 1994; Ysseldyke, Thurlow, McGrew, & Vanderwood, 1994a) indicated that students with disabilities can participate in educational accountability systems in at least three ways:

1. in exactly the same way as students without disabilities participate.

2. with accommodations in setting, scheduling, presentation, and/or response.

3. in an alternate assessment, designed specifically for students with severe disabilities.

•• INCLUDING STUDENTS WITH DISABILITIES

The National Center on Educational Outcomes (NCEO) is exploring each of these ways to include students with disabilities in statewide assessments. In addition, both the NCEO and the Office of Educational Research and Improvement (OERI) support programs that conduct research on the technical and implementation issues related to participation of students with disabilities in statewide assessments. Research by these national agencies should provide additional reasons why administrators should include children with disabilities in statewide assessments.

In this chapter, several trends that have occurred since 1990 in practices and attitudes regarding the participation of students with disabilities in statewide assessments are described. Emerging issues and future directions are also discussed (*Nineteenth Annual Report to Congress*, 1997).

•• NUMBER OF DISABLED STUDENTS PARTICIPATING IN STATEWIDE ASSESSMENTS

Since 1990, the goals of statewide assessment systems have broadened. Most administrators are cognizant of the fact that in addition to providing information on the performance of students, assessments are used to help design instructional change and assign educational accountability (Bond et al., 1996). States have also begun to hold schools accountable for the educational outcomes of students with disabilities. Most states and districts have a difficult time saying how many students with disabilities participate in their large-scale assessments.

•• CHANGES IN PRACTICES AND ATTITUDES

Evidence that practices and attitudes concerning the participation of students with disabilities in statewide assessments are changing comes primarily from analyzing state policies concerning assessment. In 1992, 28 states indicated they had participation guidelines; in 1993, 34 states indicated they had guidelines; in 1994 and again in 1995, 45 states indicated they had participation guidelines (Thurlow, Scott, & Ysseldyke, 1995b). Written guidelines provided by 34 states in 1996 showed that many factors are considered when making decisions about the participation of students with disabilities in statewide assessments. The IEP team decides whether or not to include and to what degree children with disabilities will be included in the assessment process. Participation decision is included in the written guidelines of nearly every state's guidelines. In many states, participation decisions take into consideration curricular alignment (i.e., how well the assessment is aligned with what the student is learning). A few states include consideration of the physical placement of the student (that is, the percentage of time the student is mainstreamed or whether content is received in a special education or general education class). Finally, a few states consider whether the resulting score will affect the validity or reliability of the measure.

Figure 3 illustrates comparisons of the bases for decisions in state-written guidelines on participation of students with disabilities in statewide assessments. From 1992 to 1995, there was an increased use of three of the four indicators used. The greatest increase has been in using the IEP team's recommendation when deciding whether an individual child should participate in statewide assessments.

Figure 3: *Changing Bases for Making Decisions about Participation of Students with Disabilities in Assessments*

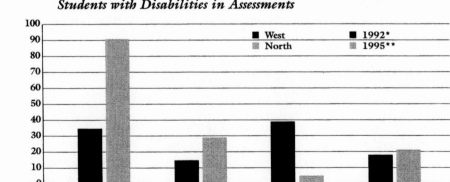

* Results based on 28 states.
** Results based on 34 states.
Source: Thurlow, Seyfarth, Scott. and Ysseldyke (1996); Thurlow, Ysseldyke, and Silverstein (1993).

•• USE OF ACCOMMODATIONS

Changing practices and attitudes about the participation of students with disabilities in statewide assessments also are reflected in state policies for using accommodations in assessments. Many students with disabilities can participate in state assessments only if appropriate accommodations are provided. Concerns about technical issues, such as whether scores of students who use assessment accommodations are comparable to scores of students who do not use accommodations, often lead to restrictive accommodation policies, even when the research data necessary to assess the effects of accommodations instruments validity has not been collected.

In 1992, 21 states indicated they had accommodations guidelines; in 1993, 25 states indicated they had guidelines; in 1994 and again in 1995, 39 states indicated they had accommodations guidelines (Thurlow, Scott, & Ysseldyke, 1995a). Analysis of written guidelines provided by 33 states in 1996 show that many kinds of accommodations are considered when making decisions about the use of accommodations by students with disabilities. Refer to chapter 8 for a comprehensive view of accommodations. Although various states have different guidelines for accommodations, administrators should be apprised of the most frequently used accommodations in the states. They are classified into one of four areas:

1. setting (taking the test in a separate room, a carrel, or a small group)

2. scheduling (extended time, breaks during testing, or testing on certain days)

3. presentation (using Braille or large print, sign language presentation of directions, or tape recording directions)

4. responses (computer-generated and scribe-recorded answers, point to answers, mark in booklet).

The specific assessment being administered often influences the type of accommodations that may be used. That is, an accommodation allowed during a norm-referenced assessment might not be appropriate for a criterion-referenced assessment.

More often in 1995 than in 1992, states' guidelines contained more specific language in terms of when certain accommodations might not be allowed. (For example, the guidelines might specify that a reading test could not be read to the student.) Figure 4 provides comparisons of the types of allowed accommodations described in the written guidelines of 33 states. Although there has been an increase in all four types of accommodations measured, the greatest increase has been in the use of extended time and reading items to students.

Figure 4: Changes in Policies for Accommodations Allowed in State Assessments

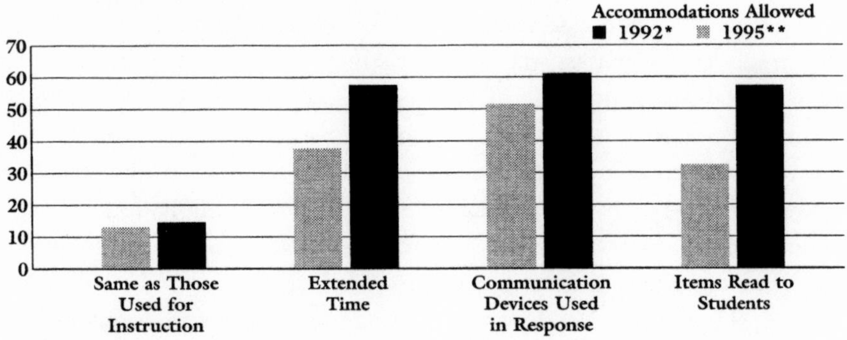

* Results based on 28 states.
** Results based on 34 states.
Source: Thurlow, et al., and Ysseldyke (1996); Thurlow, et al. (1993).

States educational agencies (SEAs) have come to realize that determining the participation rate of students with disabilities in states' assessments is actually quite complex (Erickson, Thurlow, & Ysseldyke, 1996). Participation rates may vary for different assessments and at different grade levels. In addition, children may be counted at one time of the year but have transferred out of the school, district, or state by the time the assessment is administered.

Evidence suggests that in many cases, state personnel can only give general estimates of participation rates. In 1992 and 1993, 55 states and outlying areas reported overall participation rates ranging from less than 10 percent to more than 90 percent (Shriner & Thurlow, 1993). However, in 1994, when states were asked by NCEO to provide the participation rates of students with disabilities for each assessment the states administered, states were able to provide estimates for only 49 of the 133 assessments administered that year (Erickson et al., 1995, 1996). The estimates proved ranged from 4 to 100 percent.

Since 1991, most state educational agencies have come to realize they have not defined their data elements in a way that facilitates collection or analysis of quality data on students with disabilities. During the past few years, SEAs have begun to add data elements to their files that will enable them to identify students with disabilities. Some states are requiring a test form be completed for every student in a school so participation rates are based on actual school enrollments at the time of testing. States have also started to investigate the use of accommodations, which will help special educators and administrators learn about the types of accommodations actually used.

•• CHALLENGING ISSUES

States have made much progress in implementing statewide assessment systems that include students with disabilities. However, at least three challenging issues remain unresolved. The first question is how states can continue to maintain student confidentiality when including data from students with disabilities with data from other students. This question is most pertinent for schools and districts in which the number of students with disabilities may be small, and it is therefore relatively easy to match students with learning problems to a particular score.

Second, it is not clear that the scores of students with disabilities who were provided accommodations can be compared with those of students who did not use accommodations. Are these scores similar? Are the scores of students who use accommodations valid? Intensive research must be done to study the effects of accommodations on test validity.

Third is the inevitable struggle with how best to report data. In the past, states often did not report statewide assessment data for students with disabilities, even though the data were available. Data from these students were removed from aggregated scores, were not reported separately from aggregated scores, and still yet were not reported separately to provide information on the status of students with disabilities.

These challenges are being addressed as states begin to evaluate systematically the effect of including students with disabilities in assessments. It is hoped these efforts will increase the educational systems' and administrators' accountability for all students and that more comprehensive information on how well special education services are meeting the needs of students with disabilities will become available (*Nineteenth Annual Report to Congress,* 1997).

•• ALTERNATE STATEWIDE ASSESSMENTS FOR STUDENTS WITH DISABILITIES

Including a statewide assessment for students with disabilities who are unable to participate in the regular assessment is an important part of designing statewide accountability systems that will include all students. However, states have little experience in designing such assessments, and areas of research are still being identified and refined.

Whether or not students with disabilities should take part in assessments (testing) conducted across the states or district has been an area of controversy over the years among administrators of special education programs. If these students are included, what type of modifications and accommodations, if any, should be made to ensure their disabilities do not get in the way of their demonstrating what they know or can do?

As most administrators are aware, IDEA 1997 explicitly requires states to include children with disabilities, with accommodations when necessary, in state and districtwide assessment programs. For children who cannot participate in regular assessments, states must develop alternative assessments by 2000 (see chapter 8 for additional details).

•• PURPOSE AND NATURE OF ALTERNATE ASSESSMENTS

The purpose of an alternate assessment system is to measure the learning of those students who are not working toward the standards assessed by the general assessment system. Typically, only students with severe cognitive disabilities who are working on educational goals more closely aligned with independent functioning skills should participate in alternate assessments. Chapter 8 surveys the various types of alternate strategies. At present, only three states have developed, or are developing, an alternate assessment for students unable to participate in the regular state assessment. Kentucky has an alternate assessment it has already implemented. Scores obtained on the alternate portfolio assessment used in Kentucky contribute to overall accountability scores, just as scores on the general assessment do. Maryland is field-testing an alternate assessment system it has developed. Texas is currently developing an alternate assessment system.

•• CHALLENGING ISSUES

IDEA 1997 has challenged administrators of special education programs to develop alternate statewide assessment. Research and experiences to date show that at least three types of challenges will have to be addressed at the very onset of system development.

First, exactly who should participate in the alternate assessment will have to be determined. Too many students with disabilities might be administered the alternate assessment when they could take the regular assessment, either with or without accommodations.

Second, the skills or goals to be assessed by the alternate assessment must be defined. If the alternate assessment is to be used for accountability purposes, scores need to be aggregated. In order to aggregate the scores, some common core of learning will have to be identified. A group of stakeholders that includes educators, parents, and policymakers should reach consensus on the domains of learning that are important for all students in the alternate system.

Third, a way must be found to integrate results from the alternate assessment into the accountability system, which includes results from the regular assessments as well as other types of information, such as dropout rates.

The results of the alternate assessment will also have to be reported. The methods used to resolve the three issues described here will probably also provide a framework for the appropriate reporting of results (*Nineteenth Annual Report to Congress*, 1997).

•• SUMMARY

Increasing numbers of students with disabilities are being included in statewide assessments. As clearer guidelines on participation criteria and the use of accommodations are developed, the educational system is likely to be held increasingly accountable for the educational results of students with disabilities. Five developments should be of particular interest to state departments of education and administrators of special education programs.

First, efforts to identify the effects of including students with disabilities in statewide assessment and accountability systems will increase.

Second, accommodations will become more available, and there will be increased scrutiny of certain accommodations, such as reading aloud, using scribes, clarifying directions, and others.

Third, alternate assessments will be developed and implemented. Once this takes place, the educational system can begin to be held accountable for the educational results of the students with disabilities who take alternate assessments.

Fourth, state assessments are being revised in response to changes in the law, public challenges, and national initiatives. Assessment results will assist policymakers in improving educational programs. Students with disabilities must participate in the assessment process. This participation will assist the schools in addressing the learning needs of children with disabilities.

Fifth, results of assessments that include students with disabilities, and of alternate assessments, will be increasingly included in assessment reports. Evidence indicates that it is still a widespread practice to exclude results for students with disabilities from score summaries and reports, even when the students take part in regular assessments. The entire educational system will assume greater responsibility for the education of students with disabilities when these students' scores are reported and as measurements of their performance become part of the state accountability system (*Nineteenth Annual Report to Congress*, 1997).

•• REFERENCES

Bond, L. A., Braskamp, D., & Roeber, E. (1996). *The status report of the assessment programs in the United States.* Oak Brook, IL: North Central Regional Educational Laboratory and Council of Chief State School Officers.

Colby, S. (1999). Grading in a standards-based system. *Educational Leadership, 56*(6), 52–55.

Doyle, W. (1992). Curriculum and pedagogy. In P. W. Jackson (Ed.), *Handbook of research curriculum.* New York: Macmillan.

Elliott, J. L., Thurlow, M. L., & Ysseldyke, J. E. (1996). *Assessment guidelines that maximize the participation of students with disabilities in large-scale assessments: Characteristics and considerations.* (ERIC Document Reproduction Service No. ED 404803) Washington, DC: U.S. Department of Education.

Erickson, R.N., Thurlow, M.L., & Thor, K. (1995). *State special education outcomes.* (ERIC Document Reproduction Service No. ED 404 749) Washington, DC: U.S. Department of Education.

Erickson, R. N., Thurlow, M. L., Thor, K. A., & Seyfarth, A. (1996). *State special education outcomes* (ERIC Document Reproduction Service No. ED 385 061).

Erickson, R. N., Thurlow, M. L., & Ysseldyke, J. E. (1996). *Neglected numerators, drifting denominators, and fractured fractions: Determining participation rates for students with disabilities in statewide assessment programs* (Synthesis Report 23). Minneapolis: University of Minnesota, National Center on Educational Outcomes.

Kearns, J. F., Kleinert, H. L., & Kennedy, S. (1999). We need not exclude anyone. *Educational Leadership, 56*(6), 33–38.

McGrew, K. S., Thurlow, M. L., Shriner, J. G., & Spiegel, A. N. (1992). *Inclusion of students with disabilities in national and state data collection programs* (Technical Report 2). Minneapolis: University of Minnesota, National Council on Educational Outcomes.

Nineteenth Annual Report to Congress on the Implementation of The Individuals with Disabilities Education Act. (1997). Washington, DC: Department of Education, U.S. Printing Office.

Rosenholtz, S. J. (1991). *Teacher's workplace: The social organization of schools.* New York: Teachers College Press.

Schmidt, W. H., McKnight, C. C., & Raizen, S. A. (1996). *Spintered vision: An investigation of U.S. science and mathematics education: Executive summary.*

Lansing: U.S. National Research Center for the Third International Mathematics and Sciences Study, Michigan State University.

Schmoker, M., & Marzano, R. J. (1999). Realizing the promise of standard-based education. *Educational Leadership, 56*(6), 17–21.

Shriner, J. G., & Thurlow, M. L. (1993). *State special education results.* Minneapolis: University of Minnesota, National Center on Educational Outcomes.

Thurlow, M. L., Scott, D. L., & Ysseldyke, J. E. (1995a). *Compilation of states' guidelines for accommodations in assessments for students with disabilities* (Synthesis Report 17). Minneapolis: University of Minnesota, National Center on Educational Opportunities.

Thurlow, M. L., Scott, D. L., & Ysseldyke, J. E. (1995b). *Compilation of states' guidelines for learning students with disabilities in assessments* (Synthesis Report 18). Minneapolis: University of Minnesota, National Center on Educational Opportunities.

Thurlow, M. L., Seyfarth, A., Scott, D., & Ysseldyke, J. E. (1996). *State assessment participation criteria and accommodations guidelines: 1996 analysis.*

Thurlow, M. L., Ysseldyke, J. E., & Silverstein, B. (1993). *Testing accommodations for students with disabilities: A review of the literature* (Synthesis Report 4). Minneapolis: University of Minnesota, National Center on Educational Outcomes.

Ysseldyke, J. E., & Thurlow, M. L. (1994). *Guidelines for inclusion of students with disabilities outcomes in large-scale assessments* (Policy Directions 1). Minneapolis: University of Minnesota, National Center on Educational Outcomes.

Ysseldyke, J. E., Thurlow, M. L., McGrew, K.S., & Shriner, M. (1994a). *Recommendations for making decisions about the participation of students with disabilities in statewide assessment programs* (Synthesis Report 15). Minneapolis: University of Minnesota, National Center on Education Outcomes.

Ysseldyke, J. E., Thurlow, M. L., McGrew, K.S., & Vanderwood, M. (1994a). *Making decisions about the inclusion of students with disabilities in large-scale assessments: A report on a working conference to develop guidelines on inclusion and accommodations.* (ERIC Document Reproduction Service No. ED 372 652) Washington, DC: U.S. Department of Education.

Ysseldyke, J. E., Thurlow, M. L., McGrew, K.S., & Vanderwood, M. (1994b). *Making decisions about the inclusion of students with disabilities in statewide assessments* (Synthesis Report 13). Minneapolis: University of Minnesota, National Center on Education Outcomes.

CHAPTER 8

Assessment

Assessment is a process of collecting relevant individual information in order to make valid decisions in the areas of learning and human functioning. It is a multifaceted process, that involves more than the use of standardized or informal tests. The process includes assessing individuals on a variety of mental, physical, and social tasks (see appendix B for additional detail). This chapter addresses the use of tests by administrators of special education programs and offers assistance on making sound educational decisions, which may be used to make valid instructional decisions (Salvia & Ysseldyke, 1998; Taylor, 1997; Witt, Elliott, Daly, Gresham, & Kramer, 1998).

Assessing, identifying, and placing children in the least restrictive environment requires knowledge of the use of nondiscriminatory and multidisciplinary assessment (Taylor, 1998; Thurlow, Elliott, & Ysseldyke, 1998). Once educational need is established through formal and informal testing, the student should be referred to a multidisciplinary team. Based on the type of data assessed by the team, the student's disability is defined and classified.

•• MULTIDISCIPLINARY TEAM MEMBERSHIP AND RESPONSIBILITIES

The team must include a "teacher or other specialist with knowledge in the areas of suspected disability" (34 CFR 300.533). In practice, diagnosticians and parents are usually members of the multidisciplinary team (MDT). Salvia and Ysseldyke (1998) wrote that the team is responsible for gathering information and making a recommendation about a student's disability. In theory, the decision-making process is direct. The MDT assesses the student's performance to see whether it meets the criteria for a specific disability. It must collect information required by the definition of exceptionality. Federal regulations (34 CFR 300.533) also require the teacher to do the following:

- Draw on information from a variety of sources, including aptitude and achievement tests, teachers' recommendations, physical conditions, social or cultural background, and adaptive behavior.

- Ensure that information obtained from all of these sources is documented and carefully considered.

School administrators should examine records of each team member and make sure they are competent in the areas being assessed. They should be certified or licensed in their respective disciplines. It should be clear that the focus of assessment is to determine the nature and type of disability, type of placement, how well the student is meeting the stated goals and objectives, and related services needed as reported by the team.

•• MAJOR TYPES OF ASSESSMENT DEVICES AND STRATEGIES

Several types of assessment instruments and devices are used to make decisions relevant to students' abilities (Browder, 1991; McLoughlin & Lewis, 1991). They are too numerous to be listed in this chapter. Observation, anecdotal records, self-assessment, portfolio assessment, recordings, and a brief summary of types of tests employed to assess human behavior are addressed here.

Observation

Observation is a prime assessment strategy and should be an essential part of all assessment practices. Of utmost importance is a predetermined system or structure to guide the observational process. School administrators and school personnel must define the behaviors to be observed as well as the place, time, and duration of the behavior to be observed. Once the school administrator has selected the types of behavior to be observed, it is necessary to develop or use some type of recording instrument to record the observations as illustrated in figure 5.

Anecdotal Records

Anecdotal records provide a written account of the child's behavior. Data from rating scales and checklists may be used to validate narrative statements in anecdotal records. Administrators of special education programs should exercise caution in recording events and separating facts from their interpretations of behaviors. For validity, data should be kept over a period of time to note trends.

Biases known or unknown tend to influence the information contained in anecdotal records. There is both observer bias and observed bias. *Observer bias* may be evident from recording invalid behaviors because of some like or dislike of a special characteristic of the observed. Observed bias may result because the

Figure 5: Observation Checklist

Teacher _____   Observer _____

Lesson _____   Date _____   Time _____

KEY: A = Always   F = Frequently   N = Never

Behaviors	A	F	N
Student deals positively with accusations.			
Student accepts apologies from others.			
Student respects the feelings of others			
Student knows how to avoid fights and conflicts and displays good humor.			
Student deals effectively with teasing.			
Student moves about room independently to perform routine tasks.			
Student stays away from troublesome situations			
and accepts cultural values of other pupils.			
Student verbally shows appreciation when assisted.			
Student gives praise or compliments to other students.			
Student accepts complients from othrs.			
Student apologizes for inappropriate behavior.			
Student expresses anger in a positive way.			
Student attempts to understand another's anger without getting angry.			
Student shows affection and appreciation toward others.			
Student asks permission to borrow or use other's belongings.			
Student does not lose control when left out of group activities.			
Student practices self-control.			
Student disagrees in an acceptable manner.			
Student accepts losing without becoming upset.			

Source: G. R. Taylor (in press). Informal classroom assessment strategies for teachers. Blue Ridge Summit, PA: Scarecrow Press.

observed may behave differently simply because he or she is aware of being observed. Unobtrusive observations are valuable and must be updated and kept over a period of time and used to strengthen the instructional program by programming the student's strengths and weaknesses into the curriculum (Rhodes & Nathenson-Mejia, 1992). The issue of collecting and organizing information in anecdotal records must be carefully considered. Some type of systematic plan should be evident. A simple three-ring binder sectioned off alphabetically by students' last names, a separate notebook on each content area, or a card file system may be used.

Self-Assessment

Using self-assessment data can yield valuable information on how the child feels about educational issues. Self-assessment data may come from a variety of sources, such as interviews, journals, log questionnaires, checklists, and rating scales. Construction of instruments used in self-assessment must consider the development level of the child in the principal areas of mental, social, and physical development. In the case of disabled children, the type of disability must be carefully considered. In some instances, school personnel will have to assist the child in completing his or her self-assessment (Davison & Pearce, 1992).

Portfolio Assessment

The values of using portfolios in assessing the strengths and weaknesses of children with disabilities have been well documented in the professional literature (Pike & Salender, 1995; Salinger, 1991; Wolfe, 1989). Effective portfolio assessment requires a cooperative effort on the part of school administrators and school personnel, children, and sometimes parents. The assessment should reflect the learning as well as the products of learning. Teacher should develop scoring rubrics with input from school administrators and students. Instruct students on how to use the scoring rubrics. Objective information should be reviewed periodically by school administrators, school personnel, and parents to update or delete documents or expand information items selected for inclusion in portfolios. Items should be directly related to objectives specified in the student's instructional program and to the IEP strategies developed. Develop captions to (1) identify the document, (2) show a description of the content, (3) explain why items were included, and (4) summarize and synthesize information.

Types of Recordings

Several types of recordings are necessary to record information from assessment instruments and devices. *Event recording* involves recording specific behaviors that occur. *Duration recording* is done on a continuous basis and all behavior are recorded. *Interval recording* is reserved for specific times to record behaviors. In general, short observations conducted over a period of time are frequently the best method. This approach appears to provide a better sample of the child's behavior. Rotate the time of observations to reduce the risks of biased behavior of results.

Use check marks to observe the occurrence of the behaviors or simply write yes or no to each behavior as shown in figure 5. These observational data may be used to determine strengths and weaknesses in various areas and indicate where intervention will be needed. As indicated, students may be observed in different settings. The teacher should choose those settings and times when the behaviors are most likely to occur. Certain types of behaviors may manifest themselves at certain times in the day. Several types of recording systems may be used such as event, duration, and interval recording (Pike & Salend, 1995).

•• MAJOR TYPES OF ASSESSMENT TESTS

Assessment tests and instruments have been developed to assess and evaluate all aspects of human behavior. Some are paper-and-pencil tests; others are tests administered by specialists. Some are norm referenced, and others are criterion referenced. Norm- and criterion-referenced tests are chiefly used by administrators and school personnel. These tests are based on norms of a particular age group. Criterion-referenced tests are based on the curriculum or objectives of a school district.

•• NORM-REFERENCED TESTS

Norm-referenced tests (NRT) are based on the average performance of a typical age group using standardized procedures. Items in the tests provide a sample of curriculum content that students should have had in a certain age group or subject area. For example, a fifth grade student should have been taught multiplication; test items are constructed to measure this skill. School administrators may use these scores to determine who is on or below grade levels. In essence, NRT scores show how students' scores compare with each other within school districts and across the country. NRT scores typically do not fall below the established norm or school (Salvia & Ysseldyke, 1998).

Types of interpretive scores given on norm tables are grade equivalent, intelligence quotients, mental ages, percentile ranks, and stanines. Sometimes raw scores are converted to standard scores or weighted scores. Standardized or norm-referenced scores are the most objective instruments available for measuring factual recognition, certain skills, concepts, understanding, problem solving, and sometimes personality traits such as interests and attitudes.

Standardized or norm-referenced tests should possess the following characteristics:

1. They should be available in at least two equivalent forms. It is best to use a different form when pre- and posttesting pupils.

2. They should have acceptable face validity. The tests should look valid.

3. They should use symbols and pictures that are familiar to pupils from various cultures.

4. They should reflect descriptive normative data on pupils selected for the normative groups. Educators can match and compare characteristics of the normative group with their pupils before selecting tests.

5. They should have tables reflecting appropriate standard scores to which the raw scores are transposed. School administrators may use these tables to convert raw scores to standard scores.

Statistical properties of standardized tests include the mean, the median, the standard deviation, the standard error, reliability, validity, norms, percentile, developmental scores, and standard scores (Taylor, 2000).

Mean

The mean is the arithmetic average of scores in a distribution. It is a simple way of finding the average performance of a group or an individual.

Median

The median, like the mean, gives information relevant to the central tendency. It is the middle score, commonly referred to as the 50th percentile or the 2nd quartile. The median may be used to show the performances of individuals at various grade levels.

Standard Deviation

The standard deviation is a unit of measurement that shows the spread of scores in a distribution. It also shows the standing of a score in terms of the percentage of scores or units from the mean.

Standard Error

The standard error shows the amount of error in a score. It shows the band of confidence within which an individual's score may be expected to fall. The greater the standard error, the greater the variation in the estimated score and the less confidence there is in the score.

Reliability

The reliability of a test refers to whether the test consistently yields the same results on repeated administration of a test. The greater the consistency in a test, the greater the reliability. Reliability is usually expressed as a correlation coefficient. Reliability coefficients range from .00 to 1.00. The higher the coefficient, the greater the reliability.

Validity

The validity of a test is the degree to which the test measures the concept it purports to measure. Validity is difficult to determine because educators are not always sure a trait really exists or they are not sure the instrument is measuring the stated trait. Validity is also expressed in correlation coefficients ranging from .00 to 1.00. As in reliability, the higher the coefficient, the greater the validity.

Norms

Norms are the average performances of a typical age group. They are usually established for select age groups. Norms are part of the process used in standardizing a test. They are established by using the same age group in the standardization of the norms as the group intended to take the test. Many standardized tests do not include minorities or children with disabilities in constructing norms. These tests are frequently not fair to them because they generally do not reflect their cultural and other experiences.

Percentiles

Percentiles enable educators to rank individual scores in a distribution of scores. It can be easily explained and interpreted to parents and some students. A score at the 70th percentile implies the performance of a student is equal to or greater than 70 out of 100 individuals tested.

Developmental Scores

Developmental scores are usually reported as chronological or mental ages and grade equivalents. The grade equivalent score is commonly used to determine a student's grade level. A grade equivalent score of 4.0 may be interpreted as the student performing at the fourth grade level.

Standard Scores

The many types of standard scores are mostly used to interpret raw scores and include deviation IQ scores, Z-scores, T-scores, and stanine scores. Most test manuals include tables for use in interpreting the various standard scores.

Criterion-Referenced Tests

Unlike norm-referenced tests, criterion-referenced tests may be locally normed. They provide information to determine how well students are performing based on school districts' goals and objectives in various subject areas. They are designed to compare an individual's performance to some criterion or behavior. Test items are constructed to measure the attainment of the stated objectives. Students not performing up to the criterion will probably have difficulty mastering the next instructional sequence. These test items may be constructed in several basic domains from the curriculum. For more information on strategies employed in constructing criterion-referenced tests, see Wiersman and Jurs (1990).

These tests are commonly used to determine how well students have mastered the domains outlined in the curriculum (Witt et al., 1998). Several states have begun to employ criterion-referenced testing. They are designed more for individualized instruction than norm-referenced tests. Specific standards have been set for mastery of the curriculum domains. Students not meeting the standard or criterion are judged as working below grade level. The state of Maryland has adapted criterion-referenced testing statewide. The use of criterion tests, as with most assessment devices, requires some accommodations when assessing children with exceptionalities based on the nature and extent of the exceptionality. Many of these tests have to be modified and adapted for children with disabilities. Suggestions for modifying and adapting tests are discussed later in the chapter.

•• ADVANTAGES OF USING STANDARDIZED AND CRITERION-REFERENCED TESTS

Generally, standardized and criterion tests are used to assess students' abilities in various subject areas and to compare results to a national normative or local sample. Results may be used to adapt or modify the instructional program, addressing the strengths and weaknesses of students. Parents can also be apprised of their children's achievement in various subjects. Standardized and criterion test results can show a progression or a regression of a student's progress over time in various subject areas. Maker (1993) found that standardized tests assess students in real lifelike and complex situations concerning both process and product. These tests may be group or individual, with a preponderance being group. They are less expensive than individual tests and may be administered to groups. Standardized and criterion results may be valuable in providing information relevant to how well expected outcomes for students have been achieved. They may provide a source for grading students and pointing out their progress. Many federally funded programs require school districts to report progress of students using standardized test scores.

Disadvantages of Using Standardized and Criterion-Referenced Tests

The disadvantages of using standardized and criterion measures include the following:

1. The tests reflect a mismatch between what is taught in the various school districts and test items.

2. The item pool of test questions in certain areas is too small to make a meaningful comparison of students' achievement.

3. The tests measure students' abilities in academic subjects or curricula only. Test items do not effectively measure the various types of intelligence or out-of-school learning of students. Several authors have criticized the use of standardized and criterion-referenced tests with culturally diverse groups and individuals with disabilities (McLoughlin & Lewis, 1991; Salinger, 1991; Salvia & Ysseldyke, 1998).

4. The criterion-referenced tests are expensive and time consuming to administer.

5. The criterion-referenced tests do not identify accurately the presence of disabilities in children with behavioral and learning problems.

6. Too much attention is focused on weaknesses as revealed by test results rather than the strengths of children with disabilities.

7. Specific accommodation criteria should be in place to implement, as well as techniques for alternate assessment strategies. We address these issues in greater detail later in the chapter.

8. Standardized tests are not a fair way to judge the educational effectiveness of schools.

Another major disadvantage of standardized and criterion-referenced tests is that the items most often used fall within the middle difficulty level (40 to 60 percent). Similarly, items answered correctly by 80 percent or higher by students are not normally included. Moreover, these tests do not consider the native intellectual abilities of the students being tested. Many of the items on standardized and criterion-referenced tests are quantitative or they are verbal tasks. Many children with disabilities do not have skills in these areas; consequently they perform poorly. Other aspects of intelligence should be considered in constructing standardized tests.

The premise in constructing standardized and criterion-referenced tests is based on the concept that major learning occurs inside the school. This focus on of out-of-school learning can be a serious disadvantage to many children from deprived backgrounds. Many culturally deprived children have not been exposed to the out-of-school experiences and are at a marked disadvantage (Popham, 1999).

•• TEACHER-MADE AND INFORMAL TESTS

Teacher-made and informal tests may be used to supplement or compare results from standardized tests. They may also be employed when standardized tests are not adequate for reasons of content, difficulty, scope, or sensitive cultural materials. The addition of teacher-made tests based on the objectives of the course will yield better results. One of the first things to consider in constructing a test is the type of test format. There are several types of testing formats: true-false, multiple choice, matching, completion, and essay. The type of format chosen depends greatly on the disabling conditions of the children being tested. For example, an essay-type test may not be suited for a child with cerebral palsy. Several adaptations and modifications may need to be made in the testing command and response.

Observations, questionnaires, interviews, and inventories are available. These informal assessments provide information relevant to the students' current level of performance and assist in specifying goals, objectives, and needed adaptations and modifications in the instructional program. Student performance is compared to specific learning tests or objectives within the curricula. These techniques permit the direct assessment of student behavior that may be compared with norm-referenced test data. They may be adapted for use with children who have disabilities.

•• QUESTIONNAIRES

Questionnaires may be developed to fit different formats including surveys, checklists, rating scales, multiple choice, matching, completion, and true/false items. Questionnaires are designed to collect specific information from students. Little training is needed in constructing questionnaires. The only requirement is knowledge of the content being solicited. They are relatively easy to administer and score.

•• INTERVIEWS

For many children with disabilities, an alternate means must be available for collecting information other than by questionnaires. Their disabilities frequently prohibit them from responding to questionnaires appropriately. Interviews may be substituted to elicit information. The teacher may control the length, time, and provide directions during the interviewing process. Frequently, teachers need detailed information that students can provide. Parents and school administrators must be interviewed to secure the necessary information. The validity of information secured from interviews greatly depends on the accuracy of the information provided by the interviewee. Administrators and related school personnel must be aware and proceed with caution when interpreting information.

•• INVENTORIES AND SUBJECT MATTER TESTS

Inventories and subject matter tests may be used to assess a variety of skills in curricula areas for children with exceptionalities. These techniques provide information on children's present levels of functioning in the curriculum. Inventories may be developed by the teacher or purchased commercially for many subject areas. In designing inventories and subject matter tests, school administrators and teachers should be knowledgeable about the following:

1. The curriculum area being assessed

2. Developmentally appropriate skills

3. Breaking tasks or skills into small manageable parts

4. Preparing test items for each subtest of the curriculum being assessed

5. Adapting and modifying the number of test items based on the exceptionality of the children

6. Sequencing the test items from easiest to degree of difficulty.

Other Factors to Consider

The purpose of the test must be clearly articulated and specified for the test developed. Steps include arranging items in order of difficulty, preparing directions for administering the test, setting the time limit, conducting an item analysis, constructing a scoring system, and establishing the reliability and validity of the test.

•• COMMONLY USED TESTS IN SPECIAL EDUCATION

The validity and reliability of the tests used to assess children with disabilities should be firmly established before use in order to make appropriate decisions relevant to assessment, classification, placement, intervention, and educational strategies. School administrators must know the limitation of standardized tests and the competencies of the staff who administer and interpret the results.

Tests of Cognitive Abilities

There is no universal agreement concerning the definition of intelligence. Historically, Binet defined intelligence as a collection of faculties, including judgments, practical sense, initiative, and the ability to adapt to circumstances. The multifactor theory of intelligence included such mental abilities as verbal, number, perceptual speed, reasoning, memory, word fluency, and spatial visualization (Wallace, Larsen, & Elksnin, 1992). Wechsler (1958) stated that intelligence is the ability of the person to act purposefully, to think rationally, and to deal effectively with one's environment.

School administrators should be aware of the many uses and definitions of tests to measure intelligence and the equity of using them with minority populations before selection.

The Stanford-Binet

The Stanford-Binet Test (fourth edition) is a valuable asset to educational achievement and testing. It assists in validating severe reading disability, physical disability, and emotional problems, and it provides a detailed and comprehensive assessment of intellectual level. The test is a powerful tool used to diagnose and predict intellectual levels. There are two equivalent forms based on different age levels. The items requires verbal and numerical manipulation, reasoning, and logical selection, choice, and good judgment.

The latest revision assesses cognitive abilities in individuals with disabilities from ages 2 through 23 years (Thorndike, Hagen, & Sattler, 1986). The test contains fifteen subtests that assess and evaluate four broad areas of intellectual functioning: verbal reasoning, abstract/visual reasoning, quantitative reasoning, and short-term memory. Fifteen subtests evaluate cognitive abilities.

Assessing and Diagnosing Behavior

The Stanford-Binet Test provides a cross-sectional view of the child's mental abilities. Test results can provide educators and mental health specialists with detailed information relevant to the child's performances and physical disabilities and academic skills. The Stanford-Binet Test is not designed to assess social and interpersonal skills.

The Wechsler Intelligence Scale III (WISC-III)

The WISC-III is the third revision of the scale originally published in 1949. It is individually administered to children ages 6 through 16, 11 months, to assess cognitive abilities. According to Wechsler (1991), the WISC-III can be used for a number of purposes, including psychoeducational assessment, diagnosis of exceptional needs, and clinical and neuropsychological assessment.

The test is divided into two major scales, verbal and performance. The verbal scale contains six subtests and the performance scale contains seven subtests. The total scores on the verbal subtests yield a verbal IQ score; the total scores on the performance subtests yield a performance IQ score. The scores on both tests are combined to yield a full IQ score.

The WISC-III's twelve subtests may be grouped into four factor-based index scores: (1) verbal comprehension contains information, similarities, vocabulary, and comprehension, (2) perceptual organization contains picture, completion, arrangement, block design, and object assembly, (3) freedom from distractability contains arithmetic digit and span, and (4) processing speed contains coding, symbol, and search.

Assessing and Diagnosing Behavior

The WISC-III has been used successfully to assess the intelligence of gifted, retarded, learning disabled, behavior disorders, epilepsy, speech language delays, and hearing impairment (Cohen & Spenciner, 1998).

Wechsler Preschool and Primary Scale of Intelligence–Revised (WPPSI–R)

The Wechsler Preschool and Primary Scale of Intelligence–Revised (Wechsler, 1967) is a revision of the Wechsler Preschool and Primary Scale (Weschler, 1967). It is an individually administered test of intelligence for children ages 3 to 7 years. The WPPSI–R is similar in format and content to the WISC-III. The WPPSI contains twelve subtests, two of which are optional, arranged in two scales: verbal and performance. Individual scores can be obtained for each of the subtests. Verbal, performance, and full-scale IQ scores are calculated from the subtest scores.

Assessing and Diagnosing Behavior

The WPPSI-R is widely used with children with disabilities. Children who are mentally disabled, learning disabled, and speech impaired tend to score higher on the WISC than the Stanford-Binet because their performance IQ appear to be higher than their verbal skills. In essence, their performance IQ raises their total performance. A sample of sixteen gifted children who had been tested with the Stanford-Binet test showed that some of these children would not be classified as gifted based on their performance on the WPPSI–R. Due to the limited number of samples included, additional research is recommended (Cohen & Spenciner, 1998).

Woodcock-Johnson Psychoeducational Battery–Revised

The Woodcock-Johnson Psychoeducational Battery–Revised (WJ–R) is an individually administered battery that assesses cognitive and academic abilities in individuals ages 2 years through adulthood. The battery consists of two tests, Woodcock-Johnson Tests on Cognitive Ability (WJCOG–R) and the Woodcock-Johnson Tests on Achievement (WJ-RACH). Each standard battery contains a standard battery and a supplementary battery. Each standard battery can be administered alone or with the supplemental batteries. The WJ–R has the following purposes: (1) diagnosis, (2) determination of psychoeducational discrepancies, (3) program placement, (4) individual program planning, (5) guidance, (6) assessing growth, (7) program evaluation, and (8) research.

The WJ-COG is based on the Horn-Cattel theory of cognitive processing. The abilities measured by the WJ-COG are fluid reasoning, comprehension knowledge, visual processing, auditory processing, processing speed, long-term retrieval, and short-term memory. The subtest, which includes at least two measures of each factor, forms clusters for each of these abilities.

Assessing and Diagnosing Behavior
The WJCOG–R is a norm-referenced, individually administered battery that assesses cognitive abilities in individuals ages 24 months through adulthood. The battery consists of two parts, cognitive and achievement. Reliability information is lacking. Additional investigation of validity is needed, especially regarding the use of this battery with young children with disabilities.

•• ASSESSING SENSORY AND MOTOR ABILITIES

Chapter 3 addressed the causes, identification, characteristics, diagnosis, and needs of children with disabilities in the areas of vision, hearing, and mobility. The chapter overviews assessment strategies for this group. Because of the sensory limitations among this group, assessment must be multifaceted: school administrators must identify, employ, and involve numerous professionals and specialists skilled in the areas of sensory and motor functioning in the assessment process.

Assessing Individuals with Visual Impairments

Assessing individuals with visual needs requires many assessment strategies and many specialists to administer them. Assessment processes commonly used include (1) collecting information about the nature and extent of the vision loss, (2) Braille reading and writing, (3) listening skills, (4) orientation and mobility, and (5) social and recreational skills (Silberman, 1996; Taylor, 1999). There are only a few current norm-referenced instruments that are valid to assess the visually impaired.

The Oregon Project for the Visually Impaired and Blind Preschooler is a criterion-reference instrument. It is used to assess children up to age 7 in the areas of cognitive, language, self-help, socialization, fine-motor, and gross-motor abilities. Some items were designed specifically to assess individuals with vision problems. Results are used to modify the instructional program.

Three commonly used tests assess achievement of the visually impaired. The Stanford Achievement Test, the Iowa Tests of Basic Skills, and the Brigance Comprehensive Inventory of Basic Skills are available in Braille from the American Printing House for the Blind. An important caution: Approval of the use of these instruments should be made only with the knowledge that these instruments were normed for normal children and may not be appropriate for children with visual impairments unless accommodations are made.

Assessing and Diagnosing Behavior

Multi-interdisciplinary teams are frequently needed to assess individuals with visual impairments because many of them have other disabilities. At least one member of the team should be competent in assessing visual impairment (Barraga & Erin, 1992). Assessing data relevant to visual functioning aids in educational programming and provides critical information that may assist the student in his or her ecological environment. The types of accommodations the student will need should be addressed during the assessment process.

Assessing Individuals with Hearing Impairments

Assessment batteries for students with hearing disabilities consists of several domains such as communication skills, cognitive functioning, academic achievement, and social and emotional skills (Mayer, 1996). Using standardized instruments that do not include the hearing impaired in the standardization sample will require making accommodations in the test stimulus and response.

Assessing and Diagnosing Behavior

The test examiner must be competent in the area of hearing impairment. He or she must be knowledgeable and able to communicate with the hearing impaired. Frequently, it is the examiner who will modify administration and response procedures to accommodate the student who is hearing impaired. Professionals who are not directly involved in the school should be consulted when assessing medical, physical, and social deficits outside of the auspices of the school.

Assessing Students with Physical Disabilities

Assessment information for individuals with physical disabilities comes from a variety of sources, including observational standardized instruments and non-standardized testing procedures (Pike & Spencer, 1991). The Denver Developmental Screening Test II, the AGS Early Screening Profiles, the Bruininks-Oseretsky Test of Motor Proficiency, and the Peabody Development Motor Scales and Activity Cards are recommended for assessing motor problems.

The Bruininks-Oseretsky Test of Motor Proficiency assesses motor function of children 4.6 to 14.6 years of age (Bruininks, 1978). The test assesses motor development for the purposes of making decisions about physical education programming, gross- and fine-motor skills development, and developing and evaluating motor training programs. The text consists of two forms: the short from uses 14 items from the complete battery, which consists of 8 subtests with a total of 46 items:

1. Running speed and agility

2. Balance

3. Bilateral coordination

4. Strength

5. Upper-limb coordination

6. Response speed

7. Visual-motor control

8. Upper-limb speed and dexterity. (Bruininks, 1978)

The test is norm referenced, and raw scores are converted to standard scores, percentile ranks, and stanines.

Assessing and Diagnosing Behavior

The norms on the Bruininks-Oseretsky Test are dated; therefore, school administrators should exercise caution in its use. The test is in need of revision. Both validity and reliability are below recommended standards of use.

Peabody Developmental Motor Scales and Activity Cards

The contents of this test are standardized with an instructional packet of activity cards (Folio & Fewell, 1983). The test assesses fine- and gross-motor skills in children 1 month to 7 years of age. This instrument is designed to be used with individuals who are chronologically older than 7 but with motor development in the birth to 7 developmental age range. The test includes the assessment of fine motor skills and has 112 items grouped into four skill clusters: grasping, hand use, eye/hand coordination, and manual dexterity.

Gross motor skills have 170 items, grouped into five skill clusters: reflexes, balance, nonlocomotor, locomotor, and receipt and propulsion.

Assessing and Diagnosing Behavior

Rigid standardization procedures have not been established in this test. Small samples were used. The test should be standardized using appropriate sampling and techniques. Examiners may need to modify or adapt the instrument to accommodate the many disabling conditions of individuals with physical disabilities (Gleckel & Lee, 1996).

Individuals with sensory, motor, and social deficits run the gamat of human behavior. Disabilities range from simple to complex. A variety of assessment strategies will be needed. Specialists from various areas will be needed to assist educators in assessing the diverse abilities of the children. Accommodation needs of the children must be considered (Cohen & Spenciner, 1998). Many individuals who have sensory deficits also have perceptual problems, which may affect their sensory acuity.

•• PERCEPTUAL ABILITIES

Perceptual abilities determine how individuals perceive information and how they respond. These abilities can be subdivided into at least four general areas: (1) visual-perceptual, (2) auditory-perceptual, (3) perceptual-motor, and (4) attention. Assessing a student in these areas is intended to determine strengths and weaknesses in information and sensory processing and can provide the assessment team an understanding of how the child learns best (Waterman, 1994).

The idea of perceptual deficits has long been linked to learning disabilities. Research results in this area have been mixed and controversial and offer only meager support for including evaluation of perceptual abilities in any assessment battery or approach (Overton, 1992). Linguistic issues, rather than perceptual abilities, may more often explain learning deficits. Nevertheless, because assessing perceptual abilities continues to be part of the evaluation process, we briefly discuss them here.

Visual-Perceptual Ability

Visual perception includes the ability to discriminate between two or more visual stimuli, locate a particular figure within a larger scene, and understand position in space. Perceptual skills include detecting specific colors, shapes, and sizes. In reading, it requires the ability to detect the visual features of a letter or word so the twenty-six letters of the alphabet can be distinguished from each other. The student must also discriminate among ten written digits.

Auditory-Perceptual Ability

Auditory perception includes the ability to detect certain auditory features such as changes in volume, discrimination of vowel or consonant sounds, and non-phonemic sound discrimination (e.g., the sound of a bell from the sound of a buzzer). In a school setting, then, the student would need the ability to discriminate between different sounds, identify spoken words that are the same or different, and hear sounds in order.

Perceptual-Motor Ability

Most assessments include one or more measures of perceptual-motor ability. It has long been assumed that perceptual-motor or visual-motor problems are associated with learning problems and therefore should be included in most assessment batteries (Salvia & Ysseldyke, 1991). Historically, tests of perceptual-motor skills have been second only to intelligence tests in terms of use in the assessment of school-aged children. Tests of perceptual-motor skills or perceptual-motor integration most often ask students to copy geometric designs that are placed in front of them. This requires the child to see the design, attend to and remember the relevant features, and then carry out the motor actions necessary to reproduce the design on paper.

•• ASSESSING PERCEPTUAL ABILITY

As mentioned, assessing perceptual abilities is controversial. The first issue relates to the importance of ensuring that a student's apparent perceptual difficulties are not actually the result of a lack of visual or auditory acuity (as opposed to a difficulty with processing stimuli). Before beginning an assessment of perceptual ability, the student's eyesight and hearing should be tested (Overton, 1992). This can be part of the assessment process, with the school referring the student to the appropriate facilities for such screenings.

The second issue is related to the relevance of such measures to the goals of assessment. There has been little to suggest that direct training in perceptual skills improves academic performance (Salvia & Ysseldyke, 1991). If there is little applicability, it seems reasonable to question whether formal tests of perceptual skills are necessary as part of the assessment battery.

The third issue relates to the validity and reliability of the perceptual test measures. Tests purported to measure perceptual abilities may actually measure other factors such as language or verbal memory skill. Information gained from tests thought to measure perceptual processing may actually result in incorrect explanations for learning problems. This may lead those working with the child toward strategies that are not useful (perceptual training such as copying design) and away from ones that may be helpful, such as training in phonological processing. Many school administrators are concerned the instruments currently available do not meet acceptable standards of reliability and validity (Swanson & Watson, 1989), making their use of questionable value.

•• ATTENTION

The ability to focus on a given activity for the required period is important if a student is to take in information or complete the day-to-day tasks in school. The three phases of attention are the ability to come to attention, focus attention, and maintain attention. The issues of "selective" attention must also be considered here. Students must be able to attend, and they must be able to sustain attention on the most relevant stimuli. Difficulties in any of the three phases of attention can interfere with a student's ability to learn or share what he or she knows in a consistent fashion. Although the ability to attend effectively is seldom assessed through a formalized instrument, information related to attention can be gathered through classroom observations and observations of test behaviors.

•• PREREFERRAL ACTIVITIES

School administrators should be directly involved in prereferral activities. Some recommended approaches are that regular teachers assess children before they are referred for special class placement. The regular classroom teacher should attempt to remediate the problem in the classroom prior to referral. A number of strategies and techniques as outlined throughout this chapter can be used by the regular classroom teacher to provide activities that will minimize or reduce the deficiencies. Devices such as observations, tests (both formal and informal), interviews, and services from professional staff members may be considered. Based on the assessment strategies described here, the regular classroom teacher should structure instructional interventions to reduce or eradicate the deficiency. If the deficiency still exists, the regular classroom teacher may refer the child for formal study. Prereferral is an alternative to referring children to special classes by providing realistic and functional instruction to at-risk children placed in special classes (Salvia & Ysseldyke, 1998).

If findings are confirmed, a formal assessment may be completed. Additional testing and assessment may be conducted after parental permission has been obtained. A vision, hearing, physical, language and speech, and psychological evaluation should be made.

•• ASSESSMENT ACCOMMODATIONS

New regulations of the Individuals with Disabilities Education Act (IDEA) mandate that students with disabilities be included in general state and districtwide assessment programs with accommodations if needed. An assessment accommodation is designed to permit students with exceptionalities to show what they know without the impediment of the exceptionality (Elliott, Ysseldyke, Thurlow, & Erickson, 1998). In essence, accommodations make the playing field equal for students with exceptionalities.

Most norm-referenced tests (NRTs) are normed on children without disabilities and do not permit modifications or adaptations to accommodate children with exceptionalities. Without accommodations in NRTs, children with exceptionalities most likely will score lower on the test. The new IDEA makes it abundantly clear that school districts must describe in the student IEP what accommodations will or will not be used. Thurlow et al. (1998) have developed a checklist for teachers, educators, and the IEP team to employ in making decisions to determine what accommodations are valid in altering the testing format in norm-referenced tests. School administrators should be familiar with the many forms that accommodations take, such as (1) extending time, (2) reduced stimulus response, and (3) the use of assistive devices. Alternative assessment is another technique that school administrators can employ in adapting and modifying assessment devices.

•• ALTERNATIVE ASSESSMENT

Elliott et al. (1998) stated that alternative assessment is a substitute way for school administrators to gather meaningful information on students' learning for those who are unable to take, even with accommodations, the regular assessment. Many children with disabilities in the cognitive, social, and physical domains are enrolled in different courses of study, because their exceptionalities will not permit them to complete the regular curriculum. Typically, these students are working on life skills curricula, which are designed to prepare them for supported or competitive employment, sheltered workshops, group homes, or supervised independent living situations.

Alternative assessment may involve using several formats. Portfolio assessment is commonly used in conducting alternative assessment. As indicated earlier in this chapter, portfolio assessments may include summaries and examples of all of the student's learning, which is checked by the teacher and updated frequently. Other informal types of assessment instruments such as rating scales, checklists, questionnaires, surveys, interviews, and self-report inventory strategies may be used to implement alternative assessment strategies (Witt et al., 1998).

•• SUMMARY

School administrators can make many uses of assessment data; however, the major purpose is to document strengths and weaknesses of children in the basic domains. For the purpose of this text, assessment data supply the necessary information needed to make decisions about children with exceptionalities relevant to (1) strengths and weaknesses in the areas of human functioning, (2) categorizing areas of exceptionalities, (3) identifying appropriate instructional and related services needed, (4) formulating the IEP, and (5) making appropriate placement decisions.

Standardized and criterion-referenced tests are rigidly constructed, field-tested, validated, and reliability established. The item analysis conducted is based on predetermined standards during the standardized process. The major types of standardized tests addressed in this chapter are (1) norm- and criterion-referenced tests, (2) achievement tests, (3) individual intelligence tests, (4) formal and informal assessment tests, and (5) sensory acuity tests.

Medical treatment plays a major role in the treatment of individuals with sensory and motor disabilities. Several specialists may be involved in the initial screening and the medical assessment of these children depending on the area or areas affected. These areas of exceptionality cover a wide range of children with disabilities in the areas of visual, hearing, and motor disabilities.

We have summarized some standardized instruments and procedures that may be used to assess sensory deficits. We addressed the issue of accommodation and the vital role of nonstandardized procedures in assessing sensory deficits. Educators are also encouraged to use accommodation with nonstandardized procedures (addressed in chapter 7).

School administrators should be aware of certain facts relevant to the use of standardized and criterion tests: (1) the range of skills to be expected in the classroom, (2) the dependence to be placed on the skills measured, (3) the diagnostic value of the test, and (4) the limitations of the test and precautions employed in making interpretations relevant to the test results.

Factors that may affect the reliability of the tests range from physical conditions of the children through environmental conditions. Physical conditions include deficits in sensory acuity and childhood diseases. The personal traits and competencies of the examiner may have an impact on the performance of the children. The physical atmosphere of the examination room, such as the temperature, or the structural arrangement of the furniture, may have adverse affects on the performance of children. The ecological environment will markedly affect test performances such as deprived conditions at home, at school, and in the community.

The administrative structure of the school should support and mandate that competent and unbiased specialists are used to assess children with disabilities. These specialists must also assist in providing education and other strategies to minimize or reduce the effects of the disabling conditions. They should also make recommendations relevant to the type and extent of related services needed. Finally, specialists should be available to interpret and assist the schools by examining technical data in their reports (Taylor, 1999).

Due to the many disabling conditions of children with disabilities, accommodations and modifications are frequently needed in the testing format. School administrators must ensure that appropriate accommodations and modifications are made in the testing program. Without these modifications, many children with disabilities will not be successful. Federal laws permit this modification. School districts must report in IEPs what, if any, modifications or accommodations have been made. The assessment strategies and tests discussed in this chapter are some of the testing strategies that school administrators can recommend or suggest to teachers, school-related personnel, and various specialists to use in assessing the abilities and disabilities of children with disabilities.

•• REFERENCES

Barraga, N. C., & Erin, J. N. (1992). *Visual handicaps and learning*. Austin, TX: Pro-Ed.

Browder, D. M. (1991). *Assessment of individuals with severe disabilities: An applied behavior approach to life skills assessment* (2nd ed.). Baltimore, MD: Brookes.

Bruininks, R. H. (1978). *Bruininks-Oseretsky test on motor proficiency*. Circle Pines, MN: AGS.

Cohen, L. C., & Spenciner, L. J. (1998). *Assessment of children and youth*. New York: Addison Wesley Longman.

Davison, D. M., & Pearce, D. L. (1992). The influence of writing activities on the mathematics learning of Native American students. *Journal of Educational Issues of Language Minority Students, 10*, 147–157.

Elliott, J. L., Ysseldyke, J., Thurlow, M., & Erickson, R. N. (1998). What about assessment and accountability? Practical implications for educators. *Teaching Exceptional Children, 31*(1), 20–27.

Folio, M. R., & Fewell, R. (1983). *Peabody developmental motor scores and activity cards*. Chicago: Riverside.

Gleckel, L. K., & Lee, R. L. (1996). Children with physical disabilities. In E. L. Meyen (Ed.), *Exceptional Children in Today's Schools* (3rd ed.). Denver, CO: Love.

Maker, C. J. (1993). Creativity, intelligence, and problem solving: A definition and design for cross-cultural research and measurement related to giftedness. *Gifted Education International, 9*(2), 68–77.

Mayer, R. H. (1996). Children who are deaf or hard-of-hearing. In E. L. Meyen (Ed.), *Exceptional Children in Today's Schools* (3rd ed.). Denver, CO: Love.

McLoughlin, J., & Lewis, R. (1991). *Assessing special students: Strategies and procedures* (3rd ed.). Columbus, OH: Merrill.

Overton, T. (1992). *Assessment in special education: An applied approach*. New York: Macmillan.

Pike, K., & Salender, S. (1995). An authentic assessment strategy. *Teaching Exceptional Children, 28*(1), 15–19.

Popham, W. J. (1999). Why standardized tests don't measure educational quality. *Educational Leadership, 56*(6), 8–15.

Rhodes, L. K., & Nathenson-Mejia, S. (1992). Anecdotal records: A powerful tool for on-going literacy assessment. *The Reading Teacher, 45*(7), 502–509.

Salinger, T. (1991). *Getting started with alternative assessment methods*. Workshop presented at the New York State Reading Association Conference, Lake Kiamesha, New York.

Salvia, J., & Ysseldyke, J. E. (1991). *Assessment in special education and remedial education* (5th ed.). Boston: Houghton Mifflin.

Salvia, J., & Ysseldyke, J. E. (1998). *Assessment*. Boston: Houghton Mifflin.

Silberman, R. K. (1996). Children with visual impairments. In E. L. Meyen (Ed.), *Exceptional Children in Today's Schools* (3rd ed.). Denver, CO: Love.

Swanson, H. C., & Watson, B. L. (1989). *Educational and psychological assessment of exceptional children* (2nd ed.). Columbus, OH: Merrill.

Taylor, G. R. (1997). *Curriculum strategies: Social skills intervention for your African-American males.* Westport, CT: Praeger Press.

Taylor, G. R. (1998). *Curriculum strategies for teaching social skills to the disabled.* Springfield, IL: Charles C Thomas.

Taylor, G. R. (1999). *Curriculum models and strategies for educational individuals with disabilities in inclusive classrooms.* Springfield, IL: Charles C Thomas.

Taylor, G. R. (2000). *Integrating quantitative and qualitative research methods.* Latham, MD: University Press.

Taylor, G. R. (in press). *Informal classroom assessment strategies for teachers.* Blue Ridge Summit, PA: Scarecrow Press.

Thorndike, R. L., Hagen, P., & Sattler, J. M. (1986). *Guide for administering and scoring the fourth edition.* Chicago: Riverside.

Thurlow, M. L., Elliott, J. L., & Ysseldyke, J. E. (1998). *Testing students with disabilities: Practical strategies for complying with district and state requirements.* Thousand Oaks, CA: Corwin Press.

Wallace, G., Larsen, S. C., & Elksnin, L. K. (1992). *Educational assessment of learning problems: Testing for teaching.* Boston: Allyn & Bacon.

Waterman, B. (1994). Assessing children for the presence of a disability. *National Information Center for Children and Youth with Disabilities, 4*(1), 1–22.

Wechsler, D. (1958). *The measurement and appraisal of adult intelligence* (4th ed.). Baltimore, MD: Williams & Wilkins.

Wechsler, D. (1967). *Manual of the Wechsler Preschool and Primary scale of intelligence.* San Antonio, TX: The Psychological Corporation.

Wechsler, D. (1991). *Wechsler Intelligence Scale for Children III.* San Antonio, TX: The Psychological Corporation.

Wiersman, W., & Jurs, S. (1990). *Educational measurement and testing.* Boston: Allyn & Bacon.

Witt, J. C., Elliott, S. N., Daley, E. J., Gresham, F. M., & Kramer, J.J. (1998). *Assessment of at-risk and special needs children.* Boston: McGraw-Hill.

Wolf, D. P. (1989). Portfolio assessment: Sampling student work. *Educational Leadership, 46*(7), 35–39.

CHAPTER 9

IEP Requirements

Several federal laws and regulations govern individualized education programs (IEPs). An IEP, defined by Section 614(d) of IDEA, refers to a written statement for each child with an exceptionality that is developed, reviewed, and revised in accordance with the section cited. The regulations further state that the IEP should also designate responsibilities, tasks, and time lines for implementation. The regulations in PL 94-142, PL 101-476, and PL 105-17 are specific in describing what the IEP must include and the manner in which it must be developed (refer to Chapter 6). Some flexibility is permitted in developing, formalizing, and monitoring the IEP. The basic legal requirements to consider in writing IEPs are as follows:

1. All of a student's unique needs must be addressed, not only academic needs.

2. The availability of services may not be considered in writing the IEP. If a service is needed it must be written on the IEP. If the district does not have it available, the service must be provided by another agency.

3. The IEP is a firm, legally binding "commitment of resources." The district must provide the services listed or the IEP must be amended.

4. IEPs must be individualized. Unfortunately, the same goals, same content areas, same discipline, or the same amounts of therapy have been documented on many IEPs. The Office of Special Education Programs (OSEP) and federal legislation have directed school districts to implement the procedures outlined here.

Statements regarding the student's present levels of educational performance, annual goals, special educational performance, special education and related services to be provided, projected dates for the beginning and end of services, and transition services for youth are all mandated by law to be included in the IEP. The chief modification made to these familiar components has been to place more emphasis within the law on involving students with exceptionalities in the general curriculum and into the general education classroom, with supplementary aids and services as appropriate. The new emphasis on participation in the general curriculum is intended to produce attention to the accommodations and adjustments necessary for children with exceptionalities to access the general education curriculum and the special services that may be necessary for appropriate participation in particular areas of the curriculum. Effective school administrative leadership can facilitate compliance with the IEP requirements (Committee on Labor and Human Resources, 1997).

The IEP concept is a major improvement over most instructional planning centered on placement decisions. The improvement comes largely from requiring a written plan. Components of the IEP did undergo significant changes effective July 1998. We address only those changes here.

•• INDIVIDUALIZED EDUCATION PROGRAM REQUIREMENTS

For specific strategies and examples of IEP development, see Taylor (in press).

Each student's Individualized Education Program, or IEP, is a vital document, for it spells out the special education and related services he or she will receive. The IEP is developed by a tem that includes parents and school professionals, and, when appropriate, the student. The new IDEA maintains the IEP as a document of central importance and, in the hope of improving compliance, moves all provisions related to the IEP to one place in the law—Section 614(d). Under the prior law, IEP provisions were found in several different places.

At the same time, several key changes have been made to what information the IEP must contain and the way in which the IEP is developed. The exception is provisions related to children with exceptionalities who have been convicted as adults and incarcerated in adult prisons. These provisions take effect immediately (National Information Center of Children and Youth with Disabilities [NICHCY], 1997).

Administrators of special education programs must be knowledgeable about the modifications in the IEP requirements. The IEP retains many familiar components from previous legislation, such as statements regarding the student's present levels of educational performance, annual goals, special education and related services to be provided, projected dates for the beginning and end of services, and transition services for youth.

For example, "present levels of educational performance" must now include a statement of how the child's disability affects his or her involvement and progress in the general curriculum. Similarly, the IEP must contain a statement of supplementary aids and services that the child or youth needs in order to be involved and progress in the general curriculum and to participate in extracurricular and other nonacademic activities, and to be educated and participate with other children with exceptionalities and nonexceptional children.

With these new IEP requirements there is a clear intent to strengthen the connection between special education and the general education curriculum (Committee on Labor and Human Resources, 1997). The new emphasis on participation in the general education curriculum is intended to draw attention to the accommodations and adjustments necessary for children with exceptionalities to access the general education curriculum and the special services that may be necessary for appropriate participation in particular areas of the curriculum (Sack, 1997).

Along the same lines is the requirement that the IEP include an explanation of the extent to which the student will not be participating with nonexceptional children in the general education class and in extracurricular and nonacademic activities. This explanation of the extent to which the child will be educated separately is a new component of the IEP, yet is clearly in keeping with the changes noted here.

Other aspects of the IEP are entirely new as well. For example, each student's IEP must now include a statement of how the administration of state or districtwide assessments will be modified for the student so he or she can participate. If the IEP team determines that the student cannot participate in such assessments, the IEP must include a statement of (1) why the assessment is not appropriate for the child, and (2) how the child will be assessed. These changes work in tandem with changes elsewhere in the IDEA requiring that students with disabilities be included in state and districtwide assessments of student achievement.

Other new IEP requirements are statements on (1) informing the student about the transfer of rights as he or she approaches the age of majority; (2) how parents will be regularly informed of their child's progress toward meeting the annual goals in the IEP; (3) where services will be delivered to the student; and (4) transition service needs of the student beginning at age 14.

•• DEVELOPING THE IEP

The new IDEA maintains essentially the same process for developing the IEP, namely the document is developed by a multidisciplinary team, including the parents. However, the new legislation increases the role of the administrator on the IEP team, to include, when appropriate, helping to determine positive behavioral interventions and appropriate supplementary aids and services for the student.

Also added to the IEP process are "special factors" that the IEP team must consider:

- Behavior strategies and supports, if the child's behavior impedes his or her learning or that of others

- The child's language needs (as they relate to the IEP) if the child has limited English proficiency.

•• PROVIDING FOR INSTRUCTION

The use of Braille may be used to improve the communication skills of children who are deaf, hard of hearing,and require assistive devices and services.

•• REVIEWING AND REVISING THE IEP

The language in the new IDEA emphasizes periodic review of the IEP (at least annually, as previously required) and revision as needed. A new and separate requirement exists: schools must report to parents about the progress of nondisabled children, which seems likely to affect the revision process for IEPs. If it becomes evident that a child is not making "expected progress toward the annual goals and in the general curriculum," the IEP team must meet and revise the IEP.

IDEA 1997 specifically lists a variety of other circumstances under which the IEP team would also need to review and revise the IEP, including the child's anticipated needs, the results of any reevaluation conducted, or information provided by the parents.

•• PARENT PARTICIPATION IN ELIGIBILITY AND PLACEMENT DECISIONS

Under the old IDEA, parent participation was not required for making decisions regarding a student's eligibility for special education and related services. As mentioned earlier, under the new legislation, parents are specifically included as members of the group making the eligibility decision.

Parent participation in placement decisions is similarly required. Under the old legislation, parent involvement in deciding the placement of their child was not required. The new IDEA clarifies the parents' right to be involved in such decisions.

•• REEVALUATIONS

Under the previous law, each exceptional student receiving special education and related services was reevaluated every three years in all areas related to his or her disability. The purposes of this evaluation were to determine if the child continued to be a child with a disability (as defined within IDEA) and his or her present levels of educational performance and educational needs.

Under IDEA 1997, a Local Education Agency (LEA) must ensure that a reevaluation of each child with a disability is conducted if "conditions warrant a re-evaluation of the child's parent or teacher requests a re-evaluation, but at least once every 3 years" (Section 614[a][2][a]). The new law, however, has streamlined the reevaluation process. Many of the aspects described here under initial evaluation apply as well to reevaluation. Now, at least every three years, the IEP team and other qualified professionals, as appropriate, must review existing evaluation data on the child and, based on that review and on input from the parents, the team must identify what additional information (if any) is needed to determine: (1) if the child continues to have particular category of disability (as described within IDEA) and continues to need special education and related services; (2) what the child's present levels of performance and educational needs are; and (3) whether any additions or modifications to the special education and related services are needed to enable the child to meet the goals set out in the IEP and to participate, as appropriate, in the general curriculum.

As members of the IEP team, parents participate in the review of existing data. If IEP team members and school administrators feel they do not have enough information to answer the questions just listed, the LEA must administer such tests and other evaluation procedures as may be needed to produce the information identified by the team. Parents must give informed consent before their children are reevaluated. The need for informed parental consent for reevaluation is new to the law; previously such consent was only needed for initial evaluations. If parents fail to respond to the LEA's request for consent to reevaluate the child, the LEA may proceed without it, if the LEA can demonstrate that it took reasonable measures to obtain the consent and the parents failed to respond.

Or school administrators may determine that sufficient data are available to determine whether the child continues to be a "child with a disability." In this case, the LEA is not required to conduct additional assessment. Parents must be notified of the determinations and the reasons for it, as well as their rights to request that their child be assessed to determine whether the child continues to be a "child with a disability" as defined by IDEA. If parents request such an assessment, the LEA must conduct it. As with initial evaluation, a copy of the evaluation report and the documentation determining eligibility must be given to the parent. The report provides an explanation regarding the changes IDEA 1997 brings to the entire evaluation process—both initial evaluation and reevaluation.

•• TRANSITION SERVICES

An administrative structure should be in place to address the new requirements for transition, mediation services, and discipline of children with disabilities. The requirements for providing transition services for youth with exceptionalities have been modified in IDEA 1997. Although the definition of transition services remains the same, two notable changes have been made to IEP requirements:

1. Beginning when a student is 14, and annually thereafter, the student's IEP must contain a statement of his or her transition service needs under the various components of that IEP that focus on the student's course of study (e.g., vocational education or advanced placement).

2. Beginning at least one year before the student reaches the age of majority under state law, the IEP must contain a statement that the student has been informed of the rights under the law that will transfer to him or her upon reaching the age of majority (National Information Center for Children and Youth with Disabilities, 1997).

•• MEDIATION

IDEA 1997 establishes mediation as a primary process to be used in resolving conflicts between schools and the parents of a child with a disability. Although prior legislation permitted mediation, the new legislation explicitly outlines states' obligations for creating a mediation system in which parents and schools may voluntarily participate. Among states' obligations are the following:

• Ensuring that the mediation process is voluntary on the part of the parties, is not used to deny a parent's right to due process, and is conducted by a qualified and impartial mediator trained in effective techniques.

• Maintaining a list of qualified mediators.

• Bearing the cost of the mediation process.

Some parents may choose not to use mediation, and states may establish procedures requiring parents to meet with an impartial party who would explain the benefits of mediation and encourage them to make use of the process.

•• DISCIPLINE OF CHILDREN WITH DISABILITIES

Some of the most sweeping and complicated changes in the new IDEA are in the area of disciplining children with disabilities. To assist schools in understanding and complying with these new requirements, the Office of Special Education

Programs (OSEP), U.S. Department of Education, released initial guidance on September 19, 1997. (You can obtain this guidance from NICHCY or on the Internet at *www.ed.gov/offices/OSERS/IDEA/memo.htm.*) An essential means of developing an accurate understanding of IDEA 1997's disciplinary requirements is to read the law itself. As requested by OSEP, the discussion of discipline in this *News Digest* is kept to providing verbatim quotations from PL 105-17.

The requirements of the law are found in Section 615 (k), "Placement in Alternative Educational Settings." This section is divided into ten subparagraphs (e.g., authority of school personnel, authority of setting, manifestation determination review, and so on).

There is no substitute for reading exactly what the law says. To obtain additional information concerning information on disciplining children with exceptionalities, read Section 615 (k) of IDEA 1997 in its entirety.

•• THE NEXT STEPS

Laws passed by Congress provide a general framework of policy related to a particular issue. Once a law is passed, Congress delegates the task of developing regulations to guide the law's implementation to an administrative agency within the executive branch. These federal regulations are published in the Code of Federal Regulation (CFR). The CFR interprets and further explains the law.

Regulations exist for the old IDEA, in CFR Title 34 Parts 300 to 338. Proposed regulations for IDEA 1997 were published in the Federal Register on October 22, 1997. A ninety-day period of public comments followed the publication of these proposed regulations, in which individuals and groups provided feedback and identified concerns regarding what was proposed. Comments were reviewed and appropriate revisions were made. Final regulations were implemented in the spring of 1998.

In our opinion, the new IEP regulations will create additional paperwork for school districts and administrators of special education programs. We are proposing forms to assist them. The forms are recommendations only, as indicated districts will have the flexibility to develop their own forms. We recommend these forms be computerized in order to reduce the amount of manual labor involved in their completion. These forms will need to be modified based on the various states' classification systems.

Placement decisions are made by the IEP committee based upon the assessment and evaluative data submitted. Table 2 shows the various types of public school placements for exceptional individuals. Both noncategorical (generic) classifications, which imply all mild to moderate disabled individuals, and categorical classifications, which imply severe to profound disabled individuals, are included.

•• SUMMARY

A major part of PL 94-142 and PL 105-17 mandates that an individual education program be developed for every disabled individual at a meeting that includes administrators, teachers, resource personnel, parents, and, in some instances, the children themselves. The IEP should also designate responsibilities, tasks, and time lines for implementation. The regulations of PL 94-142 and PL 105-17 are specific in describing what the IEP must include and the manner in which it must be developed. State and local educational agencies have the flexibility to develop procedures for implementing, formulating, and monitoring IEP designs. Formats differ from state to state and frequently within different school districts or the same state. Chiefly due to broad governmental regulations concerning the structure of IEP development, the following steps are usually addressed by the states:

Step 1. Identification of problems to determine whether or nor students' problems are brought to the attention of appropriate personnel.

Step 2. Referrals by appropriate school personnel.

Step 3. Evaluation that includes an extensive review of the available services and alternatives required to meet the student's needs.

Step 4. During the IEP conference, previously collected data and program needs are presented. A written plan is prepared.

Step 5. Implementation of the plan must be disseminated to all persons who will participate in the student's program. Each participant is required to monitor the student's performance and to make any necessary modification to the plan.

Step 6. Evaluation is repeated as a final step. The intent is to determine student progress and the IEP's general effectiveness. Based on evaluative results, the IEP committee may request additional information or request modifications during the instructional plan.

School administrators may find the summary of IDEA 1997 useful in developing, executing, monitoring, and revising IEPs. The IDEA 1997 maintains essentially the same process for developing the IEP—namely the document is developed by the team, including the parents, and when appropriate, the child (see appendix D).

Table 2: Placement Criteria for Each Level of Service

Level of Service	Service	Staff		Students Served
		Elementary	Secondary	
Level I (Noncategorical)	• Consultation to regular class teachers • Diagnostic services (academic, behavioral, psychology, psychiatric)	• Social worker • Psychologist	• Counselor or social worker • Psychologist	• Students mainstreamed from more intense level of service (monitoring). • Students reentering from hospitalization or out-of-city placements who require monitoring.
Level II (Noncategorical)	• Resource rooms/average of five hours per week • Behavior management strategies • Contracting • Remedial instruction • Counseling/individual or • Case conferences for regular or resource teachers • Family services	• Resource teacher • Social worker or counselor • Psychologist	• Resource teacher • Social worker or counselor • Psychologist	• Students mainstreamed from more intense level of service. • Students requiring direct service to improve and/or maintain performance in regular education. • Students requiring individual group counseling to succeed in school. • Students requiring specific behavior management plans in regular class.
Level III (Noncategorical)	• Resource room/up to fifteen hours per week • Behavior management strategies • Contracting	• Resource teacher • Social worker or counselor • Psychologist	• Resource teacher • Social worker or counselor • Psychologist	• Students mainstreamed from more intense level of service. • Students requiring direct service to improve and/or maintain performance in regular education.

Table 2: Placement Criteria for Each Level of Service (continued)

Level of Service	Service	Staff		Students Served
		Elementary	Secondary	
Level III (Noncategorical)	• Class meetings • Remedial instruction • Counseling/group or individual • Case conference • Family services			• Students requiring individual group counseling to succeed in school. • Students requiring specific behavior management plans in regular classes.
Level IV (Categorical)	• Self-contained class/up to ten students • Potential for full-day programming in special classes • Regular curriculum with remedial instruction • Behavioral management system • Behavioral management strategies • Class meeting • Crisis intervention and support • Counseling/group and individual	• Self-contained teacher • Paraprofessional • Social worker or counselor • Psychologist	• Students who are able to interact appropriately in lunchroom, halls, or auditorium, but require a full-time special education program to succeed in school. • Students requiring intense academic instruction. • Students requiring a structured consistent behavior management system throughout their school day.	

Table 2: Placement Criteria for Each Level of Service (continued)

Level of Service	Service	Staff Elementary	Secondary	Students Served
Level IV (Categorical)	• Home/school contact/ communication system • Family counseling • Case conferences on weekly basis • Psychological services as needed • Psychiatric consultation services			
Level V (Categorical)	• Self-contained class in separate facility or wing of a comprehensive building/ six to nine students • Regular or modified curriculum based on student needs • Behavior management system • Behavior management strategies • Class meetings • Crisis intervention and support	• On-site administrator • Self-contained teacher • Paraprofessional • Social worker or counselor • Psychologist • Music therapist • Art therapist • Auxiliary paraprofessional	• On-site administrator • Self-contained teacher • Paraprofessional • Social worker or counselor • Psychologist • Physical education teacher • Auxiliary paraprofessional	• Students who are unable to interact appropriately in the halls, cafeteria, or auditorium and require intense supervision even when not in the classroom. • Students requiring ration to control behavior. • Students requiring a highly structured, consistent behavior management system throughout their school day. • Students requiring crisis intervention and counseling available at all times.

Table 2: Placement Criteria for Each Level of Service (continued)

Level of Service	Service	Staff		Students Served
		Elementary	Secondary	
Level V (Categorical)	• Home/school/contact communication system • Family counseling • Case conferences on weekly basis • Psychological services as needed • Psychiatric consultation services • Self-contained class in separate facility or wing of a comprehensive building/six to nine students • Regular or modified curriculum based on student needs • Behavior management system • Behavior management strategies • Class meetings • Crisis intervention and support • Counseling/group and individual	• On-site administrator • Self-contained teacher • Paraprofessional • Social worker or counselor • Psychologist • Music therapist • Art therapist • Auxiliary paraprofessional • Physical education • Psychiatrist (consulting)	• On-site administrator • Self-contained teacher • Paraprofessional • Social worker or counselor • Psychologist • Physical education teacher • Auxiliary paraprofessional • Vocational education opportunity (senior high)	• Students who are unable to interact appropriately in the halls, cafeteria, or auditorium and require intense supervision even when not in the classroom. • Students requiring ration to control behavior. • Students requiring a highly structured, consistent behavior management system throughout their school day. • Students requiring crisis intervention and counseling available at all times. • Students requiring individual counseling.

Table 2: Placement Criteria for Each Level of Service (continued)

Level of Service	Service	Staff		Students Served
		Elementary	Secondary	
Level V (Categorical)	• Home/school contact communication system • Family counseling services • Weekly case conferences	• Reading/math specialist	• Industrial arts/home economics (junior high) • Psychiatrist (consulting) • Reading/math specialist	• Students requiring direct and family involvement in consulting to succeed in school. • Students requiring direct and frequent home/school contact to succeed in school.

•• REFERENCES

Committee on Labor and Human Resourcess. (1997). Washington, DC: U.S. Government Printing Office.

Gearheart, B., Mullen, R., & Gearheart, C. (1993). *Exceptional individuals: An introduction.* California: Brooks/Coles.

National Information Center for Youth and Children with Disabilities (NICHCY). (1997). *News Digest,* pp. 1–4, p. 26.

Sack, J. L. (1997). Educational officials cite concerns about implementing IDEA rules. *Education Week,* pp. 1–4.

Taylor, G. R. (2002). *Individualized education program: Perspective and strategies.* New York: Mellon Press.

CHAPTER 10

Inclusion

Inclusion is an important issue because it affects virtually all stakeholders in education, including children with and without disabilities and their families, special and general education teachers, administrators, related services personnel, school staff, and the general public (Alper, Schloss, Etscheidt, & MacFarlane, 1995). Inclusion, a grassroots movement driven by parental dissatisfaction with the current delivery system and the conviction that all children should be educated together, has captured the attention of administrators and the general public alike. According to Aefsky (1995), inclusion is turning the tables after fifteen unsuccessful years of teaching children in a fragmented school society. We are asking professionals, teachers, administrators, and support staff to change their roles.

Historically, this issue, debated in the 1970s, was whether disabled children learn best in integrated or segregated classes. Most of the research indicates that prior to 1975, most disabled children with mild exceptionalities were educated in integrated classes; those with severe to profound disabilities were educated in segregated classes. Federal legislation, PL 94-142, changed this concept and gave all children with disabilities equality of educational opportunities with the concept of the least restricted environment (LRE), which provides all exceptional children opportunities to be educated with their peers (Taylor, 1999). The law provides for both types of placements: integration and segregation.

•• INCLUSION DEFINED

Inclusive education has been defined in as many ways as there are attitudes toward this educational concept. For instance, Roach (1995) defined the term as serving students with a full range of abilities and disabilities in the general classroom, with appropriate in-class support. According to Brown et al. (1991), inclusion is a way to implement the least restricted environment (LRE); however, it is not necessarily the regular classroom view advanced by Bennett,

Deluca, and Burns (1997). Scruggs and Mastropieri (1996) defined inclusion as the integration of students with disabilities into a heterogeneous classroom the entire school day, in which special education services would be received. This inclusive model is typically referred to as the regular education initiative (REI).

It is the attitude of those involved in or affected by inclusive education that defines and determines the impact of this practice on the individuals who will be placed in this setting. For example, Berger (1995) asserted that the process of including individuals with special needs into the mainstream classroom has become a pressing issue for administrators.

Teaching students with disabilities in inclusive settings is a multifaceted task that cannot be accomplished by the administrator alone. Inclusive education happens when administrators form a team of mutually supportive members who pledge to provide the best possible practices for children with disabilities. Inclusive education focuses on combining the best practices in education, including cooperative learning, peer tutoring, and community building in classrooms and schools. Aefsky (1995) contended that teaching strategies for inclusive settings are synonymous with effective teaching strategies used in any area of education. Depending on the disability and level of student need, an administrator needs a team with unique but complementary skills to guide, advocate for, and implement each student's educational program. More than any other element, the administrator needing such a team is a drastic change for regular educators. Administrators with the assistance of competent team members must develop a plan to integrate the lifelong goals and special needs of students with disabilities within the context of the regular classroom (Filbin, J. Connolly, T., & Brewer, R., 1996).

Research results in the field have endorsed educating disabled children in both inclusive and separate special classes. The preponderance of research tends to support placing exceptional children in inclusive settings (Alper, et al., 1995; Banerji & Dailey, 1995; Giangreco, Dennis, Cloninger, Edelman, & Schattman, 1993; Mills & Bulach, 1996; Roberts & Mather, 1995; Sharpe, York, & Knight, 1994; Staub & Hunt, 1993).

Inclusion offers the nondisabled student an opportunity to develop an appreciation for the complexity of human characteristics as well as an appreciation for individual differences. Students who have not had these experiences may be surprised to learn, for example, that speech problems accompanying cerebral palsy do not necessarily indicate limited intelligence, cognitive impairment need not affect social development, and sensory limitations need not interfere with motor skills. Additionally, students with exceptionalities may teach nonexceptional learners to go beyond dysfunctional stereotypes. All students with behavior disorders are not aggressive, and students with learning exceptionalities can be highly capable in some academic areas.

Advocates for full inclusion of disabled children indicate that it is their democratic right to be educated with peers, and integration of exceptional children with nonexceptional children enhances interpersonal skills. Other studies indicate that curricula in inclusive schools should be appropriate for different levels of exceptionalities and sensory acuity. There is no separate knowledge base for teaching exceptional children. Teachers must be innovative and employ creative teaching strategies, such as learning centers, cooperative learning, concept teaching, directed teaching, and team teaching. Many adaptations and modifications are needed in the instructional process, depending on the amount and degree of disabling conditions present. To the extent possible, disabled children should be included in the regular learning process (Baker, Wang, & Walberg, 1995; Barry, 1995; Johnston, Proctor, & Carey, 1995; Staub & Peck, 1995; Wang, Reynold, & Walbert, 1995).

•• ADVOCATES' VIEWS ON INCLUSION

A significant number of studies and research support the idea that most children with disabilities should be placed in inclusive classrooms. The research has created some controversy regarding inclusive versus special class placement for children with disabilities (Baker et al., 1995; Waldron & McLeskey, 1998). Some of the controversy may be attributed to federal legislation, PL 94-142. This law gave all children with disabilities equality of educational opportunities with the concept of the least restrictive environment (LRE), which provided all children with disabilities an opportunity to be educated with their nondisabled peers, however, a privision in the Individual with Disability Education Act indicates that students with disabilities should be removed from regular education classes when the nature and severity of the disability is such that education in regular classes with the use of supplementary aides and services cannot be successfully achieved. Isolating children with disabilities may cause them to experience low self-esteem and may reduce their ability to deal effectively with other people. In addition, nondisabled children can learn much about a person's courage and perseverance from children with disabilities (Taylor, 1999).

Data from the *Sixteenth Annual Report to Congress on the Implementation of IDEA* (1995), reveals that school districts are not generally following the least restrictive mandate (LRE). The percentage of learning disabled children educated in regular classes ranges from a low of 20 percent to a high of 35 percent. These percentages represent an increase in the number of learning disabled children educated in regular classes in comparison to 1979 (McLeskey & Pacchiano, 1994; Waldron & McLeskey, 1995).

According to Taylor (1999, 2000), collective research in support of inclusion is based on:

1. Federal legislation in support of educating children with disabilities in regular classes. See Chapter 6 for a comprehensive review of the impact of federal legislation on inclusion.

2. Research findings tend to support that children with disabilities perform academically as well in inclusive classes as in separate classes.

3. When provided with support, many children with disabilities are able to succeed in regular education classrooms.

4. The continuum of service model is not needed in inclusive settings, and most children with disabilities should be placed in regular classes full time.

5. Children with disabilities benefit immeasurably from associating with their nondisabled peers.

6. Inclusion reduces labeling of disabled children.

7. Inclusion tends to increase interaction between disabled children and their nondisabled peers.

Through using the vast amount of research available, administrators of special education programs can plan effectively to incorporate a significant number of children with disabilities into the mainstream of education. In our opinion this will provide educational opportunities for all children.

•• OPPONENTS' VIEWS ON INCLUSION

Opponents of full inclusion believe a one-size-fits-all approach will be disastrous for disabled children, and it is not only unrealistic but also unjust. To correct this injustice, according to Shanker (1995), public laws addressing inclusion need to be rewritten to fund the cost of inclusion and provide adequate training for all teachers. To give equal weight to requests from parents and referrals by teachers, teachers must be totally involved in writing the IEP, and alternative arrangements should be made to temporarily place disabled children who are violent or disruptive in secure settings. The National Association of State

Boards of Education voiced that many special education programs are superior to regular classrooms for some types of disabled children. Baker and Zigmond (1990), Fuchs, Fuchs, and Bishop (1992), and Fuchs and Fuchs (1995) reported that individualizing strategies employed in special classes are superior to the one-size-fits-all approach observed in many regular classrooms. They support the view that separate is better for some disabled children and claim that to abolish special education placement in the name of full inclusion is to deprive many disabled children of an appropriate education.

Although the preponderance of research supports the concept of inclusion, administrators should be informed about some researchers' questions concerning whether or not children with disabilities can receive an adequate education in regular classroom settings (Fuchs & Fuchs, 1994; Borthwick-Duffy, Plamer, & Lane, 1996).

In summary, most of the research in opposition to inclusion states that inclusion will not work for disabled children because of the following observations:

1. Children with disabilities with serious problems tend to perform better in separate classes.

2. There is a need to preserve the continuum of specialized programs and placement options.

3. Disabled children enrolled in special classes perform as well as those in regular classes on curriculum-based measures.

4. Disabled children interfere with the progress of regular students.

5. Placing children with disabilities in regular classes can lead to stigmatized labels.

6. Some regular students may begin to mimic inappropriate behaviors of some disabled children, thus affecting learning.

7. Some parents fear that services for their disabled children will not be available under inclusion.

8. Parents of nondisabled children fear their children would be neglected in the classroom because of special attention required for disabled children.

9. Segregated schools are considered safe havens for some parents because they provide the specialized services needed for their disabled children. (Taylor, 1999)

The common consensus of these researchers indicated that the concept of inclusion is an excellent idea; however, it may not work for all children all the time. Although the preponderance of research supports the concept of inclusion, some researchers question whether or not children with disabilities can receive an adequate education in a regular classroom setting (Fuchs & Fuchs, 1994; Borthwick-Duffy et al., 1996).

•• PARENTAL VIEWS ON INCLUSION

Today, administrators of special education see the importance of parental involvement in inclusion education. Parental reactions toward having their children placed in inclusive or segregated classrooms parallel the views of advocates and opponents of the movement, which is multidimensional. In essence, parental perceptions support the statement that inclusion is no panacea for educating all of their disabled children. Their perceptions vacillate greatly between inclusion and special education placement. The disability is not the major reason why some parents do not want their children in inclusive settings. Issues such as instructional objectives, competent personnel, instructional strategies, delivery models, resources, and related services take precedent over placement (Taylor, 2000). Because the issue of parental involvement is so critical to the inclusion process, you may want to refer to Taylor (2000).

•• SERVICE DELIVERY MODELS

Recently the schools have made significant progress toward including disabled children in the regular classroom. This move has resulted in fewer disabled children being placed in special schools and classes. Data from reports to Congress support this trend. Table 3 provides data regarding the percentage of students in each disability category who were served in each of four placement settings in 1988–1989, and again in 1994–1995. Data in table 3 and figure 6 identify disabled individuals across all disability categories in the least restricted environment.

Figure 7 on page 150 reflects the changes in the percentage of exceptional children in each category who were served in the regular classroom in 1994–1995. The figure also shows the change in the percentage of students served in regular classroom school settings by disability categories in 1994–1995.

Statistics in Figure 6 reveal that students with speech/language impairments comprise the largest group of children with disabilities. A variety of service delivery models are used to educate children with disabilities. Placing children in various structures should depend on which model will best serve the needs of the child. The cascade of service model developed by Deno (1970) has been widely used. The model has the following levels: (1) regular classroom, (2)

Table 3: Percentage of Children with Various Disabilities by Setting, 1988–1989

	Separate Classes	Public Separate Facilities	Private Separate Facilities	Home Hospital
Specific Learning Disabilities	19.6	58.0	21.0	1.4
Mentally Retarded	6.2	23.1	60.4	10.3
Serious Emotional Disturbance	14.2	36.2	36.4	19.2
Speech/Language Impairments	75.9	19.9	3.7	1.5
Other Health Impairments	31.0	20.8	19.3	28.9
Orthopedic Impairments	30.4	20.8	19.3	28.9
Multiple Disabilities	7.5	15.1	47.3	36.1
Visual Impairments	40.8	25.8	29.3	13.1
Hearing Impairments	27.7	21.0	34.0	17.3
Deaf-Blindness	13.3	6.1	31.5	49.1

Note: Percentages of school day apart in separate, special education settings.

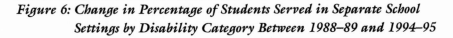

**Figure 6: Change in Percentage of Students Served in Separate School
Settings by Disability Category Between 1988–89 and 1994–95**

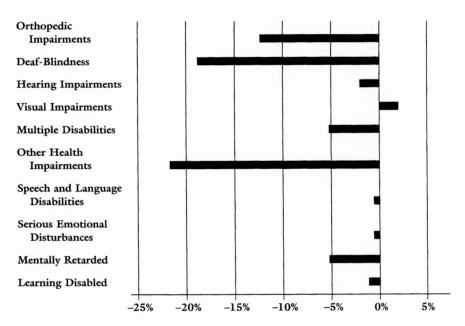

Source: Annual Reports to Congress on the Implementation of the Individuals with Disabilities
Education Act, 1991 and 1997, by the Office of Special Education Programs, Washington, DC:
U.S. Department of Education.

itinerant model, (3) consultant model, (4) resource room model, (5) resource
center, (6) special class, (7) special school, and (8) residential school. We do not
discuss these models in detail for two basic reasons: (1) The use of these models
has been well publicized in the professional literature for three decades. You
may refer to any basic book on special education for a comprehensive view of
the models. (2) The inclusion model and the LRE will significant reduce the
levels in the model because a significant number of children will be in regular
classes. Administrators will need to adjust and modify service delivery models
to accommodate the inclusion model.

Data provided by the Office of Special Education Programs clearly show the
following trends:

1. There has been a steady increase in the number of disabled children served
in inclusive settings.

Figure 7: Disabled Students Educated in General Education Classrooms, 1994–1995

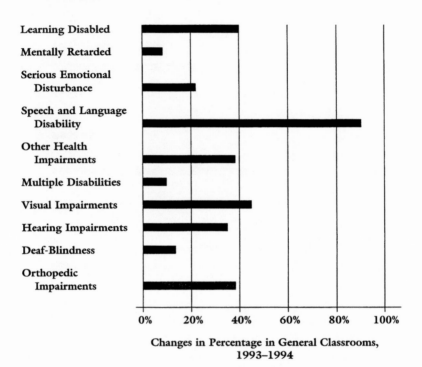

Changes in Percentage in General Classrooms,
1993–1994

Source: Annual Reports to Congress, 1991, 1997.

2. Disabled children with serious types of exceptionalities such as emotional disturbance, visual impairments, hearing impairments, mental retardation, and deaf-blindness have been educated in inclusive settings to some degree; however, most of them are educated in separate school settings.

3. Disabled children having multiple disabilities show the poorest record when educated in inclusive classrooms.

Nationally, the schools are making significant progress in educating disabled children in inclusive settings. Those trends are not universal across all states and can vary significantly. These data also show that disabled children receive services outside of the regular classroom less than 21 percent of the school day. The percentages significantly increased from 21 percent to 60 percent in the resource room. Students in special classes receive more than 60 percent of their service outside the regular class. Students in special classes receive 50 percent of the school day in separate day schools and the same percentage was listed for residential facilities and homebound/hospital settings (*Annual Report to Congress*, 1991, 1997).

•• CRITICAL ISSUES IN INCLUSION

Inclusion has proved to be a powerful tool in educating children with disabilities. This trend is supported by the voluminous research reviewed in this chapter. Jorgensen (1985) supports the notion that inclusion versus special placement is not the critical issue for administrators of special education programs, but rather whether there are well-defined goals and objectives, instructional strategies, competent personnel, supportive services, related resources, community and parental support, successful delivery models, and positive attitudes of staff members toward children with disabilities. For specific examples and factors relevant to inclusion, see appendix B.

When there is no consensus on goals or objectives, there is no logical means for choosing one approach over another, one kind of staff over another, one program component over another. It would not make sense for administrators to initiate an experimental effort unless goals and objectives were made explicit and a set of priorities were chosen. Clearly stated educational goals for disabled children would minimize the conflict in the field. On the other hand, an avoidance of clearly stated goals will not allow administrators to develop beneficial objectives unique for a particular exceptionality. It is true that although behavioral objectives of classroom instruction have been fairly well defined in most disability areas, with the exception of the retarded and learning disabled, clearly defined objectives will emphasize expected behaviors of children as well as skills and activities needed to reach the objectives (Taylor, 1999).

To achieve these goals for exceptional children, administrators should have scientific objectives in mind, as well as a plan for sequencing steps or tasks that will lead to desired behaviors. Steps that administrators may take to assume that objectives and goals are met are as follows:

1. Understanding and categorizing the objectives of the school's curriculum.

2. Defining the objectives or goals in terms of expected behaviors, based on observable and measurable data.

3. Developing instruments, materials, and activities to assess or determine if desired behaviors have been met.

4. Instituting changes at any point in the instructional process if it appears that objectives are not being achieved.

5. Sequencing tasks so exceptional children can experience success. This involves moving from known to unknown experiences, from concrete to abstract levels.

By defining goals on a continuum of levels of difficulty, administrators accomplish a twofold purpose. First, the administrator establishes objectives for each class in such a way that they are sequential in an ascending order of difficulty, and they are also achievable in a foreseeable future. Second, because individual capabilities and competencies vary among children with comparable measurable abilities, such as sequencing permits some to advance more rapidly than others in a single class.

Because some goals for disabled children are essentially short range, in contrast with the traditional concept of short- and long-range plans, the stated objectives must be precise and clear cut. In addition, administrators must frequently evaluate progress made, together with reviewing the child's potential in relation to his or her attainment. Finally, a limited capacity in mental, physical, and social growth should not imply engaging in meaningless, unproductive activities.

Another crucial problem that communities and administrators must face before they elect to choose a plan for their disabled children is that of sequencing instructional tasks. Administrators of special education program must consider life adjustment out of school-in essence, what the final result will be. Before a plan is adopted, however, those behaviors the pupil must master for successful living must be identified and programmed in sequential steps for the goals and instruction to be useful. These procedural changes should take priority over the inclusion versus special class placement controversy (Taylor, 1999).

Administrators must develop more effective tools and new curricula to measure the characteristics of disabled pupils, emphasizing needs and characteristics, rather than placement. The curriculum for disabled children should be based on realistic goals and approaches. These approaches in turn should be formulated on the basis of needs, capacities, and interests.

Individual differences and program scope must be recognized when planning an instructional program for disabled children. Program scope includes the totality of experiences and activities to which an individual is exposed during a specified period of time. Therefore, administrators must be skilled in informal assessment procedures so both the general and specific characteristics of the children can be described and reacted to in the instructional program. The evaluation of an instructional program includes evidence that the program has or has not reached its objectives; it should also provide the basis for conclusions and recommendations for improving the program. All relevant data should be matched or developed to meet the program's objectives; data and information not germane to the objectives should not be included in the instructional process.

Recognition of the disabled child as a whole, from the time of his or her identification to the time of discharge, requires methods of instruction that take into account all of his or her general and specific behaviors. These behaviors include the development of desirable general personality characteristics and the acquisition of specific knowledge and skills that should emulate from the instructional program. In essence, the instructional program should be directly associated with its goals and objectives. The instructional program should be functional and include both literacy skills, problem-solving techniques, and communication skills.

Professional preparation of school personnel is desperately needed. High standards are essential in the selection of administrators and teachers of disabled children. Ideally, before placing a special child into any class, the training, attitudes, and values of the teacher should be carefully and precisely delineated. Discovering a pupil's characteristics, which a given teacher will accept or reject, becomes a critical administrative duty. The nature of the teacher's response to expressed hostility, physical attributes, and academic skills should be included in the placement decision. Questions of this nature are critical and have more relevancy than inclusion versus special class placement. Solutions are not easy, but revision in teacher training is key: teachers must be trained to seek, identify, and demand the assistance needed to educate disabled children.

Administrators and teachers must be trained to initiate new teaching strategies, as well as cooperating with other teachers, parents, and the community. As much as their mental, physical, and social disabilities permit, teachers should actively involve disabled children in the instructional process. Collaboration among administrators and teachers is necessary to provide the best possible education for disabled children. Joint planning, modifications, and adaptation in the instructional program are essential to assure quality of education opportunities for children with disabilities.

If proper support services are not provided for disabled children, no degree of placement will be successful. Special helping teachers, (itinerant or school based), a resource room, and other well-known educational manipulations are needed if any plan is to be successful.

•• SUMMARY

Effective inclusion necessitates the involvement of parents in the planning process, and parental involvement in IEPs is mandated by law. However, many parents of children with disabilities have concerns related to inclusion. They have voiced concerns about their children in integrated classrooms. Some parents are not sure their children with disabilities are receiving appropriate services; consequently, some have elected to have their children educated in segregated classrooms (Hanline & Halvorsen, 1989; Hobbs & Westling, 1998). Most of the studies relevant to parental perceptions on inclusion dealt with children with mild to moderate disabilities. A study conducted by Borthwick-Duffy et al., (1996) was designed to assess parental perceptions of children with severe disabilities. Parental reactions of these parents were similar to those of parents with children with mild to moderate disabilities. Regardless of the levels of disabilities, parents' views of inclusion are more related to well-defined goals and objectives, the personality traits of the teachers, attitudes of staff members toward disabilities, supportive services, competent personnel, innovative instructional strategies and delivery models, and resources and related services. Administrators must find innovative ways of involving parents if inclusion is to be successful.

The research cited here and the federal and state legislation discussed in chapter 6 combine to have a significant impact on parental perceptions toward inclusion. Perceptions toward inclusion are multidimensional and differentiated by several factors (Anotonak & Larriver, 1995; Schmelkin, 1981; Wilczenski, 1992).

Integration of disabled children into the regular classroom and elimination of separate educational classrooms have been issues of major concern in the field of special education for administrators for well over two decades (Baker et al., 1995; Borthwick-Duffy et al., 1996; Fuchs & Fuchs, 1994; Katsiyannis, Conderman, & Franks, 1995). A multitude of conditions and trends have attributed to the controversy. As indicated, federal legislation generally supports educating exceptional children in regular classes; a provision in the Individuals with Exceptionalities Education Act indicates that students with disabilities should be removed from regular education only when the nature and severity of the disability is such that education in regular classes with the use of supplementary aides and services can not be achieved successfully (Taylor, 1999).

In comparing the research over the last two decades, data still support that inclusion placement is no panacea for educating all disabled individuals. The public school record on behalf of students with exceptionalities is best characterized as one of exclusion, separation, and absence of services. In growing numbers, however, disabled learners are receiving at least a portion of their instruction alongside their classmates (Baker et al., 1995; Borthwick-Duffy et al., 1996; Fuchs & Fuchs, 1994). A multitude of conditions and trends have attributed to the controversy as articulated in this chapter.

•• REFERENCES

Aefsy, F. (1995). *Inclusion confusion: A guide to educating students with exceptional needs.* Thousand Oaks, CA: Corwin Press.

Alpher, S., Schloss, P. J., Etscheidt, S. K., & MacFarlane, C. A. (1995). *Inclusion: Are we abandoning or helping students?* Thousand Oaks, CA: Corwin Press.

Annual Report to Congress on the Implementation of the Individuals with Disability Education Act. (1991). Washington, DC: U.S. Department of Education.

Annual Report to Congress on the Implementation of the Individuals with Disability Education Act. (1997). Washington, DC: U.S. Department of Education.

Anotonak, R. F., & Larriver, B. (1995). Psychometric analysis and revisions of the opinions relative to mainstreaming scale. *Exceptional Children, 62,* 139–149.

Baker, E. T., Wang, J., & Walberg, H. C. (1995). The effects of inclusion on learning. *Educational Leadership, 50*(4), 33–35.

Baker, J., & Zigmond, N. (1990). *Full time mainstreaming: Are learning disabled students integrated into the instructional program?* Paper presented at the Annual Meeting of the American Educational Research Association, Tampa, FL: ERIC Document Reproduction Service No. ED 32-373.

Banerji, M., & Dailey, R. (1995). A study of the effects of an inclusion model on students with specific learning disabilities. *Journal of Learning Disabilities, 28,* 511–522.

Barry, A. L. (1995). Easing into inclusion classrooms. *Educational Leadership, 52*(4), 4–6.

Bennet, R., Deluca, D., & Burns, D. (1997). Putting inclusion into practice. *Exceptional Children, 64*(12), 115–131.

Berger, R. S. (1995). Inclusion: A legal mandate: An educational dream. *Updating School Board Politics, 26*(4), 104.

Borthwick-Duffy, S. A., Palmer, D. S., & Lane, K. L. (1996). One size doesn't fit all: Full inclusion and individual differences. *Journal of Behavioral Education, 6,* 311–329.

Brown, L. P., Schwartz, A., Unvari-Solner, E. F., Kampshroer, F., Johnson, J., Jorgensen, J., & Greenwald, L. (1991). How much time should students with severe disabilities spend in regular classrooms and elsewhere? *Journal of the Association of Persons with Severe Disabilities, 16,* 39–47.

Deno, E. (1970). Special education as developmental capital. *Exceptional Children, 37*(3), 229–237.

Fiblin, J., Connolly, T., & Brewer, R. (1996). *Individualized learner outcomes: Infusing student needs into the regular education curriculum.* Tampa, FL: (ERIC Document Reproduction Services No. ED 400 641) Washington, DC: U.S. Department of Education.

Fuchs, D., & Fuchs, L. (1994). Inclusive school movement and the radicalization of special education reform. *Exceptional Children, 60,* 294–309.

Fuchs, D., & Fuchs, L. (1995). Sometimes separate is better. *Educational Leadership, 50*(4), 22–26.

Fuchs, D., Fuchs, L., & Bishop, N. (1992). Teacher planning for students with learning disabilities: Differences between general and special education. *Learning Disabilities Research and Practice, 7,* 120–128.

Giangreco, M., Dennis, R., Cloninger, C., Edelman, S., & Schattman, R. (1993). I've counted JON: Transformation experiences of teachers educating students with disabilities. *Exceptional Children, 59,* 359–371.

Hanline, M. F., & Halvorsen, A. (1989). Parent perceptions of the integration transition process: Overcoming artificial barriers. *Exceptional Children, 55,* 487–492.

Hobbs, T., & Westling, D. L. (1998). Promoting successful inclusion. *Teaching Exceptional Children, 31*(1), 12–19.

Johnston, D., Proctor, W., & Carey, S. (1995). Not a way out: A way in. *Educational Leadership, 50*(4), 46–49.

Jorgensen, C. M. (1995). Essential questions-inclusive answers. *Educational Leadership, 50*(4), 52–55.

Katsiyannis, A., Conderman, G., & Franks, D. L. (1995). State practices on inclusion: A national review. *Remedial and Special Education, 16,* 279–287.

McLeskey, J., & Pacchiano, D. (1994). Mainstreaming students with learning disabilities: Are we making progress? *Exceptional Children, 60,* 508–517.

Mills, D., & Bulach, S. (1996). *Behavioral disordered students in collaborative/ cooperative class: Does behavior improve?* Tampa, FL: ERIC Document Reproduction Services No. ED 394 224.

Roach, V. (1995). Beyond rhetoric. *Phi Delta Kappan, 77,* 295–299.

Roberts, R., & Mather, N. (1995). The return of students with learning disabilities to regular classrooms: A sellout? *Learning Disabilities Research and Practice, 10*(16), 46–58.

Schmelkin, L. P. (1981). Teachers' and non-teachers' attitudes toward mainstreaming. *Exceptional Children, 48,* 42–57.

Scruggs, T. E., & Mastropieri, M. A. (1996). Teachers perceptions of mainstreaming/inclusion: A research synthesis. *Exceptional Children, 63*(1), 59–74.

Shanker, A. (1995). Full inclusion is neither force nor appropriate. *Educational Leadership, 50*(4), 18–21.

Sharpe, M. N., York, J. L., & Knight, J. C. (1994). Effects of inclusion on the academic performance of classmates with disabilities. *Remedial and Special Education, 15*, 281–287.

Staub, D., & Hunt, P. (1993). The effects of social interaction training on high school peer tutors of schoolmates with severe disabilities. *Exceptional Children, 60*, 41–47.

Staub, D., & Peck, C. (1995). What are the outcomes for non-disabled students? *Educational Leadership, 50*(4), 36–39.

Taylor, G. R. (1999). *Curriculums models and strategies for educating individuals with disabilities in inclusive classrooms.* Springfield, IL: Charles C Thomas.

Taylor, G. R. (2000). *Parental involvement: A practice guide for collaboration and teamwork for students with disabilities.* Springfield, IL: Charles C Thomas.

Waldron, N. L., & McLeskey, J. (1995). The effects of an inclusive school program on students with mild and severe learning disabilities. *Exceptional Children, 64*(3), 395–405.

Wang, M. C., Reynold, M. C., & Walberg, H. J. (1995). Serving students at the margins. *Educational Leadership, 50*(4), 12–17.

Wilczenski, F. L. (1992). Measuring attitudes toward inclusive education. *Psychology in the Schools, 29*, 306–312.

CHAPTER 11

Promoting Cultural Awareness

By 2020, an estimated half of the school-age population will be African Americans, Hispanic Americans, or Asian Americans (Pallas, Natriello, & McDill, 1989). Our educational system is characterized as basically Eurocentric. A Eurocentric model will not address or meet the needs of this projected diverse population. Administrators must prepare school personnel to teach students who cannot adequately respond to a Eurocentric model because of language and ethnic backgrounds.

•• COURT CASES

The Civil Rights Act of 1964 banned discrimination based on race, color, or national origin in any program receiving federal funding. In reference to the language of minority children, the U.S. Supreme Court ruled that "There is no equality of treatment merely by providing students with the same facilities, textbooks, teachers, and curriculum, for students who do not understand English are effectively foreclosed from any meaningful education" (*Lau v. Nichols*, 1974).

The major implication of this ruling implied that for students who do not understand English, school districts must find alternate forms of communication, such as providing bilingual education. Several court cases have addressed the issue of bilingual education. In *Dyrcia, S., et al., v. Board of Education of the City of New York* (1979), the court directed that students be evaluated by school-based teams using bilingual evaluation procedures in the students' own environment. It also required a Spanish-version booklet of parents' rights and hiring neighborhood workers to facilitate parental involvement in both evaluation and development of the IEP. Finally, it ordered appropriate bilingual programs, available on a full continuum of placement options, for children with limited English proficiency and disabilities. In a consent decree, the San Francisco School District provided a bilingual bicultural program for minority students in the district (Gearheart, Mullen, & Gearheart, 1993).

Several court cases have determined that certain assessment instruments frequently discriminated or were biased against children from diverse backgrounds. *Diana v. State Board of Education* (1970, 1973) and *Larry P. v. Riles* (1979), found that Hispanic and African American students' evaluations were discriminatory. *Diana v. State Board of Education* concluded that children tested for potential placement in special education must be assessed in their native or primary language, and children can not be placed in special education classes on the basis of culturally biased test results.

The courts have consistently directed school districts to provide bilingual education and unbiased testing for minority children. They have also ruled that bilingual students with disabilities must receive assistance from both bilingual and special education programs. In order to meet these court directives, administrators of special education programs must consistently take into account the assessment of non-English-speaking children. Language diversity must be considered a major factor in assessing and placing minority children in special education settings (Diaz-Rico & Weed, 1995; McMillan, 1997). Regular classroom teachers must use prereferral assessment strategies to assist minority children in the regular classroom (Katsiyannis, 1994).

•• ASSESSING MINORITY DISABLED CHILDREN

This chapter summarizes specific problems in assessment as they relate to assessing the disabled. Several authors have indicated the importance of assessing students for special education (Kauffman, Hallahan, & Ford, 1998; MacMillan, Gresham, Lopez, & Bocian, 1996; MacMillan & Reschly, 1998). Collectively, these authors indicated that the major problem lies in the use of standardized tests. Traditional standardized tests do not include many of the cultural experiences the children face; thus a significant number of them are biased. Many of these tests are based on the defect model, and using the result in educational planning is questionable.

Assessment constitutes more than standardized testing. It may include informal tests, observations, interviews, surveys, questionnaires, rating scales, checklists, and tests administered by specialists in various fields. If conducted properly, assessment data can provide realistic and functional data that may be used in placing and educating minority children. Administrators must monitor the assessment program in their schools to ensure it is fair, reliable, accurate, and used directly in the instructional program. Curriculum and performance-based assessment appear to be two strategies that will reduce bias in assessment data. Additional research is needed to validate these strategies to assess minority children.

•• SPECIAL EDUCATION PLACEMENTS

Because of bias in assessment instruments, lack of prereferral activities by regular classroom teachers, language differences, and negative attitudes toward children from diverse backgrounds, minority children are prime candidates for special education placements. This statement was confirmed by a U.S. Department of Education Report (1977), which found a disproportionate number of children from diverse backgrounds in special education programs. Podemski, Marsh, Smith, and Price (1995) attribute this large number to factors such as inadequate assessment procedures, lack of trained assessment personnel, lack of trained special educators, and gaps between knowledge and practice. Administrators of special education programs serving children from diverse backgrounds should ensure these factors are not responsible for placement in special education programs. Additionally, they should not allow the lack of English to become a criterion for placing students in special education classes. Objective decisions must be made, based on objective data and the type of services needed.

Many disabled children from culturally diverse populations do not need a formal bilingual program but rather special program planning related to their disabilities and to their cultural background. Their academic needs may be the development of additional competence in English and broadened exposure to and experience with cultures other than their own. Multicultural education and values provided by the school will enhance the education of minority children (Gearheart et al., 1993).

Administrators must exercise caution before placing minority children in special education programs, as outlined under the court and federal mandates we addressed earlier. Additionally, administrators should make sure diversity is not equated with disability, and develop or have an understanding of the cultural values and characteristics of a group and how these characteristics and values are similar and different between and among various cultural groups. Having a knowledge of various cultural groups might have an impact on reducing the high percentage of minority children in special education classes. Refer to chapter 10 for recommended service delivery models for placing children with disabilities.

•• STRATEGIES FOR IMPROVING PARENTAL INVOLVEMENT

Administrators need strategies that permit families with different cultural and linguistic backgrounds, having children with disabilities, to fully participate in the schools. Variables such as socioeconomic status, education level, and length of residence in the country should not promote sterotyping beliefs relevant to cultures (Wayman, Lynch, & Hanson, 1990). Hyun and Fowler (1995) provided examples of how cultural awareness can be enhanced by exploring one's own cultural heritage and examining the attitudes and behaviors associated with it. Administrators must become familiar with the child's culture and community.

If limited English is spoken, the administrator should have an interpreter present. An ideal person may be a leader in the cultural community, providing the individual can speak and interpret both languages. In planning for meetings and conferences, the following steps are recommended by researchers (Hyun & Fowler, 1995; Landon & Novak, 1998):

1. Decide with the parents who will participate.

2. Encourage parents to bring people who are important to them.

3. Send a written notice of the meeting in the parents' native language.

4. Determine whether families need assistance with child care or transportation.

By adhering to these steps, administrators show respect for the parents and recognize their individual differences and cultural values. Parents need to feel their cultural styles and languages are valuable knowledge and this knowledge is needed and welcomed in the school. The school can assist those parents by providing training programs to assist them in understanding their roles in planning and understanding their rights as mandated under federal legislation. Any training programs, to be successful, must incorporate the language and culture of the parents in order to prepare them to participate and contribute to the educational planning of their children (Gorman & Balter, 1997; Thorp, 1997).

Creative and innovative ways relevant to family involvement must be tried to improve parental involvement, especially for parents of children with disabilities (Mansbach, 1993; Edwards, 1995). Factors such as (1) diverse school experiences, (2) diverse economic and time constraints, and (3) diverse linguistic and cultural practices all combine to inhibit parental involvement. Diversity should be recognized as a strength rather than a weakness.

•• DIVERSE SCHOOL EXPERIENCES

Parents whose home language or culture differs substantially from the norm may be exposed to conflicting expectations about acceptable modes of behavior. This is particularly true for parents of children with disabilities. Some culturally shaped learning is now within the acceptable ranges for most schools. Creative administrators should not permit this type of bias learning to occur within the school. Parents confronted with so-called normal behaviors frequently remark that their behaviors are not acceptable by the schools. If the schools are to serve the needs of parents from diverse cultures effectively, radical reforms and strategies must be developed to address the following as advocated by Cross (1988):

- An awareness and acceptance of ethnic differences

- Self-awareness of one's personal culture

- Recognition of the dynamics of differences

- Knowledge of the family culture

- Adaptation of skills.

According to Cross (1988), changes are needed in how administrators define cultures. Strategies are also needed to address ways of adapting one's perception toward various cultures. Administrators must develop sensitivity to parents who exhibit behaviors foreign to them and modify and adjust the academics to compensate for cultural differences. The school must change the basic Eurocentric model in use out of respect for cultural diversity (Masten, 1994).

The statement advanced by the American Association on Colleges for Teacher Education (1973) is a way for administrators of special education programs to deemphasize the Eurocentric model. The statement reads as follows:

> Multicultural education is education which values cultural pluralism. Multicultural education rejects the view that schools should seek to melt away cultural differences or the view that schools should merely tolerate cultural pluralism. Instead, multicultural education affirms that schools should be oriented toward the cultural enrichment of all children and youth through programs rooted to the preservation and extension of cultural diversity as a fact of life in American society, and it affirms that major education institutions should strive to preserve and enhance cultural pluralism. (p. 264)

Multicultural education should be designed to teach all students about differences in cultures. Children's feelings and beliefs about diverse cultures are partly shaped by their classroom experiences. A complete education must include the contributions that members of various cultures have made to humankind. Contemporary multiculture education promotes recognition and respect for cultural differences (Hardman, Drew, & Egan, 1999; Kitano, 1997). Hallahan and Kauffman (2000) have provided us with three general purposes of multicultural education that administrators may employ in developing or promoting multicultural education in their schools: (1) to promote pride in one's own cultural heritage and understanding of microculture differences from one's own culture, (2) to foster positive attitudes toward cultural diversity, and (3) to ensure equal educational opportunities for all students.

In order for these purposes to become realities, administrators must plan multicultural experiences that teach about the values and contributions that various cultures have made to our knowledge base, as well as providing models of acceptable types of cultural activities. The types of cultural awareness activities will greatly depend on the number and types of minority children in the school as well as the resources to support them (Finn, 1993). Administrators must address many issues before starting a multicultural program, such as (1) the influence of gender and religion, (2) experiences that are offensive to the group, (3) the use of dialects, (4) types of activities that should not be considered, and (5) views concerning disabilities. Administrators may want to consider expert opinions relevant to developing a program, and an excellent approach would be to consider using community resources.

Banks (1997) Tiedt and Tiedt (1995), and Gollnick amd Chinn (1994) voiced a similar definition of multicultural education. They articulated that

> There is strength and value in promoting culture diversity. Schools should be models for the expression of human rights and respect for culture differences. Social justice and equality for all people should be of paramount importance in the design and delivery of curricula. Attitudes and values necessary for the continuation of a democratic society can be promoted in schools. Schooling can provide the knowledge and skills for the redistribution of power and income among cultural groups. Administrators working with families and communities can create an environment that is supportive of multiculturalism.

These definitions denote that multiculture education is designed to develop understanding and to expose students to different cultures and their values. Administrators must make sure that schools under their supervision reflect positive knowledge about diverse groups and their roles in shaping our society and the world. A successful multicultural program must involve all parents, and administrators must consider the diverse conditions under which many of them operate.

•• DIVERSE ECONOMIC AND TIME CONSTRAINTS

Many families and children with disabilities, because of the high cost of health care and maintenance, have limited funds. One major factor is the one-family income. Because of the constant care and needs of a disabled child, only one parent can work, which is usually the father, if one is present within the home. Another factor deals with the type and nature of the employment. Many parents of children with disabilities hold low-paying jobs, chiefly due to their lack of educational training. Money earned is used to maintain the family from day to day. These economic conditions in the family frequently take priority over concerns related to the child's education. Thus activities related to school, such as homework, attending meetings, volunteering, or involvement in any school activities are not considered important by some parents. In essence, many parents feel the time spent with academic matters is secondary to employment. Administrators should take these factors into account and attempt to structure activities that include parents in the schools. The notion of employing some of these parents as lunch aides, crossing guards, paraprofessionals, consultants, and resource individuals should be considered.

•• DIVERSE LINGUISTIC AND CULTURAL PRACTICES

Many parents from diverse backgrounds are accustomed to certain ways of acquiring and transmitting information. These methods are usually different from those expected by the school or less adaptive in different cultural contexts. Parents may be relatively unprepared to learn new ways of expressing themselves in language and cultural experiences different than their own. Administrators should recognize and appreciate the cultural and linguistic styles of parents. Misunderstood cultural and linguistic practices can lead to misjudging the parents' language and culture style as inappropriate (Taylor, 1997).

•• PARENTAL INVOLVEMENT

Each culture and language has made significant contributions to humankind. Establishing relationships and activities for parents from diverse cultural and language heritage should be encouraged and supported by the school. Multiculturalism and diversity should be accepted and respected (Atkinson & Juntunen, 1994; Casas & Furlong, 1994; Taylor, 1997, 1998).

•• PROMOTING CULTURAL AWARENESS

According to Hyun and Fowler (1995), cultural understanding and awareness may be expedited by the school. Administrators should examine their own attitudes and values associated with their own and other cultures to reinforce the concept that cultures are more alike than different. Administrators may develop specific strategies to improve cultural awareness of parents with children with disabilities. Some strategies may include interviewing parents and family members, examining their official records to verify experiences and competencies, clarifying one's attitudes toward diverse cultures and resources relevant to various cultures, and developing associations with various groups and members of diverse culture groups.

Administrators should stress that each cultural style is different; however, similar characteristics operate across all cultures. It is incumbent on the school to recognize cultural styles and how styles determine behavior. School activities should reflect the richness and contribution each culture has made to improve the human condition.

Norton and Drew (1994) wrote that people of diverse cultural backgrounds have perspectives and beliefs regarding disabling conditions that may differ from those of the cultural majority. Their research also indicated that parents from some cultures have great difficulty accepting disabling because of religious beliefs and values. Administrators must take these factors into consideration when planning educational activities for children from diverse backgrounds. The role of higher education will play a major role in promoting cultural awareness.

•• ROLE OF INSTITUTIONS OF HIGHER EDUCATION

The role of institutions of higher education in preparing future teachers is uncertain. Much of the doubt may be attributed to the institutions' lack of collaboration with other professions, combined with slowness and inability to respond to criticisms from all segments of society. These criticisms indicate that institutions of higher education are not training teachers properly to teach and suggest that other organizations should take over teacher training, such as district-based or state-based training centers or professional associations.

In order to respond to the negative criticisms launched at institutions of higher education, school districts and administrators of special education programs need to join with institutions of higher education to train teachers. Historically, institutions of higher education have provided the teaching profession with a knowledge base, which is required as a point of reference. What is also needed is the practical application of this knowledge base in the classroom. Institutions of higher education have not moved as expeditiously as school districts in these areas. The union of professional development schools with institutions of higher education might be the answer to this pressing dilemma in teacher education.

•• SUMMARY

Administrators of special education programs instructing children from diverse backgrounds are required by law to provide equal educational opportunities for these children. Types of assessment techniques used should be examined and biased instruments should not be used to assess children from diverse backgrounds. Cultural experiences enrich all children and should be viewed by administrators as a strength rather than a weakness.

Many strategies can be developed and implemented by administrators of special education programs to promote cultural awareness in the school. Being sensitive to the needs of children from diverse backgrounds can be demonstrated through recognizing their cultural values. Involving parents, the community, and institutions of higher education in school activities infuses cultural values into the instructional program and recognizes that individuals from all cultures have made significant contributions to improve the human condition.

•• REFERENCES

American Association of Colleges for Teacher Education: Commission on Multicultural Education. (1973). No one model. *American Journal of Teacher Education, 4*, 264.

Atkins, D. R., & Juntunen, C. S. (1994). School counselors and school psychologists as school-home-community liaisons in ethnically diverse schools. In P. Pederson and J. C. Carey (Eds.), *Multi-cultural counseling in schools: A practical handbook*. Boston: Allyn & Bacon.

Banks, J. A. (1997). Multicultural education: Characteristics and goals. In J. A. Banks & C. A. M. Banks (Eds.), *Multicultural education: Issues and perspectives* (3rd ed.). Boston: Allyn & Bacon.

Casas, M., & Furlong, J. J. (1994). School counselors as advocates for increased Hispanic parent participation in schools. In P. Penderson and J. Carey (Eds.), *Multi-cultural counseling in schools: A practical handbook*. Boston: Allyn & Bacon.

Cross, T. (1988). Services to minority populations: What does it mean to be a culturally competent professional? *Focal Point, 2*(4), 1–3.

Diana v. State Board of Education. C-70, RFP (N.D. Calif. 1970, 1973).

Diaz-Rico, L. T., & Weed, K. Z. (1995). *The cross-cultural language and academic development handbook*. Boston: Allyn & Bacon.

Dyrcia, S. et al. v. Board of Education of the City of New York. 79c.2562 (E.D. N.Y. 1979).

Edwards, P.A. (1995). Combining parents' and teachers' thoughts about storybook reading at home and school. In L. M. Morrow (Ed.), *Family literacy: Connections in schools and communities.* College Park, MD: International Reading Association.

Finn, J. D. (1993). *School engagement and students at risk.* Washington, DC: National Center for Education Statistics.

Gearheart, B., Mullen, R. C., & Gearheart, C. J. (1993). *Exceptional individuals: An introduction.* Pacific Grove, CA: Brooks/Cole.

Gollnick, D. M., & Chinn, P. (1994). *Multicultural education in a pluralistic society* (4th ed.). Columbus, OH: Merrill.

Gorman, J. C., & Balter, J. (1997). Culturally sensitive parent education: A critical review of quantitative research. *Review of Educational Research, 67,* 339–369.

Hallahan, D. P., & Kauffman, J. M. (2000). *Exceptional learners: Introduction to special education.* Boston: Allyn & Bacon.

Hardman, M. L., Drew, C. J., & Egan, M. W. (1999). *Human exceptionality: Society, school, and family.* Boston: Allyn & Bacon.

Hyun, J. K., & Fowler, A. (1995). Respect cultural sensitivity and communication. *Teaching Exceptional Children, 28*(1), 25–28.

Katsiyannis, A. (1994). Pre-referral practices: Under Office of Civil Rights Recruiting. *Journal of Developmental and Physical Disabilities, 6,* 73–76.

Kauffman, J. M., Hallahan, D. P., & Ford, D. Y. (1998). Editor's introduction. *Journal of Special Education, 32,* 3.

Kitano, M. K. (1997). A rationale and framework for course change. In A. I. Morey & M. K. Kitano (Eds.), *Multicultural course transformation in higher education: A broader truth.* Boston: Allyn & Bacon.

Langdon, H. W., & Novak, J. M. (1998). Home and school connections: A Hispanic perspective. *Educational Horizons, 1,* 15–17.

Larry, P. v. Riles. 343 F. Supp. 1306, 502, F. 2d 963 (N.D. Calif. 1979).

Lau v. Nichols. 414 U.S. 563 (1974).

Lynch, E. W., & Stein, R. (1987). Parent participation by ethnicity: A comparison of Hispanic, Black, and Anglo families. *Exceptional Children, 54,* 105–111.

MacMillan, D.L., Gresham, F. M., Lopez, M. F., & Bocian, K. M. (1996). Comparison of students nominated for pre-referral intervention by ethnicity and gender. *Journal of Special Education, 30,* 131–151.

MacMillan, D. L., & Reschly, D. J. (1998). Over-representation of minority students: The case for greater specificity or reconsideration of the variables examined. *Journal of Special Education, 32,* 15–24.

Mansbach, S. C. (1993). We must put family literacy on the national agenda. *Reading Today,* 37.

Masten, A. (1994). Resilience in individual development: Successful adaptation despite risk and adversity. In M. C. Wang & E. W. Gordon (Eds.), *Educational resilience in inner-city America*. Hillsdale, NJ: Erlbaum.

McMillan, J. H. (1997). *Classroom assessment: Principles and practice for effective instruction*. Boston: Allyn & Bacon.

Norton, P., & Drew, C. J. (1994). Autism and potential family stressors. *American Journal of Family Therapy, 22*, 68–77.

Pallas, A. M., Natriello, G., & McDill, E. L. (April 1989). The changing nature of disadvantaged population: Current dimensions and future trends. *Educational Leadership*, pp. 16–22.

Podemski, R. S., Marsh, G. E., Smith, T. E., & Price, B. J. (1995). *Comprehensive administration of special education*. Englewood Cliffs, NJ: Merrill.

Taylor, G. R. (1997). *Curriculum strategies: Social skills interventions for young African-American males*. Wesport, CT: Praeger.

Taylor, G. R. (1998). *Curriculum strategies for teaching social skills to the disabled: Dealing with inappropriate behaviors*. Springfield, IL: Charles C Thomas.

Thorp, E. K. (1997). Increasing opportunities for partnership with culturally and linguistically diverse families. *Intervention in School and Clinic, 32*, 261–269.

Tiedt, P. L., & Tiedt, I. M. (1995). *Multicultural teaching: A handbook of activities, information, and resources* (4th ed.). Boston: Allyn & Bacon.

U.S. Department of Education. (1997). *Nineteenth Annual Report to Congress on the Implementation of the Individuals Disability Education Act*. Washington, DC: Author.

Wayman, K. L., Lynch, E. W., & Hanson, M. J. (1990). Home-based early childhood services: Cultural sensitivity in a family systems approach. *Topics in Early Childhood Special Education, 10*, 56–75.

CHAPTER 12

Reporting Progress to Parents

The importance of student files and records for both administrative and legal purposes cannot be overemphasized. The special education administrator must establish and monitor procedures regarding the use, access, care, and storage of student records. All school districts must maintain student records and files as required by state and federal regulations (Podemski, Marsh, Smith, & Price, 1995). An educational accessible record is defined by the Department of Health and Human Services as directly related to a student and maintained by an educational agency. Accessible records include test results and any assessment information used for decision making. Information kept by an individual for private use is not regarded as an accessible record (*Federal Register*, 1977).

Podemski, et al. (1995) summed up the importance of special education administrators safeguarding records. They commented,

> In recent years, access to students records has become a somewhat sensitive issue among parents as well as administrators. School administrators have reported instances of teachers misplacing records and sharing confidential data in inappropriate situations. As a result of litigation regarding the use of such records, some administrators have become extremely protective. There are even reported instances in which teachers are not allowed to view the student folders, but must rely instead upon summaries prepared by administrators, school counselors, or others. And some school policies stipulate that teachers can examine records only in the administrator's office.

In order to resolve this dilemma, administrators, and teachers must develop trust and collaborative agreements concerning records. Teachers and school staff members need to understand that administrators by law must adhere to the local, state, and federal policies to protect the interest of students. However, teachers and related school staff members must have access to records in order to plan functional and realistic instructional programs and services for children with disabilities. In using accessible information, administrators should make clear to teachers and related school staff members the importance of storage, transfer, and confidentiality of student records.

•• STORAGE AND TRANSFER OF STUDENT RECORDS

Federal and state regulations mandate that student records be safely stored and parental permission be obtained when records are transferred. There are numerous ways of storing records, such as in folders, file cabinets, and computerized data storage. Regardless of the method of storage, administrators should have a plan for safeguarding them. This plan should reflect local, state, and federal guidelines as well as procedures outlining how school staff members can modify the files. Additionally, procedures should be adjusted based on new policies, litigation, and legislation at the local, state, or federal levels.

The *Federal Register* (1977) states,

> Federal regulations specify the requirements relating to school records. First, the school must inform the parents when personally identifiable information is no longer needed to provide educational services to the child. Second, such information must be destroyed at the request of the parents. However, a record of the student's name, address, phone number, grade, attendance record, classes attended, grade level completed, and year completed must be maintained without these limitations.

Parental permission is needed to destroy school records associated with the education of their child. Parents may request the destruction of records for a variety of reasons, including safeguard measures, confidentiality, and use of records. These reasons are not inclusive. Administrators should caution parents concerning the long-term consequences of destroying records and employ specific criteria for destroying records based on local, state, and federal policies.

•• GRADING PRACTICES AND REPORTING TO PARENTS

Several research studies have examined the grading practices of schools related to children with disabilities. Generally, these studies have shown that the reform movement and the public outcry for improved grading practices have had a significant impact. When standard grading practices are employed, children with disabilities are most likely graded lower. A study of mainstream children with disabilities in the sixth and eighth grades concerning letter grades revealed these children felt helpless in attempts to earn higher grades, but blamed themselves for the low grades (Selby & Murphy, 1992). Normal standards were applied in grading these students. Putman (1992) found that teacher-made tests in the sciences, social studies, math, and English did not address higher thinking or critical thinking skills. The questions were frequently written using the multiple-choice format and asked at the knowledge level. Questions written at this level do little to stimulate critical thinking skills for children, especially those with disabilities. The major question that administrators of special education programs may face concerning grading students with disabilities is whether or not a different standard should be used in grading them. In our opinion, grading children with disabilities and reporting progress of children with disabilities to parents may require some modification in the regular grading procedures. Administrators can make modifications based on the unique disability and interest of the child if needed. Many children with disabilities do not need any modifications in the grading procedures used. Any modifications made should resemble the regular grading system as much as possible. Strickland and Turnbull (1993) concluded that maintaining similar grading procedures for all students can serve to protect the student's right to confidentiality. State guidelines contain little information on grading. Most states give local school districts the authority to decide on how children with disabilities will be graded. However, some states are reviewing their grading policies.

Administrators must develop effective reporting procedures for informing parents of the progress of their children with disabilities. A first step will be for administrators to examine state and local regulations concerning grading practices. Reports to parents can also improve communication between the home and school. There are several reporting techniques that administrators and teachers can employ to inform parents. These techniques are chosen based on the disabilities, needs, and interests of the children with disabilities and are by no means inclusive:

1. *Anecdotal records.* Anecdotal records may be used to show progress. A permanent type of folder should be used such as a spiral notebook to keep information. All relevant information concerning the student can be listed and categorized. Information listed in anecdotal records may provide information needed to justify a change in the student's academic program. Teachers should attempt to control subjectivity in their interpretation of behaviors.

2. *Work samples.* Work samples are an excellent way to compare a student's performance between time periods on any area or areas in his or her academic program. Students can use self-recording and plot their own progress by using work samples. Parents can also have an objective method to gauge their children's progress in school.

3. *Checklist.* The teacher records critical behaviors he or she has observed in the educational setting. Information is forwarded home to the parents. The parents' signature indicates they have read the information included in the checklist. Collective strategies can be developed by the teacher and parents to reduce or eliminate the undesirable behavior or in some instances to promote possible behavior.

4. *Newsletters.* A newsletter is an excellent way to apprise parents of school issues and special events at the school. The newsletter is an effective device for seeking cooperation from parents in conducting certain school functions.

5. *Daily or weekly report cards.* These report cards inform parents about the academic progress of their children. Parents have an opportunity to respond to the report cards and to indicate ways in which they can assist the child or to make other relevant comments.

6. *Telephone calls.* Most telephone calls to parents are negative. Thus more often the teacher should have positive remarks to make.

7. *An award system.* This system awards children for their accomplishments. The nature of the disability and the interests and needs of the children are considered. No group standards are employed. The child becomes his or her own yardstick and is awarded based on achieving his or her own individualized behavior.

8. *Use of cameras and videotapes.* The behaviors of students are recorded. The recordings and pictures may be used with the permission of parents. The recordings and pictures may be used by the teacher and parent to reinforce positive behaviors or to remediate negative behaviors.

9. *Use of computer technology.* This technology affords rapid reporting to parents, providing the parents have the necessary computer hardware and software and are versed in their uses.

10. *Home visits.* Conditions in some communities do not make home visits an attractive option for many teachers. Some teachers, in spite of poor com-

munity conditions, visit homes. It is recommended if home visits are conducted in most urban communities that homes be visited before dark and another person accompany the teacher.

One of the first strategies advocated by Shea and Bauer (1991) is that administrators and teachers contact the family as soon as possible using some of the techniques listed here. The benefits of this contact can be immeasurable. Parents can (1) inform the teacher about performance, (2) assist the teacher in understanding the student's performance outside of school that may have an impact on performing in school, (3) shed light on cultural differences that may be impeding the instructional program, and (4) assist in reinforcing skills learned at school, including monitoring homework. Reporting data recorded and forwarded to parents should provide for parental disagreement. Any disagreements can be addressed at conference time (James, 1996).

•• CONFIDENTIALITY

PL 94-142 and the Buckley Amendments, Section 513 of PL 93-380, mandate that information collected related to children with disabilities be treated in a professional and confidential manner and not be distributed without parental permission (*Federal Register*, 1977). Access to records by school personnel must conform to the confidentiality safeguards:

1. An administrator should be appointed to monitor the use of student records and must develop safeguard procedures for protecting them.

2. Training should be provided for all school personnel regarding the use of confidentiality of using student records.

3. A list indicating all professionals in the school district who have access to confidential information must be developed and maintained.

4. Records must be made available for auditing and inspection as required by school policies and parental permission. (Strickland & Turnbull, 1993)

5. Information stored electronically on children with disabilities can easily be retrieved by individuals other than school or community personnel. This may create some problems for administrators charged with protecting confidential information. Consequently, administrators must make ethical and logical decisions about data collection and storage to assure as much as possible the confidentiality of information entrusted in their care.

When the school or agency no longer needs the information, administrators must inform the parents they have the option to request the destruction of the information. A permanent record, without regard to time constraints and containing demographic and academic information may be maintained (Taylor, 2000).

•• GRADUATION PRACTICES

Graduation requirements for children with disabilities differ from state to state. Most states award three types of certificates to signify completion of high school, according to Podemski et al. (1995): a regular diploma, a special diploma, and a certificate of attendance. The type of diploma issued is usually left up to the individual school district.

A significant number of children with disabilities at the secondary level can earn the regular diploma. For these students, awarding a special education diploma can be a source of legal dispute. A special education diploma may signify the student was not capable of meeting the graduation requirements.

•• REPORTING TO PARENTS

Parents have the right to secure information relevant to the function of their children in school. The teacher's major responsibility is informing parents how well their children have progressed within an administratively approved reporting period. Reporting should describe children's progress accurately and objectively. Teachers need to describe in narrative terms and refer to samples of classwork so the parents can make their own assessment of their children's work (Potter, 1998).

Administrators and teachers, as indicated, have several avenues for reporting children's progress to parents. Before forwarding a report home or conducting a conference, administrators should prepare an outline that includes information which will reflect significant aspects of the child's behavior. Communication should be clear and concise. Language usage must be on a level the parent can understand. If their language is not native English, attempts should be made to report to the parent in his or her native language. If this is not feasible, an interpreter should be available, so parents may participate effectively and interact with the educator. Progress reports for children with disabilities are usually long narrative descriptions of behavior, constituting significant pages. To summarize the total report would consume too much time. The administrator should select parts of the report that he or she wishes to discuss or forward home to the parents.

Frequently in conferences, administrators and teachers have special concerns. These concerns may be completely independent of the information covered in the report. To avoid this type of encounter, administrators should seek from parents their special interests. Another approach would be to have a planning meeting and to set the agenda at that time, or the administrator can seek permission to explore an issue that in his or her opinion is common to the parents (Goldring & Hausman, 1997). Parents should keep in close contact with the school, check their children's homework regularly, and send notes frequently to school inquiring about the progress of their children. Parents displaying these traits are usually familiar with the school's program. These parents do not need a full conference or reporting period. Administrators can simply review the major parts of the report and enlist comments from the parents. But parents who do not visit frequently or keep in contact with the school will need additional time and information concerning the school's program and reporting system.

Most parents like a reporting system that covers all of the aspects of human behavior in the academic, social, emotional, and physical domains. Additionally, they are seeking information relevant to classroom behavior, normative data on performance, progress report on growth in all areas, and preferred learning styles. As outlined, administrators need to provide some parents with detailed information concerning the reporting system. Others, who are well informed, will need little information. Administrators have to decide on the best structure for reporting the information to parents.

•• ACADEMIC PERFORMANCE

The administrator should decide on the frequencies of the reporting period, which may be weekly, monthly, quarterly, or every semester. As a general rule, the reporting periods for children with disabilities must be equal in number and have the same interval sequence as provided to nondisabled school-age children. Regardless of the reporting period, parents of children with disabilities, as well as other parents, are concerned about their children's academic performance in the basic skills as well as in other subjects. Administrators should provide objective information in the academic areas to parents through conferences and the reporting period. Parents should respond to the progress report. Collectively, parents, teachers, and administrators can plan to develop strategies for improving the performance or plan to upgrade or remediate the deficit areas. Planning may take place using a variety of approaches already articulated. We believe that a face-to-face conference is the better approach to take. The conference approach permits both teachers and parents to discuss their feelings openly and make a collective plan to address the problems of the child.

•• SOCIAL/EMOTIONAL DEVELOPMENT

Social/emotional competency is an important aspect of educational interrelationships (Taylor, 1998). The experience of interacting with others is necessary for the development of all children, especially for children with disabilities. These children need to be acknowledged, noticed, valued, respected, and appreciated by others and to be aware that others want the same from them. Administrators should support the concept that social/emotional competency is the sum total of one's ability to interact with other people, to take appropriate social initiatives, to understand people's reactions to them, and to respond accordingly (Taylor, 1998). Children with disabilities must learn to interact appropriately with others. Social/emotional skills are a continuous process, and parents need to know how their children's competency measures up, how they deal with their frustrations, and how they approach new learning tasks. The progress report can indicate needed interpersonal skills to encourage and those to limit. Parental responses and practicing social skills at home can do much to augment the teacher's social skills program.

•• PHYSICAL DEVELOPMENT

Many children with disabilities have severe physical problems with deficits in bones, nerves, muscles, and other organs, and their activities are restricted because of physical disabilities. Administrators should provide detailed descriptions of physical activities the child can perform and provide as many physical activities as possible to assist in maintaining and developing whatever physical strength the child has. During reporting times, the administrator and the teacher should discuss with the parents the strengths and weaknesses observed, and a unified plan should be devised for meeting the stated needs of the child (Taylor, 1999).

Once the academic, social/emotional, and physical traits have been appropriately assessed, the next step for administrators and parents is to decide what strategies are to be implemented to achieve the stated objectives in each of the three major areas. The classroom is an excellent place for the child to demonstrate behaviors in the three domains outlined (Taylor, 1999).

•• CLASSROOM BEHAVIOR

The classroom provides a structure for the child to demonstrate various behaviors in the three basic domains (Taylor, 1999). Administrators need to make known to parents the methods and procedures that will be employed to evaluate the child's behavior and performance. This assessment requires professional judgment to report the behavior accurately and objectively. Detailed knowledge of development norms in the areas of intelligence, social/emotional, and physical development are needed in order for the administrator and the teacher to make a valid report on the child's classroom behaviors. Parents should have an opportunity to observe the child in the classroom. With the teacher they should plan strategies for improving or modifying the behavior. When communicating with parents relevant to classroom behaviors, the teacher can compare performance of the child with another child of the same age. However, some caution is in order. Children of the same age with disabilities and having the same disabling conditions may perform well above or below the normative group. The recommended approach would be to use the child as his or her own yardstick and assess progress over a certain time frame.

During reporting and conference time, administrators should discuss with the parent the procedures used to evaluate the child, noting reasons why the child is performing above or below the expected age level of his or her peers and how the learning style was assessed. It is essential during the conference that the administrator accent the positive behaviors of the child and encourage the parents to reinforce those behaviors at home. For negative behaviors, strategies should be discussed to minimize or eradicate those behaviors. Before ending the discussion, reporting periods, or conference, administrators, teachers, and parents should agree on the following:

- What can be done at school and home to increase the child's performance in all academic, social/emotional, and physical development areas.

- Time lines and location for the next conference with a possible area for discussion.

- What community resources can be used to assist us in meeting the stated objectives.

- A plan for selecting a group leader, not necessarily the teacher.

- Who will report to parents and to those who were not present at the initial conference.

- A tentative progress report on how certain strategies will be achieved.

•• SUMMARY

Teachers become the central figures in grading and reporting procedures employed in the schools. They are exposed to pressures from parents, children, and the school's grading policy for children with disabilities. The teacher becomes a catalyst in the grading and reporting controversy, attempting to explain the school's reporting pattern and the unfeasibility of grading children with disabilities. Research is desperately needed in this area. However, the administrator should make sure that parents understand the grading and reporting procedures employed and attempt to seek community support concerning the system.

Reports that parents of children with disabilities receive differ from school district to school district, as well as from state to state. In addition, use of reporting and grades in evaluating the progress of children with disabilities is highly questionable. Much of the controversy lies in the fact that administrators in the past did not have an objective system to determine the achievement of children with disabilities. The lack of specificity and objectivity of outcomes to be graded and the attitudes of teachers toward pupil interest and effort reduces decidedly the validity and reliability of marks.

The value of a marking system subsequently becomes dependent on what is being marked, who is doing the marking, who is being marked, and who interprets the marks. Furthermore, marks and accompanying competitive situations can cause many undesirable traits and attitudes to develop in children with disabilities, such as insecurity, fear, anxiety, cheating, and inferiority. These factors indicate that an objective and scientific way of evaluating the growth of these children should be instituted. Rather than group evaluation, individual evaluation based on the unique interests, abilities, disabilities, and characteristics of children with disabilities will aid in their total development. It is recommended that the approach outlined better provide administrators and teachers with a model leading to an effective evaluation of the children's achievement.

There is universal agreement that parents should be regularly informed by the school concerning their children's growth and development. The major source of conflict is how progress should be reported. Administrators should explain their grading systems to parents and seek their support and approval before instituting any grading pattern. Teacher/parent conferences appear to be an opportune place to explain and seek parental approval for a marking system.

Among the many methods used to report to parents are report cards, use of descriptive words, checklists, narrative or letter reports, conferences, pupil self-appraisals, informal notes, telephone conversations, information meetings, and home visits. When parents and school administrators agree on a marking pattern and parents understand their children's achievement is evaluated in relation to their capacities, a great deal of the controversy over marking is significantly reduced. Reporting can then be viewed as a suitable method of helping parents accept their children for who they are, to understand what the school program is attempting to accomplish, and to learn how well their children are succeeding. Reporting should be a means for strengthening a sound relationship between home and school in the guidance of the child and contribute to the increased effectiveness of learning.

•• REFERENCES

Federal Register. (1977, August 23). Washington, DC: U.S. Government Printing Office.

Goldring, E. B., & Hausman, C. (1997). Empower parents for productive partnership. *Education Digest, 62*, 25–29.

James, A. B. (1996). Helping parents of a special needs child. *Lutheran Education, 132*, 78–87.

Podemski, R. C., Marsh, G. E., Smith, T. E., & Price, B. J. (1995). *Comprehensive administration of special education* (2nd ed.). Englewood Cliffs, NJ: Prentice Hall.

Potter, L. (1998). Making parent involvement meaningful. *Schools in the Middle, 6*, 9–10.

Putnam, M. L. (1992). Characteristics of questions on test administered by mainstream secondary classroom teachers. *Learning Disabilities Research and Practice, 7*(3), 29–36.

Selby, D., & Murphy, S. (1992). Graded of degraded: Perceptions of letter grading for mainstreamed learning disabled students. *B.C. Journal of Special Education, 16*(1), 92–104.

Shea, T. M., & Bauer, A. M. (1991). *Parents and teachers of children with exceptionalities: A handbook for collaboration* (2nd ed). Boston: Allyn & Bacon.

Strickland, B. B., & Turnbull, A.D. (1993). *Developing and implementing individualized education programs.* Englewood Cliffs, NJ: Prentice Hall.

Taylor, G. R. (2000). *Parental involvement: A practical guide for collaboration and teamwork for students with disabilities.* Springfield, IL: Charles C Thomas.

Taylor, G. R. (1998). *Curriculum strategies for teaching social skills to the disabled.* Springfield, IL: Charles C Thomas.

Taylor, G. R. (1999). *Curriculum models and strategies for educating individuals with disabilities in inclusive classrooms.* Springfield, IL: Charles C Thomas.

CHAPTER 13

School and Community Interactions

Research has shown that community involvement and action can be powerful allies in transforming schools. Community involvement with the schools has been credited with (1) improving the physical conditions and resources that support learning in the schools, (2) raising the attitudes and expectations of parents, teachers, and students, and (3) improving the depth and quality of the learning experiences of students through collaborative planning (Hatch, 1998; Murnane & Levy, 1996; Shirley, 1997; Cohn-Vargas & Grose, 1998). The major purpose of school/community relations is to share information about the special education program.

It is essential that administrators make parents aware and informed about progress made toward achieving reforms. Parents are more likely to become associated with the school if administrators develop a strong and trusting relationship with them. The bond can be further strengthened by making frequent contacts with the parents, conducting seminars, and sponsoring social events developed by the community. Administrators frequently deal with community groups and agencies and must possess effective interpersonal and community skills.

Because of the emotional impact of disability upon the family, parents need help from the community. Services provided by the community impact to some degree how children with disabilities develop and also provide strategies to help family members cope with the disabilities (Norton & Drew, 1994). The community's most important contribution to families is a willingness to listen and understand what they are experiencing. Parents and siblings need someone they can express their feelings to and receive support. Administrators can ensure that parents' needs are heard through school/community relations designed to share information about special education with the community.

The need for direct involvement of parents and communities has been advocated by Atkinson and Juntunen (1994). They reported that administrators must function as a school-home-community liaison. Casas and Furlong

(1994) supported the increase of parental participation and empowerment in the community and encouraging parents to visit with other parents of children with disabilities. Most communities have support groups of parents who have disabled children. Organizations dealing with the specific disability of the child can also be helpful to the family (e.g., the Association of Retarded Citizens, United Cerebral Palsy Association).

According to Lunenburg and Ornstein (1991), administrators can use the following ideas to keep parents and the community informed:

- A brochure that describes the special education program, including the district's philosophy of services to individuals with disabilities

- Specialized brochures, each describing a specific aspect of the program

- A parent handbook that describes the IEP process, forms, and the role of the parent

- Articles in the district newspaper, school building paper, or local newspaper

- A special newsletter that focuses on special education news

- Telephone contacts with individual parents and other citizens

- Speeches to community groups or civic clubs

- Annual reports, open houses, videotapes, and letters to groups

- Displays at locations, such as civic meeting places and shopping malls

- Public service announcements on radio and television describing some aspect of special education services.

Collaboration strategies can also be used effectively to promote communication. Collaborative activities can meet the needs of children with disabilities and their parents by integrating the services of both the home and school in all areas of human functioning. These activities may do much to improve culture, social, and physical problems associated with the children's disabilities. Administrators must strive to become an integral part of the collaborative efforts if they are to be successful. The following guidelines are offered as a means to improve the collaborative efforts:

1. Develop a plan to build trust and security among parents.

2. Involve parents in the school development plan and seek volunteers in all aspects of the plan to ensure that every parent contributes to the attainment of the goals and objectives.

3. Construct individual agreements with each parent so the parent will have some responsibilities in meeting the stated goals, objectives, and IEP requirements.

4. Develop strategies for identifying, assessing, using, and evaluating community resources.

5. Establish a citizen advisory committee and involve them in the planning.

Several authors have indicated disadvantages in promoting collaborative activities, especially with advisory committees (Podemski, Marsh, Smith, & Price, 1995; Podemski & Steele, 1981):

1. Advisory committees can consume a great deal of the administrator's time.

2. Committee members often lack perspective and background information about educational issues.

3. Special interests of individual committee members can dominate.

4. Committee members may not be aware of past school practices or how the school operates.

5. Committee members may not understand group dynamics or group decision-making procedures.

6. Final recommendations can exceed the committee's original charge or overstep its authority.

7. The committee may search for problems or issues to justify its existence.

We believe administrators can overcome many of the pitfalls just listed by developing small focus groups knowledgeable about the issues under discussion who are willing to reach a consensus. Members of this group should have time to commit to the issues. Additionally, administrators should apprise the group of any history or procedures that will assist them in reaching a consensus, provide as much assistance as possible to the group, and implement as much of the committee's recommendations as possible. Lack of implementing committee's recommendations will erode the relationship between the committee and administrators.

Collaborating with parents and working with families are major modifications and reforms that administrators can make in improving communication between the home and school. Much of the improvement in communication has come about due mainly to state and federal legislation, parental rights groups, parent empowerment, and the schools' recognition of the value of parental input in educating children. Administrators have become cognizant of the influence of poverty, ethnicity, family structure and transitions, parental age, and other factors that interact with children's development (Powell & Diamond, 1995). Using the vast amount of research generated in these areas, administrators have developed programs to strengthen parental behavior as well as revised programs to reflect cultural diversity.

•• PROMOTING CULTURAL AWARENESS

Promoting cultural awareness helps families with different cultural and linguistic backgrounds with children with disabilities to participate fully in the schools. Variables such as socioeconomic status, educational level, and length of residence in the country should not promote stereotyped beliefs (Wayman, Lynch, & Hanson, 1990; Gorman & Balter, 1997). Hyun and Fowler (1995) explored how cultural awareness can be enhanced by exploring one's own cultural heritage and examining the attitudes and behaviors associated with one's own culture. Administrators must become familiar with the child's culture and community (Powell, 1998). Refer to Chapter 11 for specific strategies.

•• COMMUNITY AND PARENTAL INVOLVEMENT

No school program can be completely effective without the support of parents and the community. Most administrators are acutely aware of the need for parents and active community involvement in the entire educational program for children with disabilities. When the school and community are genuinely interested in the welfare of the child and his or her parents, apathy and despair turn to hope and self-fulfillment, which can do much to ease many of the emotional problems experienced. Further, improvement in communication can do much to eliminate the negativism of many parents. This positive approach cannot help but assist the child with a disability in his or her educational pursuits.

A desirable relationship in the community is one marked by a strong bond of understanding and cooperation between parents and school personnel. Parents should have a direct share in deciding what types of instruction appear to serve their children best. Parents should be welcome to make suggestions for the guidance of their children. Through various channels the administrator should enlist the cooperation of parents and community agencies in designing and implementing educational programs for children with disabilities. In communities where educators work with parents and with religious, recreational, and social agencies in a constructive effort to help, the results are reflected in healthier personalities of boys and girls.

Communities can do a great deal to make better use of their resources through a coordination of efforts. Coordination mobilizes the skills of people to help all programs, eliminates wasteful competition, saves money, improves training opportunities, and gives invaluable assistance to the disabled child and his or her family. The school should be the key for coordinating activities in the community. Specialists in various disciplines should be consulted as needs of disabled children dictate. Some consideration should be given to the parents who may need financial assistance. Again, personnel in the schools and diagnostic centers can refer the parent to appropriate community agencies that can provide the support (Podemski et al., 1995).

Differentiation of general and specialized services is vital, not only to make ample use of community resources but to provide the disabled child with a complete diagnosis. Services provided should include both approaches. Coordinated planning should be a well-planned process that seeks to elicit cooperation and communication among various community agencies. Some of the obstacles associated with effective community planning are (1) lack of personnel with experience to conduct the planning, (2) decreased interdisciplinary communication due to lack of mutual respect among specialists, (3) facilities for the disabled failing to recognize that no one clinic or agency can provide the necessary services needed to diagnose, treat and rehabilitate the disabled child, and (4) exclusion of parents from the initial diagnostic evaluation, treatment, and follow-up procedures.

The position of school personnel on a special education team headed by noneducators and the relationship of medical personnel with other members are some specific problems that should not vary as widely as they do from program to program. Understanding the intricacies of teamwork and agreeing upon its definition might clarify areas of misunderstanding. The necessity of communication within the team, or team action with parents, community members, state departments, and other programs, as well as balancing progress, morals, and democratic ideals, constitute other areas of coordination sometimes overlooked by administrators.

•• COORDINATION OF ACTIVITIES

Coordination of the education program for children with disabilities should exist among and between all units of the school system and community (Thorp, 1997). Effective planning for coordination calls for participation of many agencies, official and voluntary, local and regional. In order for the disabled to receive maximum benefit from community programs, activities need to be closely coordinated with the schools. Until the last few decades, the responsibility for preparing the disabled youth to assume the obligations of a mature citizen was almost exclusively that of the school. Presently, certain social and vocational services external to the school, which had as their purpose the rendering of training and placement services to disabled persons of postschool age, are beginning to assist the schools in these attempts. These agencies developed separately from the school and remained at some distance until they recognized a mutuality of interests and purposes with the school. Today, the nature of the interaction between schools and other community agencies is more continuous and harmonious. The responsibility for educating children with disabilities does not rest with the elementary school alone. All levels of the public school system, parents, and community are responsible for educating all the children of all the people (Wang, et al., 1996).

Regular and continuous progress of children with disabilities through the school system requires coordination of effort on the part of the community, administrators, and teachers. The elementary and secondary schools need to be unified in purpose and procedure so that steady, continuous progress may be ensured. Despite an increase in coordination between levels of education in the public schools and a commitment to team efforts, school personnel still place too much emphasis on how to use the findings of other professionals rather than how to work to establish and improve the quality of programs for children with disabilities (Taylor, 2000).

•• STRATEGIES FOR IMPROVING PARENTAL INVOLVEMENT

Much of the interest and increase in parental involvement may be attributed to PL 94-142 and its amendments. These legislative amendments have mandated parental participation in all aspects of the child's educational program, including assessment, IEP development, placement decisions, evaluation, follow-up, and transitional services.

• *Rewarding Parents*
  Administrators need to recognize and reward parents for their involvement. Reinforcing parental efforts can make a significant impact in working with their children (Oswald & Sinah-Nirbay, 1992). Parents employ some of the same techniques that teachers use to reinforce their children. Social and academic growth of children with disabilities may be expedited through the use of reinforcement strategies. Teachers who create a positive atmosphere for communication and collaboration with parents increase the probability of the child's success in his or her academic pursuits.

- *Modeling for Parents*

  Many parents are not trained in teaching strategies. Administrators can train interested parents through observation, demonstration, and modeling. Bandura (1977) has validated the importance of these techniques. Administrators should provide ample strategies for parents to imitate. Today, administrators realize the importance of parental involvement and understand that cooperative efforts between teachers and parents benefit the children significantly.

- *Conferences*

  Both group and individual conferences have been found invaluable in improving collaboration between parents and administrators. Administrators may decide on the best type of conference needed to address the needs of the children. Some problems can be dealt with successfully in large groups, others in small groups. At any rate, confidentiality must be observed once the initial conference has been held. Future conferences should be conducted regularly, agreed on by both parent and the administrator. Timing of conferences is of prime importance. Conferences must be held at a convenient time for parents to attend. The length of the conferences must also be considered. Parents have other commitments, and to avoid conflicts, administrators should send out conference schedules and agenda items in advance. Advanced schedules should solicit parents' comments and suggestions. The final schedule should be modified to meet parental concerns. This approach will reinforce a sense of cooperation and openness between administrators and parents. Teachers and administrators must be cognizant of the individual needs of parents and plan strategies based on these needs. Various types of reinforcement strategies should be in place to reinforce parental behaviors. The type of reinforcement or reward program instituted should be conducted in concert with the individual needs of the parents.

•• IMPORTANCE OF PARENTAL INVOLVEMENT

Parental involvement is a widely accepted practice among proponents of education. Parents can serve as partners to the teacher in the child's academic program. Taylor (2000) summed up the importance of parental involvement in the schools by stating that parents are a school's best friend. He listed several statements that have major implications for involving parents in the school: (1) The immediate family, not the school, provides the first instruction for the child; (2) Parental involvement in their children's education improves the child's chances for later academic success; (3) Parental involvement is most effective when it is comprehensively planned; and (4) The earlier parents become involved in their children's education, the more likely they will be involved throughout the child's academic career.

It is incumbent on administrators to understand and appreciate the importance of parental and family involvement in order to improve family/school cooperation. Individuals with disabilities cannot reach their optimum level of functioning unless their parents become actively involved in their education (Taylor, 1998). Significant benefits can be derived from involving parents at any level.

To be effective, administrators should launch parental involvement on two fronts: the home and school. Involving parents with their children's education at home augments the learning process, providing that learning strategies are addressed collaboratively by both teachers and parents. Achievement of students tends to accelerate when both teachers and parents agree on common goals and objectives. Parents can be instructed to focus on school readiness skills and specific objectives that nurture learning (Langdon &Novak, 1990).

All children benefit when parents are involved in the school, and this is especially true for children with disabilities and minority children. The education level of parents should not be a prerequisite for involving them. Parents can perform many nonacademic tasks. All children are pleased and proud to see their parents involved in the school (Clark, 1993; Floyd, 1998; Wang et al., 1996).

Both the home and school have a significant impact on students' attitudes. Attitudes are mostly formed at home during the early years and are reinforced by the parents as the child matures. If attitudes are not reinforced by the school, negative ones may surface and impede the achievement of students.

•• DEVELOPMENT OF SCHOOL POLICY

Parental involvement in school policy is essential if the school is to meet state and federal mandates. Administrators should insist that parents serve on all the major policy-making bodies in the school, not just the PTA. Parents should be involved in choosing textbooks, developing curriculum guidelines, forming social committees, and serving as resource individuals, to name but a few. Parental involvement appears most effective when parents are directly involved in all school activities that have a direct impact on their children. Parents can be effective when they define the conditions under which they serve. Administrators should articulate specific ways parents can participate in the education program. Some in-service training may be needed for parents to participate effectively in the education program (Ohlrich, 1996; Potter, 1996; Thompson, 1998).

Administrators can promote parental involvement by adhering to strategies recommended by the Education Commission of the States (1996):

1. Listen to people first, talk later.

2. Expect to fail if you do not communicate well with teachers.

3. Make involving parents and the community a top priority.

4. Be clear about what it means to set high standards for all students and what it will take to achieve them.

5. Show how new ideas enhance, rather than replace, the old ones.

6. Educate parents about the choices available to them.

7. Help parents and other community members understand how students are assessed and what the results mean.

Sergiovanni's views (1996) supported the Education Commission of the States position. He argued that both the what and how of student learning should be decided by administrators, teachers, and parents, because that is the essence of democratic community and the give-and-take of such decisions is what produces understanding and trust. Authenticity is essential in promoting trust between stakeholders. It is what parents desire most from the school (Rich, 1998). Administrators assumed that parents expected them to be professional and businesslike, and parents actually want the opposite. Parents from all levels complained about educators talking down to them (Education Commission of the States, 1996). Information should be provided to parents in a manner they can understand. Counseling appears to be an effective technique for providing information to parents.

•• COUNSELING PARENTS

Effective counseling techniques can do much to inform parents about the nature, extent, and implication of their children's disabling conditions. Further, many of the emotional strains, unhappiness, and conflicts can be significantly reduced with professional counseling strategies. A first step should be to conduct a needs assessment of the parents. Once conducted, teachers and educators will have factual data for conducting counseling sessions to reduce, minimize, or eradicate problems.

Information sessions and conferences may be scheduled to address the problems in a variety of individual and group sessions. Administrators should provide parents with detailed information explained in lay terms on treatment, intervention, and diagnostic evaluations and etiological information concerning their children. Information relevant to community facilities and services, intervention and treatment, education, related services, and other technical services should be made readily available to them. They should be made aware that their problems are not unique. Many parents have children with disabilities and are seeking ways to manage and treat the disabilities effectively.

Diagnosis and counseling is one continuing process and should begin simultaneously. It is of prime importance that administrators involved in the diagnostic process also be included in counseling. The importance of including parents from the inception to the conclusion of the diagnostic and treatment process cannot be overemphasized. Diagnostic information is of little use to parents unless it can be adjusted to fit into their short- and long-range plans for care of the child. Parents should participate in present and future treatment plans.

Because some parents with children with disabilities suffer from emotional conflicts, guidance and counseling are deemed important if the child is to be treated effectively. Parents must either change their way of viewing the child or develop ego defense mechanisms such as denial, repression, or a guilt complex. Administrators should assist parents in dealing with their feelings. Unless professional help is given, the emotional problems of the child will most likely increase. For the best results, both parents should be included in the counseling process (Atkinson & Juntunen, 1994; May, 1991).

•• ROLES OF ADMINISTRATORS

Based on the nature and extent of the disability, many parents may be counseled by professionals from several disciplines. Administrators must be active listeners. They must give the parents sufficient time to present their cases. Parents should be encouraged to discuss their problems and areas in which they need assistance, the type of services their children have had, and the expectations they have for their children's future (Brandt, 1998; Friend & Bursuck, 1996).

Parents also need counseling in accepting their children's disabilities. Administrators should provide strategies to reduce the shame and guilt felt by many parents. Counselors and administrators should be aware of the intense social pressure experienced by these parents. Some parents may become defensive and hostile due to social pressures as well as unsympathetic counselors.

Administrators should be patient by showing understanding, acceptance, and empathy when counseling parents. By using this approach, administrators can reinforce certain behaviors of parents and reject others without forming judgmental bias or condemning relevant parental statements concerning their disabled children (Bradley, Knoll, & Agosta, 1992; Gartner, Lipsky, & Turnbull, 1991; Muir-Hutchinson, 1987; Turnbull & Turnbull, 1990, 1993).

The major role of administrators in the treatment and guidance of parents of children with disabilities is to provide correct knowledge and information. When in doubt, administrators should refer parents to appropriate professionals. The administrator's role is not to counsel parents, but merely to direct and recommend them to professionals. Administrators must establish the emotional level of parents before effective treatment can be initiated. Some parents have a high level of acceptance; others have a low acceptance level. Professionals must assess the level of acceptance and provide appropriate intervention and treatment (Dettmer, Thurston, & Dyck, 1993; Shea & Bauer, 1991). Administrators who are not certified in counseling should not attempt to conduct sessions. The administrator's role should be to provide support to the family. Coleman (1986) suggested that some parental problems are beyond the administrator's and teacher's competencies and should be referred to appropriate professionals. He listed the following conditions:

1. Parents experience a period of unusual financial difficulty, marital discord, or emotional upheaval.

2. Parents routinely express feelings of helplessness or depression.

3. Parents feel unable to control their child.

4. Parents report that the child is habitually in trouble with juvenile authorities.

5. Parents chronically appear to be under a high level of stress.

6. Parents impose on the teacher's time at home or school with their personal problems.

Although Coleman presented these conditions in 1986, they still have relevance today. Administrators should be aware that parents have varying counseling needs. Some will be defensive, and others will be resistant to treatment because of previous experiences. Counseling techniques are designed to reduce and minimize these types of behaviors.

It is incumbent on administrators that the total family be involved in any treatment. Family therapy should continue throughout the lifetime of the child, and the approach should inform parents of community resources and services in the community. The end results of counseling should be to assist the family in setting realistic goals for their children with disabilities (Cross, 1988).

•• EMOTIONAL NEEDS OF THE PARENTS

As already discussed, parents display a wide range of emotional problems. The emotional reactions of parents should be fully assessed before treatment or intervention is attempted. Frequently, parents are not aware of the consequences of their emotional reactions on the child, the school, and the family. Administrators should assist parents in understanding the nature, cause, and result of their psychological defenses, and indicate ways to minimize these defenses. The parents should be made to understand they are not alone, but many other parents have similar problems. Parents should be encouraged to participate in support groups. Parents sharing similar situations can do much to alleviate individual problems of parents (Shea & Bauer, 1991).

Parental problems may be addressed individually or in groups. Some parents might initially be treated individually, but the long-range plan should be to involve the parents in group activities where common views can be shared and discussed. Group activities have proven to be highly effective for educative and guidance sessions. Additionally, group activities may serve as a resource where valuable procedural methods are shared by each parent. They support parents who have similar problems (Atkinson & Juntunen, 1994; Bradley et al., 1992; Coleman, 1986; Muir-Hutchinson, 1987; Shea & Bauer, 1991).

Administrators may recommend a wide variety of supportive services to assist parents in dealing effectively with their children with disabilities. Groups and individual techniques may be used, based on the assessed needs of the parents, such as group and individual psychotherapy. Therapists are trained to determine the nature and extent of the psychotherapy needed to assist both the child and the parents to cope successfully with problems imposed by the disabilities.

•• SPECIAL SERVICES

Special services should be an integral part of the teaching/learning program for children with disabilities. Disability usually denotes many associated problems. Because of these problems, administrators call on specialists from other fields for purposes of evaluation and consultation. The school will not be able to provide the comprehensive array of special services required, and therefore arrangements should be made to use private and community services, in addition to those available within the school.

Many of the disabled require medical and paramedical services. The incidence of other types of disabilities is high among this group. Because many of their problems are medical, the administrator should consult each child's physician to learn how to handle all possible contingencies. The disabled child from deprived settings often needs to be referred to clinics for a variety of problems because parents are often unable to handle their medical needs (Heddel, 1998; Fowler, 1995).

Administrators should promote adequate community action to meet the total life needs of all children with disabilities. This depends on the knowledge and competencies of personnel from many disciplines, which must be coordinated and utilized, and an expanded program of information and education for the general public and pertinent professional organizations.

Agencies providing services for children with disabilities should be aware of their areas of greatest professional competencies. Implementation of this philosophy requires all persons to think beyond traditional approaches of individual agencies as they now exist. Program levels could be raised if special services were obtained from agencies best equipped to provide them. Barriers that make general community services unavailable to children with disabilities should be removed. The disabled should have access to all services applicable to his or her needs. Enriched or special services should be provided so each disabled person may develop to his or her fullest potential. Disabilities must not be seen as a single symptom, but as an array of difficulties in physical, psychological, and social areas. Because of the complexity of the problem, services should encompass a variety of professional disciplines. No single profession can meet the many needs of the disabled. The professional team should function initially as a diagnostic team, incorporating the findings of other team members in their decision process. If at all possible, the initial team should participate in the treatment and follow-up process.

Diagnostic evaluation, if broadly perceived, can play an important role in the management of disabling conditions in childhood. If the diagnostic study is carried out by experts and specialists from various disciplines, referrals can be achieved more easily. The staff of the diagnostic clinic has at its disposal the information obtained in the intake procedures as well as the information requested from other hospitals and physicians. The social worker assigned to the patient usually accompanies him or her during the history-taking session. During the physical examination, it is often possible for the social worker to develop further rapport with the family. The clinical psychologist may be introduced to the family by the social worker. A conference is held between the staff members. Plans are made for needed studies and preliminary impressions are recorded. Specialized studies, such as formal psychological, medical, and orthopedic evaluations, are scheduled when indicated.

A diagnostic evaluation almost always includes a thorough review of development, social functioning, a specific history of the presenting problems, and psychiatric, pediatric, neurological, and psychological examinations. A clinic should also maintain or have access to facilities for laboratory examinations. The public health nurse can yield valuable information regarding the child's development, general physical health, interests, abilities, and relationships within and outside the family. His or her observations frequently make it possible to assess parental reaction to the child, the level of family anxiety, and the ability of the family to carry out home training regiments. The making of a diagnostic plan and a guidance program for children with disabilities takes the combined efforts of many specialists.

Administrators of special education and vocational and/or regular counselors should also comprise the evaluation team. The administrator should work closely with school personnel in coordinating the efforts of all those who act as resource personnel for the teacher of disabled children. With the guidance of the administrators, the teacher is made more keenly aware of the factors that contribute to the growth and development of children with disabilities. The other specialists help the teacher by providing input into developing plans and activities for meeting the needs of each pupil. Joint participation of administrators, teachers, and specialists in meeting pupils' problems enables research and current findings in the field of disabilities to become a part of daily classroom teaching. Teamwork of teachers and specialists can be of major assistance to the teacher in meeting the needs of children with disabilities.

•• AN INTEGRATED APPROACH TO MEETING NEEDS

The integrated approach to learning, so necessary for children with disabilities, requires that the services of specialists be coordinated by administrators and integrated with the work of the teacher. A teacher of disabled pupils is likely to find many disabilities and maladjustments, such as speech disorders, defective hearing, poor reading ability, weak eyesight, motor disabilities, and behavioral maladjustments. The problems of disability are so intricate and extensive that many specialists will be needed in the evaluation and treatment process. Specialists in various disciplines should be consulted as the needs of the disabled child dictate.

Because variations in the severity of disabilities come about as a result of the complex interaction of biological and environmental influences, the determination of the degree of disability is a complex problem and cannot be qualified adequately on the basis of a mere test score. It must include a careful estimate of the medical aspects of the condition, a thorough estimate of the whole child—his or her social experiences, his or her family life; schooling; and social contacts—and must weigh the effects of other complicating factors such as speech disabilities or sensory or motor defects. The goals of treatment should be individual and realistic. Such goals should be based on careful evaluation. One of the major purposes of integrated services should be to improve the identification process of children with developmental problems.

Children with disabilities should be identified as early in their school life as possible by qualified experts. Early identification is necessary if the school is to give maximum help. Without early identification, many children with disabilities may be expected to fulfill unreasonable demands and expectations. Their inability to cope with situations beyond their capacities can lead to fear, anxiety, and maladjustment. When their disabilities are not known, they are likely to be misunderstood and misdirected as they attempt to meet their needs. Their behaviors may become hostile, and later tasks of helping them make better psychological and social adjustments become more difficult.

It would be helpful to everyone concerned if these children were identified during their preschool years. Many disabilities in very young children of preschool age can be identified early. Disabled children or preschool age can first be located through referrals by parents, pediatricians, public health organizations, and social agencies. They can then be referred to psychological clinics for diagnosis. Early identification can be made by a careful and thorough case study that includes the use of tests suitable for very young children. When these children enter school with their disabilities already diagnosed, the school can better meet their needs from the beginning of their school life. The possibilities of failure, anxiety, frustration, and rejection in their experience will thus be reduced.

Accurate identification of children with disabilities, whether before or after entering school, depends on thorough, complete clinical procedures. There cannot be reliance on observation and subjective judgment alone. Symptoms of disability may be false and misleading. Passivity, aggressiveness, antisocial behavior, lack of reading ability, poor health, low marks, and defective articulation do not necessarily indicate subnormal mental development. These symptoms may be the result of negative personal and environmental factors apart from subnormal intelligence. Children identified as disabled on a subject basis alone may thus be done a grave injustice.

The team concept needs a prominent place in the school's organizational pattern. How effectively the team operates by group decisions and carefully sifts evidence also depends to a great extent on the administrator's self-confidence and faith in the faculty. His or her ability to weave properly into the daily schedule all the diverse elements of medical treatment, therapies, testing, guidance, and special teaching as well as social and recreational activities needed by individuals with disabilities will test the comprehensiveness of a successful school program.

Schools can use diagnostic information to design effective programs tailored to the needs and interests of the disabled child. Evaluation findings also pinpoint modifications needed in the school curricula so the child can benefit from educational experiences. The school can plan for trained personnel, supplies, equipment, and special services based on the assessment. Teachers must employ methods and materials suited to the individual's unique pattern of needs, interests, abilities, and motivation. Properly used, this information can provide the teacher with a vehicle for individualized instruction and provide an avenue for the child to succeed in his or her educational pursuits. A first step in making diagnostic information relevant to the schools is the retrieval of accurate, descriptive data that can be used in the instructional process.

•• SUMMARY

Community groups should join together to plan for children with disabling conditions. Community organizations can greatly facilitate services to the disabled child. Effective diagnosis should be interdisciplinary and point the way to adequate treatment and evaluation. Parents are a prime concern in community planning and should be involved throughout the total process if the treatment is to be beneficial. Properly instituted, community planning can greatly aid the child with developmental and/or learning disorders.

•• REFERENCES

Atkinson, D. R., & Juntunen, C. S. (1994). School counselors and school psychologists as school-home-community liaisons in ethnically diverse schools. In P. Pederson and J. C. Carey (Eds.), *Multi-cultural counseling in schools: A practical handbook*. Boston: Allyn & Bacon.

Bandura, A. (1977). *A social learning theory*. Englewood Cliffs, NJ: Prentice Hall.

Bradley, V. J., Knoll, J., & Agosta, J. M. (1992). *Emerging issues in family support*. Washington, DC: The American Association on Mental Retardation.

Brandt, R. (1998). *Listen first. Educational Leadership 55*(8), 25–30.

Casas, M., & Furlong, M. J. (1994). School counselors as advocates for increased Hispanic parent participation in schools. In P. Pederson & J. C. Carey (Eds.), *Multi-cultural counseling in schools: A practical handbook*. Boston: Allyn & Bacon.

Clark, R. M. (1993). *Family life and school achievement.* Chicago: University of Chicago Press.

Cohn-Vargas, K., & Grose, K. (1998). A partnership for literacy. *Educational Leadership, 55*(8), 45–48.

Coleman, M. C. (1986). *Behavior disorders: Theory and practice.* Englewood Cliffs, NJ: Prentice Hall.

Cross, T. (1988). Services to minority populations: What does it mean to be a culturally competent professional? *Focal Point, 2*(4), 1–3.

Dettmer, P., Thurston, L. P., & Dyck, N. (1993). *Consultation, collaboration, and teamwork for students with special needs.* Boston: Allyn & Bacon.

Education Commission of the States. (1996). *Bending without breaking.* Denver, CO: Author.

Floyd, L. (1998). Joining hands: A parental involvement program. *Urban Education, 33,* 123–125.

Friend, M., & Bursuck, W. D. (1996). *Including students with special needs.* Boston: Allyn & Bacon.

Gartner, A., Lipsky, D., & Turnbull, A. P. (1991). *Supporting families with a child with disabilities.* Baltimore, MD: Paul H. Brookes.

Gorman, J. C., & Balter, L. (1997). Culturally sensitive parent educator: A critical review of quantitative research. *Review of Educational Research, 67,* 339–369.

Hatch, T. (1998). How community action contributes to achievement. *Educational Leadership, 55*(8), 16–19.

Heddel, F. (1988). *Children with mental handicaps.* Ramsburg, Marlborough, England: Crowood Press.

Hyun, J. K., & Fowler, A. (1995). Respect cultural sensitivity and communication. *Teaching Exceptional Children, 28*(1), 25–28.

Langdon, H. W., & Novak, J. M. (1998). Home and school connections: A Hispanic perspective. *Educational Horizons, 1,* 15–17.

Lunenburg, F. C., & Ornstein, A. C. (1991). *Educational administration.* Belmont, CA: Wadsworth.

May, J. (1991). Commentary: What about fathers? *Family Support Bulletin,* p. 19.

Muir-Hutchinson, L. (1987). Working with professionals. *Exceptional Parent, 17*(5), 8–19.

Murnane, R., & Levy, F. (1996). *Teaching the new basic skills: Principles for educating children to thrive in a changing economy.* New York: Free Press.

Norton, P., & Drew, C. J. (1994). Autism and potential family stressors. *American Journal of Family Therapy, 22,* 68–77.

Ohlrich, K. B. (1996). Parent volunteers: An asset to your technology plan. *Learning and Leading with Technology, 24*, 51–52.

Oswald, D. P., & Sinah-Nirbay, N. (1992). Current research on social behavior. *Behavior Modification, 16*, 443–447.

Podemski, R. S., Marsh, G. E., Smith, T. E., & Price, B. J. (1995). *Comprehensive administration of special education*. Englewood Cliffs, NJ: Prentice Hall.

Podemski, R. S., & Steele, R. (1981). Avoid the pitfalls of citizen committees. *American School Board Journal, 168*(4), 440–442.

Potter, L. (1996). Making schools parent-friendly. *Education Digest, 62*, 28–30.

Powell, D. R. (1998). Reweaving parents into early childhood education programs. *Education Digest, 64*(3), 22–25.

Powell, D. R., & Diamond, K. E. (1995). Approaches to parent-teacher relationship in use in early childhood programs during the twentieth century. *Journal of Education, 77*(3), 71–94.

Rich, D. (1998). What do parents want from teachers? *Educational Leadership, 55*(8), 37–39.

Sergiovanni, T. J. (1996). *Leadership for the school house*. San Francisco: Jossey-Bass.

Shea, T. M., & Bauer, A. M. (1991a). *Parents and teachers of children with exceptionalities: A handbook for collaboration* (2nd ed.). Boston: Allyn & Bacon.

Shirley, D. (1997). *Laboratories of democracy: Community organizing for school perform*. Austin, TX: University of Texas Press.

Taylor, G. R. (1998). *Curriculum strategies for teaching social skills to the disabled: Dealing with inappropriate behaviors*. Springfield, IL: Charles C Thomas.

Taylor, G. R. (2000). *Parental involvement: A practical guide for collaboration and teamwork for students with disabilities*. Springfield, IL: Charles C Thomas.

Thompson, S. (1998). Moving from publicity to engagement. *Educational Leadership, 55*(8), 54–57.

Thorp, E. K. (1997). Increasing opportunities for partnership with culturally and linguistically diverse families. *Intervention in School and Clinic, 32*, 261–269.

Turnbull, A. P., & Turnbull, H. R. (1990). *Families, professionals, and exceptionality* (2nd ed.). Columbus, OH: Merrill.

Turnbull, A. P., & Turnbull, H. R. (1993). *Participating research on cognitive coping: From concepts to research planning.* In A. P. Turnbull, J. M. Patterson, S. K. Behr, D. L.

Wang, J., & Wilderman, L. (1996). The relationship between parental influence and student achievement in seventh grade mathematics. *School Science and Mathematics, 96,* 395–399.

Wayman, K. L., Lynch, E. W., & Hanson, M. J. (1990). Home-based early childhood services: Cultural sensitivity in a family system approach. *Topics in Early Childhood Special Education, 10,* 56–75.

CHAPTER 14

Conclusion

Administrative styles and leadership abilities can impede or promote special education programs in schools. Democratic behaviors are best displayed by involving all stakeholders concerned with the education of children with disabilities. The organizational structure of the school should promote collaboration among and between all administrative units and community agencies. Any school reforms must include the support of all stakeholders from initial planning to implementation. This democratic approach will do much in reducing the problems of administering programs for children with disabilities. We have alluded to those problems throughout the text in detail; they are simply summarized here.

Vast amounts of money are being appropriated by local, state, and federal governments to support assessment, staff development, legal mandates for governing special education, and placement of children with disabilities in appropriate educational settings. These are to name but a few needs that administrators of special education programs can use appropriated funds to address the above problems. Informed administrators are aware that because of the unique needs of children with disabilities, they need to begin their school experiences early. Many require educational services well into adulthood. Services needed for children with disabilities should be closely coordinated by administrators both in school and in the community. It appears that a coordinated effort by administrators, combined with placement, facilities, equipment and supplies, competent school personnel, guidance counselors, curriculum, and special services, will do much to meet the state and federal mandates outlined in chapter 6, as well as providing equal educational opportunities for children with disabilities.

•• IMPROVING THE EDUCATION AND OUTLOOK FOR CHILDREN WITH DISABILITIES

The aim of special education programs for children with disabilities is basically the same aim as that of all education: to teach the individual how to live better, to teach him or her to use all of his or her capacities, and to teach him or her to become a useful member of a social group. The extent of disabilities limits both the amount and kind of subject matter that many disabled individuals can master successfully. Much of the personal and social progress made must be in terms of habit formation. The objectives of a public school program for children with disabilities should be to develop social competencies, occupational adequacy, and academic learning to the extent of their abilities.

Children with disabilities have mental, physical, and social limitations. Some are limited in adaptive power, in associative relationships, and in learning speed. Many children with disabilities must spend much time learning and practicing the simple things the normal child picks up casually. Administrators must realize that each disabled individual has potential and help the child grow through his or her school experiences. Additionally, the school program should continue as long as the individual benefits from it.

•• SELECTION AND PLACEMENT

The selection and placement of pupils in various classes is an important part of the total special education program. Today, most children with disabilities are placed in inclusive classes. Proper placement requires a thorough group screening, a comprehensive individual evaluation, an understanding of characteristics of the disabled, and workable criteria for placement. Much confusion and misunderstanding can be prevented by having well-defined lines of authority for making the final decision about placement of these children. Meeting the needs of children with disabilities covers a broad spectrum of services. It is generally agreed that children with special needs should be educated in the regular classroom. However, it might be necessary to place some children with disabilities in community-based programs or special classes, depending on the needs as well as the type of placement that will assure educational opportunities for them. Wherever children with disabilities are placed, they need supportive or supplementary services if they are going to reach their full optimum growth. All placement should be flexible, allowing children with disabilities to move from various educational settings as their needs dictate, if services cannot be provided in the regular classroom.

•• FACILITIES, EQUIPMENT, AND SUPPLIES

The type and variety of equipment and supplies used in teaching children with disabilities are dictated to a large degree by the budget, the age of the children, and the ability of administrators to plan appropriately. Administrators should not overlook three valuable sources for securing additional equipment and materials that the budget may not permit. The first is recognizing community organizations as a resource. In many cases, organizations have given teachers of disabled children substantial sums of money to spend for classroom materials. A second valuable source is the actual construction of materials by children, parents, members of the community, and the teacher. A third source is money provided by the federal government to support the many federal laws and mandates. Teaching materials such as educational games, doll clothes, toys, bookshelves, and furniture are examples of items that can be made, often by vocational high school students. Simpler articles can be made by the children themselves. With imagination and ingenuity, the administrator can help direct and guide a successful self-help program.

Classrooms for children with disabilities should permit them to plan, experiment, read, create, play, and share their experiences in reasonable comfort and safety. A good classroom for these children should also have an adequate amount and variety of equipment and supplies that can be used for carrying on significant real-life activities. If facilities are not provided in the school, it might be necessary for them to go to specially equipped schools elsewhere.

The location of inclusive and other classrooms is as important as their size and furnishings. An acceptable classroom is an area that is not isolated or remote from the rest of the school and one that does not imply stigmatization or discredit. The administrator should make sure the classroom has good lighting, ventilation, and general appearance. It should be at least as satisfactory as any classroom in the school.

A classroom used for general nonmanual and quieter manual activities needs suitable equipment. Individual, movable, and desks and chairs permit flexibility of classroom planning and arrangement for instruction. A large number of materials and objects needed for manual and academic experiences should be easily accessible and provide children with ample shelf and cabinet space. A sufficient number of bulletin, chalk, and exhibit boards are required for demonstration and exhibition purposes. It is important that provisions be made for a classroom book corner that pupils may use as a resource for information and pleasure. The well-equipped classroom should also include audiovisual equipment and computer technology that can widen and enrich children's experiences. Additional requirements for a classroom include ready access to laboratories and showers, a suitable nearby outdoor play area, and easy access to a garden if one can be provided.

•• COMPETENT SCHOOL PERSONNEL

Selection of qualified school personnel to teach and administer school programs for children with disabilities is of utmost importance. Personnel must be well informed and specially trained to work with children with disabilities. High standards are needed for the selection of administrators of special education programs for children with disabilities. Furthermore, an examining board that is impartial, well qualified, and capable is an essential prerequisite. With the selection of the most capable administrators possible, teachers of children with disabilities can be given maximum help in achieving the children's educational goals.

A large share of the responsibility for direct supervision of the special classes for children with disabilities lies with the principal. His or her efforts, coordinated with those of the department of special education, are directed toward studying and improving the total teaching/learning situation of which children with disabilities are a part. The principal takes into account both instructional and administrative problems, recognizing that the life-centered curriculum is affected by all factors in the school situation. The principal should act cooperatively with special class teachers to obtain a better understanding of the basic principles and policies underlying the education of children with disabilities. He or she should encourage and coordinate the creative abilities of these teachers and help them seek better ways of meeting the needs of children with disabilities.

The principal, in cooperation with the special administrator, uses both group and individual techniques in helping teachers of children with disabilities improve teaching/learning situations. The special class teachers are provided opportunities for working together both as a special-interest group and as members of other groups that include regular class teachers, depending on purposes. Group techniques may include the cooperative study of instructional and administrative problems, study groups, local workshops, and group study of the community. Individual techniques include the principal's visits to the special classroom followed by conferences, visits of teachers to other special classes both in and outside of their school, promotion of activities that capitalize on the special interests of the teachers, and stimulation of continued professional development through attendance of special teachers at colleges and universities. Special class teachers thus can have opportunities, through group and individual activities, to study and improve the teaching and learning of children with disabilities. They also have an opportunity to contribute to better understanding by regular classroom teachers of the problems faced in special education classes for children with disabilities and their relation to the total school program.

The key position of the principal in improving the educational program for children with disabilities requires that he or she have a basic understanding of the characteristics and needs of these children and of the modifications and adaptations required in the total school program for them. The professional preparation of the principal should include the area of special preparation for children with disabilities.

Teachers of children with disabilities should be carefully selected. High standards of personal fitness and professional preparation should determine selection, not mere administrative expediency. Some school districts require prospective special teachers to take examinations, together with health tests and performance tests. Many school systems require a probationary period of one or more years before permanent appointment is made. Special supervisory assistance is given during the probationary year(s).

Whatever the procedure for selection, teachers appointed should be able to give children with disabilities the best educational opportunities possible for happy, successful living. Because special education, regardless of opinions that justify or refute its existence, is an established division of public school education, and because of the critical learning factors involved, a considerable amount of money appropriated by federal and state governments is earmarked for use on special education endeavors on a pupil ratio basis. Special education personnel must possess competencies that enable them to be fluent and efficient in educational spheres. Certification and qualification should not be any different than those required of education in other fields; in many instances standards should be higher. Personnel lacking in ability and specific training for meeting the needs of children with disabilities will in all probability deprive them of the right kinds of school experiences necessary for the best possible life adjustments. Teachers and administrators require instructional skills not usually required for the regular grades. Great emphasis should be placed on the use of a variety of media in instructing children with disabilities.

•• CURRICULUM DESIGN

Curriculum means all the planned experiences provided by the school to assist pupils in attaining the designated learning outcome to the best of their abilities. It bridges the past, present, and the future. The curriculum should be designed to

1. Develop the child's mental capabilities.

2. Strengthen the child's emotional stability.

3. Fulfill the child's health and social needs.

4. Promote the child's occupational adjustment.

5. Provide prevocational skills.

6. Assist in preparing the child for the world of work.

The implementation of these objectives into practical curriculum activities is mandatory in preparing an adequate way of life for the disabled in our society. Curriculum in its development depends on numerous factors. Consideration must be given to the intellectual learning potential of the disabled as well as to aims and objectives of education.

The school must provide systematic and appropriate methods of assessing the impact of its instruction on children with disabilities through the formation of realistic objectives based on needs, capacities, and interests. Some will require considerably more drill and practice in skills and habits than is required for most children if their living is to be effective. Plentiful quantities of opportunities for making concrete applications of their ideas is important because many do not express themselves well verbally or in abstract ways. Activities must help children with disabilities gain honest and realistic appraisals of themselves so their life goals will be set neither too high nor too low.

The curriculum must be derived from the intensive study of the individual child. It must provide for the setting and climate in which the child can grow and develop to his or her capacity. To accomplish this end, school personnel must have an open and objective mind. They must be alert to even the most subtle cues as the children react to their experiences. Additionally, administrators should be flexible enough to reject their favorite theories or techniques when their application fails.

If the school is to assist children with disabilities in achieving social and vocational competencies, a special developmental curriculum must be provided for them. Activities should be sequenced into small steps so they have a chance to succeed. Because many disabled children learn best from concrete materials, as many concrete experiences as possible should be provided. Criteria for selecting curricular content should be based on an understanding of the disabled, provided through research findings and observations. Equally important will be assessing the present and future job markets in order to assure the disabled a place in the world of work after school experiences end.

•• SPECIAL SERVICES

A wide range of services should be evident for disabled children, including assistance from various disciplines, to aid school personnel in providing quality education. Many problems are too complex for the school to handle alone. The services of specialists can promote classroom enrichment activities. Services for children with disabilities should be improved in the area of diagnosis, evaluation, and treatment. Special services should be an integral part of the teaching/learning program for disabled children. A comprehensive system of services for them should be coordinated with other agencies in the community. The administrator should be the key person charged with this responsibility. Other types of services that the schools should provide are in the areas of transportation, specially designed facilities, special equipment, individualized instruction, and supportive teaching personnel. These are to name but a few services needed to meet the individual differences of children with disabilities.

•• THE ROLE OF THE SCHOOL

In summary, the schools must produce children with disabilities who have been trained and educated for special competencies and have been given some direction and preparation for occupational competency. In reviewing records of adult disabled individuals, it becomes evident that the schools have not provided many of them with the skills to compete successfully in our society. When we attempt to assess the reasons for the school's failure, it quickly becomes complex. However, in this connection, many goals and training programs implemented by the schools are selected randomly and are culturally unsuitable for children with disabilities. Another factor might be a lack of clear analysis of the tasks involved. Thus the chief aim of the school should be to shape attitudes toward goals that are acceptable to children with disabilities and reflect his or her present and future needs. It is not likely this objective can be achieved by the school alone. Parents and community agencies must be fully involved.

When followed, the strategies that have been enumerated and discussed here can help administrators achieve these major results: (1) the organization of adequately staffed and equipped classes as an outcome of careful, cooperative planning with the guidance and cooperation of a department of special education; (2) the use of sound pupil personnel procedures based on knowledge and understanding of the needs and characteristics of children with disabilities; (3) the provision of needed supervisory services to aid teachers and principals in improving instruction; (4) the development of a well-integrated program of special services to meet the individual differences of children with disabilities; and (5) the fostering of school/community relationships that will aid in the understanding and support of a special education program for these disabled pupils. Underlying the achievement of desired results should be adequate financial support, cooperative action, and continuous evaluation by the school and community.

The use of these strategies are urgent because the quality of conditions and services provided for children with disabilities by the school affects in large measure the quality of their living and learning. Thus they will be helped to grow and develop through democratic means. These pupils, from the day of their school entrance to the end of their school careers, will then receive the fullest attention and the best help the school can give. The highest quality of conditions and services will be made available to them, and to all children, for their maximum growth and development. Then the investment of public education for children with disabilities will pay rich dividends in their productive and responsible living as respected members of the community.

Parental Due Process Checklist

1. The right to examine all school records concerning your child.

2. The right to obtain an independent evaluation.

3. The right to determine whether the hearing will be closed or open to the public.

4. The right to advice of counsel and representation by counsel at the hearing.

5. The right to bring your child to the hearing.

6. The right to keep your child in his or her current educational placement until all due process hearing appeals have been completed.

7. The right to written notification about the hearing in the primary language or mode of communication of the parent.

8. The right to present evidence and testimony.

9. The right to prohibit the introduction of any evidence that has not been disclosed to parents at least five days prior to the hearing.

10. The right to cross-examine and challenge all testimony presented during the hearing.

11. The right to receive a verbatim transcript of the hearing, at reasonable cost.

12. The right to appeal the decision of the hearing officer or hearing panel.

The Manifestation Determination Review: Was the Child's Behavior a Manifestation of His or Her Disability?

When is an MDR Required?

(4) (a): "If a disciplinary action is contemplated as described in paragraph (1) or paragraph (2) [see page 6] for a behavior of a child with a disability described in either of those paragraphs, or if a disciplinary action involving a change in placement for more than 10 days is contemplated for a child who has engaged in other behavior that violated any rule of code of conduct of the local educational agency that applies to all children."

"(I) no later than the date on which the decision to take action is made, the parents shall be notified of that decision and all procedural safeguards accorded under this section; and

(ii) immediately if possible, but in no case later than 10 school days after the date on which the decision to take that action is made, a review shall be conducted of the relationship between the child's disability and the behavioral subject to the disciplinary action." [Section 615 (k) (4) (A)]

Who conducts the MDR?.....................V

(4) (B) "INDIVIDUALS TO CARRY OUT REVIEW—A review described   in subparagraph (A) [see above under "When."] shall be conducted by the IEP Team and other qualified personnel." [Section 615 (k) (4) (B)]

How is the MDR conducted?..............V

Source: Individuals with Disabilities Education Act Amendments of 1997. Washington, DC: U.S. Government Printing Office.

(4) (C) "CONDUCT OF REVIEW—In carrying out a review described in subparagraph (A), the IEP Team may determine that the behavior of the child was *not* [emphasis added] a manifestation of such child's disability only if the IEP Team—

(i) first considers, in terms of behavior subject to disciplinary action, all relevant information, including—(I) evaluation and diagnostic results, including such results or other relevant information supplied by the parents of the child; (II) observations of the child, and (III) the child's IEP and placement, and

(ii) then determines that—(I) relationship to the behavior subject to disciplinary action, the child's IEP and placement were appropriate and the special education services, supplementary aids and services, behavior intervention strategies were provided consistent with the child's IEP and placement; (II) the child's disability did not impair the ability of the child to understand the impact and consequences of the behavior subject to disciplinary action; and (III) the child's disability did not impair the ability of the child to control the behavior subject to disciplinary action." [Section 615 (k) (4) (C)]

Placement During Appeal.............V

(7) PLACEMENT DURING APPEALS—

"(A) IN GENERAL—When a parent requests a hearing regarding a disciplinary action described in paragraph (1) (A) (ii) or paragraph (2) to challenge the interim alternative educational setting or the manifestation determination, the child shall remain in the interim alternative educational setting pending the decision of the hearing officer or until the expiration of the time period for in paragraph (1) (A) (ii) or paragraph (2), whichever occurs first, unless the parent and the State or local educational agency agree otherwise.

"(B) CURRENT PLACEMENT—If a child is placed in an interim alternative educational setting pursuant to paragraph (1) (A) (ii) or paragraph (2) and school personnel propose to change the child's placement after expiration of the interim alternative placement, during the pendency of any proceeding to challenge the proposed change in placement, the child shall remain in the current placement (the child's placement prior to the interim alternative educational setting), except as provided in subparagraph (C) below.

"(C) EXPEDITED HEARING—(I) If school personnel maintain that it is dangerous for the child to be in the current placement (placement prior to removal to the interim alternative educational setting) during the pendency of the due process proceedings, the local educational agency may request an expedited hearing.

(iii) In determining whether the child may be placed in the alternative educational setting or in another appropriate placement ordered by the hearing officer, the hearing officer shall apply the standards set out in paragraph (2).

Referral to and Action by Law Enforcement and Judicial Authorities....V

(9) "(A) Nothing in this part shall be construed to prohibit an agency from reporting a crime committed by a child with a disability to appropriate authorities or to prevent State law enforcement and judicial authorities from exercising their responsibilities with regard to the application of Federal and State law to crimes committed by a child with a disability."

"(B) An agency reporting a crime committed by a child with a disability shall ensure that copies of the special education and disciplinary records of the child are transmitted for consideration by the appropriate authorities to whom it reports the crime." [Section 615 (k) (9) and (B)]

Internet Sites with Information on the IDEA Amendments of 1997

The Internet sites listed below offer information related to the IDEA Amendments of 1997 (P.L. 105-17). This list is not comprehensive.

- US Dept. of Education, Office of Special Education and Rehabilitation Services

  http://www.ed.gov/offices/OSERS/IDEA/the_law.html

  This is the origin of federal information on IDEA. It links to the text of the law (P.L. 195-17); speeches about IDEA; general information; articles; letters and memos; IDEA '97 updates; Federal Register notices; and information on training and technical assistance.

- Council for Exceptional Children (CEC)

  http://www.cec.sped.org/pp/ideahome.htm

  General and legislative information and publications

- Federal Resource Center

  http://www.dssc.org/frc/texton/idea.htm

  Includes links to P.L. 105-17; Notice of Proposed Rule Making (NPRM) for P.L. 105-17 (proposed regulations); Senate Report Language; side-by-side comparisons of IDEA '97; memos from OSEP on IEP Requirements, State Improvement Grants, Initial Disciplinary Guidance, changes in Part B of IDEA; monthly OSEP IDEA updates; questions and answers from OSEp on IDEA, and data sources.

- Great Lakes Regional Resource Center (GLARRC)

  http://www.csnp.ohio.-state.edu/GLARRC/idea.htm

  Information on State Improvement Grants/State Improvement Resources (SIG/SIP), profesisonal development, paraprofessionals, funding, alternate assessment, systems change, certification, and data sources.

- National Early Childhood Technical Assistance Center (NECTAS)
  http://www.nectas.unc.edu/idea/idea.html
  Information on IDEA '97 in relation to early childhood educational settings.

- National Information Center for Children and Youth with Disabilities (NICHCY)
  http://www.nichcy.org/textonly/ideatxt.htm
  General legislative information, publications, training material
  http://nichcy.org/Trainingpkg/order.htm
  OSEP's training package on IDEA '97 and/or Spanish overheads.

- Western Regional Resource Center (WRRC)
  Offers several documents addressing specific provisions of IDEA '97
  http://interact.uoregon.edu/wrrc/IDEEATech.html
  Assistive technology devices and services
  http://interact.uoregon.edu/wrrc/IDEAStateadvpan.html
  Establishment, membership, and responsibilities of BIA Advisory Board and State Advocacy Panels
  http://interact.uoregon.edu/wrrc.IDEADiscipline.html
  Discipline of students with disabilities
  http://interact.uoregon.edu/wrrc.CRSMemo.html
  Memorandum from the Congressional Research Service (CRS) to Rep. Robert Scott (VA) on discipline issues under IDEA '97. Scott requested this memo to answer questions from the Virginia School Boards Association
  http://itneract.uoregon.edu/wrrc/IDEACorrections.htm
  Children with discipline in adult correctional facilties
  http://interact.uoregon.educ.wrrc/IEP/iephome.htm
  Includes material initially collected for the IEP Institute Series: Training for Trainers; Individualized Education (IEP); Tool for Success in Education and Beyond.

This publication was prepared with funding from the Office of Educational Research and Improvement, U.S. Department of Education, under contract no. RR93002995. Any opinions expressed in this report do not necessarily reflect the positions or policies of OERI or the Department of Education. ERIC DIGESTS are in the public domain and may be freely reproduced and disseminated.

The IEP Process under IDEA 1997
(Effective July 1, 1998)

Components of the IEP (Effective July 1st, 1998)

Section (614(d) of IDEA begins by defining the term "Individualized Education Program":

> *The term "Individualized Education" or "IEP" means a written statement for each child with a disability that is developed, reviewed, and revised in accordance with this section and that includes . . .*

This sentence is followed by a long list of what information or components the IEP must include. Each of these components is summarized below. As part of this summary, selected comments from the Committee on Labor and Human Resources Report (1997) [to accompany S.717] are included to explain the intent behind proposed changes to the law.

- *Present Levels of Educational Performance*
  The IEP starts by stating how the child with a disability is currently doing in school. This is called the student's *present level of educational performance.* What are the student's strengths and weaknesses? What areas or skills need to be addressed? This information is drawn from recent evaluations, observations, and input from parents and school personnel. A new area of emphasis in IDEA '97 is stating "how the child's disability affects the child's involvement and progress in the general curriculum."

- *Annual Goals (and benchmarks or short-term objectives)*
  Having identified how the child is doing in school and, in particular, where he or she is having difficulty, the IEP Team focuses upon determining what educational goals are appropriate for the student, given those areas of difficulty. The goals must be annual and measurable and should be reasonable. What can the student reasonable accomplish in a year? The goals must include *benchmarks or short-term objectives.* The goals must relate to helping

the child be "involved in and progress in the general curriculum" and address other educational needs that arise due to the child's disability.

• *Special Education and Related Services*
Given the areas of need the child or youth has, and the annual goals that have been established, what special education and related services does he/or she require in order to attain those goals and address those needs? The IEP Team must consider—and specify in writing—what supplementary aids and services are necessary to enable the student to be involved in the general curriculum, to participate in extracurricular activities, and to be educated and participate with other children (those with disabilities and those without).

• *The Definition of Supplementary Aids and Services*
The term *supplementary Aids and Services* means aids, services, and other supports that are provided in regular education classes or other education-related settings to enable children with disabilities to be educated with non-disabled children to the maximum extent appropriate in accordance with Section 612(a)(5) [IDEA '97's provision on the Least Restrictive Environment].
Additionally, the IEP Team must consider—and specify in *writing—any program modifications or support for school personnel* that will be provided for the child. These will assist school personnel in helping the child progress in the general curriculum. This emphasis upon the student's involvement in the general curriculum is one of the primary areas of modification in the IDEA '97's IEP requirements. The Committee on Labor and Human Resources' (1997) remarks on this subject are presented in the box below and offer an illuminating explanation of these IEP modifications.

• *Report Language*
The following citations come from the Report [to accompany S.717] and illuminate changes IDEA '97 makes to the IEP document. On the new emphasis upon involving children with disabilities in the general curriculum: *The majority of children identified as eligible for special education and related services are capable of participating in the general education curriculum to varying degrees with some adaptations and modifications. The provision is intended to ensure that children's special education and related services are in addition to and are affected by the general education curriculum, not separate from it* (Committee on Labor and Human Resources, 1997, p. 20). On the *explanation of nonparticipation to be included in the child's IEP.*

"The law and this bill contain a presumption that children with disabilities are to be educated in regular classes . . ." This committee recognizes that every decision made for a child with a disability must be made on the basis of what that individual child needs. Nonetheless, with the decision is made to educate the child separately, an explanation of that decision will need, at a minimum, to be stated as part of the child's IEP (p. 21).

Thus, when the IEP Team specifies the special education and related services a student will receive, it must give attention to the accommodations, supports, and adjustments that the student needs in order to enable him or her to participate in the general curriculum as fully possible. When these accommodations, supports, and adjustments are necessary in order for the child to receive a FAPE (Free and Appropriate Public Education), they must be specified in the IEP.

- *Explanation of Nonparticipation*

The IDEA has always had a strong preference for children with disabilities being educated with their non-disabled peers, to the maximum extent appropriate. This preference is manifested in IDEA '97 in this new IEP requirement: *the IEP must now include an explanation of the extent, if any, to which the child or youth will not be participating with non-disabled children in the regular class, in the general curriculum, and in extra-curricular and non-academic activities.* The Report Language regarding this new requirement is provided in the box above and reaffirms both IDEA's preference for students with disabilities being educated with their non-disabled peers to the maximum extent appropriate and the importance of deciding the most appropriate educational setting for each student on an individual basis.

References

Aefsy, F. (1995). *Inclusion confusion: a guide to educating students with exceptional needs.* Thousand Oaks, CA: Corwin Press.

Alper, S., Schloss, P. J., Etscheidt, S. K., & Macfarlane, C. A. (1995). *Inclusion: Are we abandoning or helping students?* Thousand Oaks, CA: Corwin Press.

American Association of Colleges for Teacher Education: Commission on Multicultural Education. (1973). No one model. *American Journal of Teacher Education, 4,* 264.

American Institute for Research. (1999). *An educator's guide to school-wide reform.* Arlington, VA: Educational Research Service.

Anderson, R. D. (1996). *Study of curriculum reform* (ORAD-96-1309). Washington, DC: U.S. Department of Education.

Annual Report to Congress on the Implementation of the Individuals with Disability Education Act. (1991). Washington, DC: U.S. Department of Education.

Annual Report to Congress on the Implementation of the Individuals with Disability Education Act. (1997). Washington, DC: U.S. Department of Education.

Anotonak, R. F., & Larriver, B. (1995). Psychometric analysis and revisions of the opinions relative to mainstreaming scale. *Exceptional Children, 62,* 139–149.

Atkins, D. R., & Juntunen, C. S. (1994). School counselors and school psychologists as school-home-community liaisons in ethnically diverse schools. In P. Pederson and J. C. Carey (Eds.), *Multi-cultural counseling in schools: A practical handbook.* Boston: Allyn & Bacon.

Baker, E. T., Wang, M. & Walberg, H. G. (1995). The effects of inclusion on learning. *Educational Leadership, 59*(4), 33–35.

Baker, J., & Zigmond, N. (1990). *Full-time mainstreaming: Are learning disabled students integrated into the instructional program?* Paper presented at the Annual Meeting of the American Education Research Association, Boston (ERIC Document Reproduction Service No. PD 320 373).

Bandura, A. (1977). *A social learning theory.* Englewood Cliffs, NJ: Prentice Hall.

Banks, J. A. (1997a). Multicultural education: Characteristics and goals. In J. A. Banks & C. A. M. Banks (Eds.), *Multicultural education: Issues and perspectives* (3rd ed.). Boston: Allyn & Bacon.

Bannerji, M., & Dailey, R. (1995). A study of the effects of an inclusion model on students with specific learning disabilities. *Journal of Learning Disabilities, 28,* 511–522.

Barraga, N. C., & Erin, J. N. (1992). *Visual handicaps and learning.* Austin, TX: Pro-Ed.

Barry, A. L. (1995). Easing into inclusion classrooms. *Educational Leadership, 52*(4), 4–6.

Bennett, R., Deluca, D., & Burns, D. (1997). Putting inclusion into practice. *Exceptional Children, 64*(1), 115–131.

Bennis, W. (1984). The Four Competencies. *Leadership Training and Development Journal, 38*(8), 15–19.

Berger, S. (1995). Inclusion: A legal mandate—an educational dream. *Updating School Board Politics, 26*(4), 104.

Berne, R. (1988). Equity issues in school finance. *Journal of Education Finance, 14*(2), 159–180.

Blackhurst, A. E., & Berdine, W. H. (1993). *An introduction to special education* (3rd ed.). Lexington, MA: HarperCollins.

Blumberg, A. (1986). *Effective school principals.* Report of the Southern Regional Education Board. Atlanta, GA. Washington, DC: U.S. Department of Education (ERIC Document Reproduction Service No. ED 376 740).

Boath, A., & Dunne, J. (Eds.). (1996). *Family-school links: How do they affect education?* Hillsdale, NJ: Erlbaum.

Bond, L. A., Braskamp, D., & Roeber, E. (1996). *The status report of the assessment programs in the United States.* Oak Brook, IL: North Central Regional Educational Laboratory and Council of Chief State School Officers.

Booth, A., Dunne, J. (Eds.). (1996). *Family-school links: How do they affect education?* Hillsdale, NJ: Erlbaum.

Borthwick-Duffy, S. A., Palmer, D. S., & Lane, K. L. (1996). One size doesn't fit all: Full inclusion and individual differences. *Journal of Behavioral Education, 6,* 311–329.

Bradley, V. J., Knoll, J., & Agosta, J. M. (1992). *Emerging issues in family support.* Washington, DC: American Association on Mental Retardation.

Brammer, L. M., & MacDonald, G. (1998). *The helping relationship: Process and skills* (7th ed.). Boston: Allyn & Bacon.

Brandt, R. S. (1998). *Listen first. Educational Leadership 55*(8), 25–30.

Brandt, R. S. (2000). *Education in a new era.* Alexandria, VA: Association for Supervision and Curriculum Development.

Brooks, J. G., & Brooks, M. G. (1993). *In search of understanding: The case of constructivist classrooms.* Alexandria, VA: Association for Supervision and Curriculum Development.

Browder, D. M. (1991). *Assessment of individuals with severe disabilities: An applied behavior approach to life skills assessment* (2nd ed.). Baltimore, MD: Brookes.

Brown, J. L., & Moffett, C. A. (1999). *The hero's journey: How educators can transform schools and improve learning.* Alexandria, VA: Association for Supervision and Curriculum Development.

Brown, L. P., Schwartz, A., Unvari-Solner, E. F., Kampshroer, F., Johnson, J., Jorgensen, J., & Greenwald, L. (1991). How much time should students with severe disabilities spend in regular classrooms and elsewhere? *Journal of the Association of Persons with Severe Disabilities, 16,* 39–47.

Brown v. Board of Education of Topeka. 347 U.S. 483, 74 S. Ct. 689 (1954).

Bruininks, R. H. (1978). *Bruininks-Oseretsky test on motor proficiency.* Circle Pines, MN: AGS.

Cairney, T. H., Ruge, J., Buchanan, J., Lowe, K., & Munsie, L. (1995). *Developing partnership: The home, school, and community interface.* Canberra: Department of Employment, Education, and Training.

Casas, M., & Furlong, J. J. (1994). School counselors as advocates for increased Hispanic parent participation in schools. In P. Penderson and J. Carey (Eds.), *Multi-cultural counseling in schools: A practical handbook.* Boston: Allyn & Bacon.

Castetter, W. B. (1981). *The personnel function in educational administration* (3rd ed.). New York: Macmillan.

Clark, R. M. (1993). *Family life and school achievement.* Chicago: University of Chicago Press.

Cohen, L. C., & Spenciner, L. J. (1998). *Assessment of children and youth.* New York: Addison Wesley Longman.

Colby, S. (1999). Grading in a standards-based system. *Educational Leadership, 56*(6), 52–55.

Coleman, M. C. (1986). *Behavior disorders: Theory and practice.* Englewood Cliffs, NJ: Prentice Hall.

Committee on Labor and Human Resources. (1997). Washington, DC: U. S. Government Printing Office.

Conoley, J. C., & Conoley, C. W. (1992). *School consultation: Practice and training* (2nd ed.). Boston: Allyn & Bacon.

Corey, S. (1993). *Helping other people change.* Columbus, OH: State University Press.

Council for Exceptional Children. (1993). *Council for Exceptional Children (CEC) Policy on inclusive schools and community setting.* Reston, VA: Author.

Cross, T. (1988). Services to minority populations: What does it mean to be a culturally competent professional? *Focal Point, 2*(4), 1–3.

Cruickshank, W. A. (1963). *Psychology of exceptional children and youth.* Englewood Cliffs, NJ: Prentice Hall.

Daniel, P. L., & Stallion, B. K, (1996). Implementing school-based professional development in Kentucky. *Journal of Staff Development, 17*(4), 30–32.

David, J. (1995, 1996). The who, what, and why of site-based management. *Educational Leadership, 53,* 4–9.

Davison, D. M., & Pearce, D. L. (1992). The influence of writing activities on the mathematics learning on Native American students. *The Journal of Educational Issues of Language Minority Students, 10,* 147–157.

Davies, D. (1996). Partnership for student success. *New Schools New Communities, 12*(13), 14–21.

Day, C. (2000). Beyond transformational leadership. *Educational Leadership, 57*(7), 56–59.

Delbecg, A. L., Van de Ven, A. H., & Gustafson, D. H. (1986). *Group techniques for program planning: A guide to nominal group and delphi processes.* Middletown, WI: Green Briar.

Deno, E. (1970). Special education as developmental capital. *Exceptional Children*, 37(3), 229–237.

Dettmer, P., Thurston, L. P., & Dyck, N. (1993). *Consultation, collaboration, and teamwork for students with special needs*. Boston: Allyn & Bacon.

Diana v. State Board of Education. C-70, RFP (N.D. Cal, 1970, 1973).

Diaz-Rico, L. T., & Weed, K. Z. (1995). *The cross-cultural language and academic development handbook*. Boston: Allyn & Bacon.

Downing, J. E. (1999). *Teaching communication skills to students with severe disabilities*. Baltimore, MD: Paul H. Brookes.

Doyle, W. (1992). Curriculum and pedagogy. In P. W. Jackson (Ed.), *Handbook of research curriculum*. New York: Macmillan.

Dyrcia, S. et al. v. Board of Education of the City of New York. 79c.2562 (E.D. N.Y., 1979).

Education Commission on the States. (1996a). *Listen, discuss, and aid*. Denver, CO: ESC.

Education Commission on the States. (1996b). *Bending without breaking*. Denver, CO: Author.

Education Commission on the States. (1998a). *Comprehensive school reform: Allocating federal funds*. Denver, CO: Author.

Education Commission on the States. (1998b). *Comprehensive school reform: Allocating federal funds*. Denver, CO: Author.

Edwards, P.A. (1995). Combining parents' and teachers' thoughts about storybook reading at home and school. In L. M. Morrow (Ed.), *Family literacy: Connections in schools and communities*. College Park, MD: International Reading Association.

Egan, G. (1997). *The skilled helper: A systematic approach to effective helping* (6th ed.). Monterey, CA: Brooks/Cole.

Elliott, S. N., & Sheridan, S. M. (1992). Consultation and teaming: Problem solving among educators, parents, and support personnel. *Elementary School Journal, 92*, 315–338.

Elliott, J. L., Thurlow, M. L., & Ysseldyke, J. E. (1996). *Assessment guidelines that maximize the participation of students with disabilities in large-scale assessments: Characteristics and considerations*. Washington, DC: U.S. Department of Education (ERIC Document Reproduction Service No. ED 404803).

Elliott, J., Ysseldyke, J., Thurlow, M., & Erickson, R. (1998). What about assessment and accountability? Practical implications for educators. *Teaching Exceptional Children, 31*(1), 20–27.

Elsbree, W. S., McNally, H. J., & Wynn, R. (1967). *Elementary school administration and supervision.* New York: Van Nostrand Reinhold.

Epstein, J. L. (1995). School, family, community partnerships: Caring for the children we share. *Phi Delta Kappan, 77*(9), 701–712.

Epstein, M. H., Bursuck, W. D., Polloway, E. A., Cumbland, C., & Jayanthi, M. (1993). Homework, grading, and testing. National Surveys of School District Policies. *OSERS News* (in print), *5*(4), 15–21.

Erickson, R.N., Thurlow, M.L., & Thor, K. (1995). *State special education outcomes.* Washington, DC: U.S. Department of Education (ERIC Document Reproduction Service No. ED 404 749).

Erickson, R. N., Thurlow, M. L., Thor, K. A., & Seyfarth, A. (1996). *State special education outcomes* (ERIC Document Reproduction Service No. ED 385 061).

Erickson, R. N., Thurlow, M. L., & Ysseldyke, J. E. (1996). *Neglected numerators, drifting denominators, and fractured fractions: Determining participation rates for students with disabilities in statewide assessment programs* (Synthesis Report 23). Minneapolis: University of Minnesota, National Center on Educational Outcomes.

Federal Register. (1977, August 23). Washington, DC: US Government Printing Office.

Fege, A. F. (2000). From fund raising to hell raising: New roles for parents. *Educational Leadership, 57*(7), 39–43.

Fiblin, J., Connolly, T., & Brewer, R. (1996). *Individualized learner outcomes: Infusing student needs into the regular education curriculum.* Tampa, FL. Washington, DC: U.S. Department of Education (ERIC Document Reproduction Service No. ED 400 641).

Finn, J. D. (1993). *School engagement and students at risk.* Washington, DC: National Center for Education Statistics.

Fishbaugh, M. S. E. (1997). *Model of collaboration.* Boston: Allyn & Bacon.

Floyd, L. (1998). Joining hands: A parental involvement program. *Urban Education, 32,* 123–125.

Folio, M. R., & Fewell, R. (1983). *Peabody developmental motor scores and activity cards.* Chicago: Riverside.

Friend, M., & Bursuck, W. (1996). *Including students with special needs.* Boston: Allyn & Bacon.

Friend, M., & Cook, L. (1990). Collaboration as a predictor for success in school reform. *Journal of Educational Psychology Consultation, 1,* 69–86.

Friend, M., & Cook, L. (2000). *Interactions: Collaboration skills for school professionals* (3rd ed.). New York: Longman.

Fuchs, D., & Fuchs, L. (1994). Inclusive schools movement and the radicalization of special education reform. *Exceptional Children, 60,* 294–309.

Fuchs, D., & Fuchs, L. (1995). Sometimes separate is better. *Educational Leadership, 50*(4), 22–26.

Fuchs, D., Fuchs, L., & Bishop, N. (1992). Teacher planning for students with learning disabilities: Differences between general and special education. *Learning Disabilities Research and Practice, 7,* 120–128.

Fullan, M.G. (1990). Staff development innovation and institutional devleopment. In B. Joyce (Ed.), *Changing school culture through staff development: 1990 Yearbook of the Association for Supervision and Curriculum Development.* Alexandria, VA: Association for Supervision and Curriculum Development.

Fullan, M., & Miles, M. B. C. (1992). Getting reform right: What works and what doesn't? *Phi Delta Kappan, 73,* 744–752.

Gallagher, K., & Ansastasiow, N. (1993). *Educating exceptional children.* Boston: Houghton Mifflin.

Gallivan-Fenlon, A. (1994). Integrated transdisciplinary teams. *Teaching Exceptional Children, 26*(3), 16–20.

Gamble, T. K., & Gamble M. (1996). *Communication works* (5th ed.). New York: McGraw-Hill.

Garmston, R. L., & Wellman, B.M. (1992). *How to make presentations that teach and transform.* Alexandria, VA: Association for Supervision and Curriculum Development.

Gartner, A., Lipsky, D., & Turnbull, A. P. (1991). *Supporting families with a child with disabilities.* Baltimore, MD: Paul H. Brookes.

Gearheart, B., Mullen, R. C., & Gearheart, C. J. (1993). *Exceptional individuals: An introduction.* Pacific Grove, CA: Brooks/Cole.

Giangreco, M., Dennis, R., Cloninger, C., Edelman, S., & Schattman, R. (1993). I've counted JON: Transformation experiences of teachers educating students with disabilities. *Exceptional Children, 59,* 359–371.

Glatthorn, A. A. (1998). *Performance assessment and standard-based curriculums.* Larchmont, NY: Eye on Education.

Gleckel, L. K., & Lee, R. L. (1996). Children with physical disabilities. *In Exceptional Children in Today's Schools* (3rd ed.). Denver, CO: Love.

Goddard, H. H. (1913). *The Kallikak family.* New York: The Macmillan Company.

Gollnick, D. M., & Chinn, P. (1994). *Multicultural education in a pluralistic society* (4th ed.). Columbus, OH: Merrill.

Goodlad, E. (1984). *A place called school.* New York: McGraw-Hill.

Gorman, J. C., & Balter, L. (1997). Culturally sensitive parent educator: A critical review of quantitative research. *Review of Educational Research, 67,* 339–369.

Grandmont, R. P. (1995, March). Curriculum revision: A step-by-step approach. *Principal, 80*(569), 46–47.

Grasmick, N. S. (2000). How Maryland communicates change? *Educational Leadership, 57*(7), 44–47.

Hall, E. T. (1996). *The hidden dimension.* Garden City, NY: Doubleday.

Hallahan, D. P., & Kauffman, J. M. (2000). *Exceptional learners: Introduction to special education.* Boston: Allyn & Bacon.

Hanline, M. F., & Halvorsen, A. (1989). Parent perceptions of the integration transition process: Overcoming artificial barriers. *Exceptional Children, 55,* 487–492.

Hardman, M. L., Drew, C. J., Egan, M. W., & Wolf, B. (1993). *Human exceptionality: Society, school, and family.* Needham Heights, MA: Allyn and Bacon.

Harris, K. C. (1995). School-based bilingual special education teacher teams. *Remedial and Special Education, 16,* 337–343.

Hartman, W. (1988). *School district budgeting.* Englewood Cliffs, NJ: Prentice Hall.

Hatch, T. (1998). How community action contributes to achievement. *Educational Leadership, 55*(8), 16–19.

Heddel, F. (1988). *Children with mental handicaps.* Ramsburg, Marlborough, England: Crowood Press.

Helgesen, M., Brown, S., & Brown, S. (1994). *Active listening: Building skills for understanding.* Cambridge, MA: Cambridge University Press.

Heyward, W., & Orlansky, D. (1992). *Exceptional children* (4th ed.). New York: Merrill.

Hill, P. T., Foster, D. E., & Gendler, T. (1990). *High schools with character.* Santa Monica, CA: Rand.

Hilliard, A. (1997). The structure of valid staff development. *Journal of Staff Development, 18*(2), 28–34.

Hirth, M. A., & Valesky, T. C. (1990). Principal's knowledge of special education. *National Forum of Educational Administration and Supervision Journal, 6*(3), 131–141.

Hobbs, T., & Westling, D. L. (1998). Promoting successful inclusion. *Teaching Exceptional Children, 31*(1), 12–19.

Hollis, J., & Gallegos, E. (1993). Inclusion: What is the extent of a school district's duty to accommodate students with disabilities in the regular classroom? *Texas School Administrator's Legal Digest, 9*(9), 4–7.

Holloway, J. H. (2000). The promise and pitfalls of site-based management. *Educational Leadership, 57*(7), 81+82.

Hyun, J. K., & Fowler, A. (1995). Respect cultural sensitivity and communication. *Teaching Exceptional Children, 28*(1), 25–28.

Idol, L., Nevin, A., & Paolucci-Whitcomb, P. (1994). *Collaborative consultation* (2nd ed.). Austin, TX: Pro-Ed.

Jackson, S., & Taylor, G. R. (1973). *School organization for the mentally retarded.* Springfield, IL: Charles C Thomas.

Jayanthi, M., & Friend, M. (1992). Interpersonal problem solving: A selected literature review to guide practice. *Journal of Educational and Psychological Consultation, 3,* 147–152.

Johnson, D. W., & Johnson, F. (1991). *Joining together* (4th ed.). Upper Saddle River, NJ: Prentice Hall.

Johnson, L. J., & Pugach, M. C. (1996). Role of collaborative dialogue in teachers' conceptions of appropriate practice for students at risk. *Journal of Educational and Psychological Consultation, 7,* 9–24.

Johnston, D., Proctor, W., & Carey, S. (1995). Not a way out: A way in. *Educational Leadership, 50*(4), 46–49.

Jorgensen, C. M. (1995). Essential questions—inclusive answers. *Educational Leadership, 50*(4), 52–55.

Joyce, B., & Showers, B. (1995). *Student achievement: Fundamental of school renewal* (2nd ed.). White Plains, NY: Longman.

Kain, D. L. (1995). Teaming with a purpose. *Schools in the Middle, 4*(4), 6–9.

Kain, R. L., & Rosental, R. A. (1964). *Organizational stress: Studies in role conflict and ambiguity*. New York: Wiley.

Kaplan, P. (1966). *Pathways for exceptional children*. Minneapolis: West.

Katsiyannis, A. (1994). Pre-referral practices: Under Office of Civil Rights Scruiting. *Journal of Developmental and Physical Disabilities, 6,* 73–76.

Katzen-Meyer, M., & Moller, G. (1996). *Awakening the sleeping giant: Leadership development for teachers*. Thousand Oaks, CA: Corwin Press.

Kauffman, J. M., Hallahan, D. P., & Ford, D. Y. (1998). Editor's introduction. *Journal of Special Education, 32,* 3.

Kearns, J. F., Kleinert, H. L., & Kennedy, S. (1999). We need not exclude anyone. *Educational Leadership, 56*(6), 33–38.

Kitano, M. K. (1997). A rationale and framework for course change. In A. I. Morey & M. K. Kitano (Eds.), *Multicultural course transformation in higher education: A broader truth*. Boston: Allyn & Bacon.

Knapp, M. S., Adelman, N. E., Needels, M. C., Zucker, A.A., McCollum, H., Turnbull, B. L., Marder, C., & Shields, P. M. (1991). *What is taught and how to teach children of poverty* (LC 88054001). Washington, DC: U.S. Department of Education.

Kratochwill, T. R., & Bergan, J.R. (1990). *Behavioral consultation in applied settings: An individual guide*. New York: Plenum.

Lambert, L. (1998). How to build leadership capacity. *Educational Leadership, 55*(7), 17–19.

Langdon, H. W., & Novak, J. M. (1998). Home and school connections: A Hispanic perspective. *Educational Horizons, 1,* 15–17.

Larry, P v. Riles. 343 F. Supp. 1306, 502, F. 2d 963 (N.D. Calif. 1979).

Lau v. Nichols. 414 U.S. 563 (1974).

Lee, G. V., & Barnett, B. G. (1994). Using reflective questioning to promote collaborative dialogue. *Journal of Staff Development, 15*(1), 16–21.

Levey, J., & Acker-Hocevar, M. (1998). *Site-based management: Retrospective understanding and future directions*. Washington, DC: U.S. Department of Education (ERIC Document Reproductive Service No. ED 428 439).

Lewis, R., & Morris, J. (1998). Communities for children. *Educational Leadership, 55*(8), 34–36.

Little, J. W. (1992a). Norms of collegiality and experimentation: Workplace conditions of school success. *American Educational Research Journal, 5,* 325–340.

Little, J. W. (1992b). Teacher's professional development in a climate of educational reform. *Education Evaluation and Policy Analysis, 15,* 129–151.

Louis, K. S., & Miles, M. B. (1990). *Improving the urban high school: What works and why.* New York: Teachers College Press.

Lounsbury, J. H. (1991). A fresh start for the middle school curriculum. *Middle School Journal, 23*(2), 3–7.

Lunenburg, F. C., & Ornstein, A. C. (1991). *Educational administration.* Belmont, CA: Wadsworth.

Lustig, M. W., & Koester, J. (1999). *Intercultural competence: Interpersonal communication across cultures* (3rd ed.). New York: Longman.

Lynch, E. W., & Stein, R. (1987). Parent participation by ethnicity: A comparison of Hispanic, Black, and Anglo families. *Exceptional Children, 54,* 105–111.

MacMillan, D. L., Gresham, F. M., Lopez, M. F., & Bocian, K. M. (1996). Comparison of students nominated for pre-referral intervention by ethnicity and gender. *Journal of Special Education, 30,* 131–151.

MacMillan, D. L., & Reschly, D. J. (1998). Over-representation of minority students: The case for greater specificity or reconsideration of the variables examined. *Journal of Special Education, 32,* 15–24.

Magestro, P. V., & Stanford-Blair, N. (2000). A tool for meaningful staff development. *Educational Leadership, 57*(8), 34–35.

Maker, C. J. (1993). Creativity, intelligence, and problem solving: A definition and design for cross-cultural research and measurement related to giftedness. *Gifted Education International, 9*(2), 68–77.

Marsh, D. (1999). *Yearbook: Preparing our schools for the 21st century.* Alexandria, VA: Association for Supervision and Curriculum Development.

Masten, A. (1994). Resilience in individual development: Successful adaptation despite risk and adversity. In M. C. Wang & E. W. Gordon (Eds.), *Educational resilience in inner-city America.* Hillsdale, NJ: Erlbaum.

May, J. (1991). Commentary: What about fathers? *Family Support Bulletin,* p. 19.

Mayer, R. H. (1996). Children who are deaf or hard-of-hearing. In E. L. Meyen (Ed.), *Exceptional Children in Today's Schools* (3rd ed.). Denver, CO: Love.

McChesney, J., & Hertling, E. (2000). The path to comprehensive school reform. *Educational Leadership, 57*(7), 10–15.

McCloskey, W., Mikow-Porto, V., & Bingham, S. (1998). *Reflecting on progress: Site-based management and school improvement in North Carolina.* Washington, DC: U.S. Department of Education (ERIC Document Reproduction Service No. 421 766).

McDonnell, L. (1989). *Restructuring American schools: The promise and the pitfalls* (Conference paper No. 10). New York: Institute on Education and the Economy, Teachers College, Columbia University.

McGrew, K. S., Thurlow, M. L., Shriner, J. G., & Spiegel, A. N. (1992). *Inclusion of students with disabilities in national and state data collection programs* (Technical Report 2). Minneapolis: University of Minnesota, National Council on Educational Outcomes.

McLaughlin, M. W., & Talbert, J. (1993). *Contexts that matter for teaching and learning.* Stanford, CA: Stanford University, Context Center on Secondary School Teaching.

McLeskey, J., & Pacchiano, D. (1994). Mainstreaming students with learning disabilities: Are we making progress? *Exceptional Children, 60,* 508–517.

McLoughlin, J., & Lewis, R. (1991). *Assessing special students: Strategies and procedures* (3rd ed.). Columbus, OH: Merrill.

McMillan, J. H. (1997). *Classroom assessment: Principles and practice for effective instruction.* Boston: Allyn & Bacon.

Meyen, E. (1990). *Exceptional children in today's schools.* Denver, CO: Love.

Mills, D., & Bulach, S. (1996). *Behavioral disordered students in collaborative/cooperative class: Does behavior improve?* Tampa, FL. Washington, DC: U.S. Department of Education (ERIC Document Reproduction Services No. ED 394 224).

Mofett, C. A. (2000). Sustaining change: The answers are blowing in the wind. *Educational Leadership, 57*(7), 35–38.

Muir-Hutchinson, L. (1987). Working with professionals. *Exceptional Parent, 17*(5), 8–19.

Murnane, R., & Levy, F. (1996). *Teaching the new basic skills: Principles for educating children to thrive in a changing economy.* New York: Free Press.

Murphy, C. (1997). Finding time for faculties to study together. *Journal of Staff Development, 18*(3), 29–32.

National Association of State Board of Education. (1992). *Winners all: A call for inclusive schools.* Alexandria, VA: Author.

National Education Goals Panel. (1992). *World class standards for American education.* Washington, DC: U.S. Department of Education.

National Information Center for Youth and Children with Disabilities (NICHCY). (1997). *News Digest,* pp. 1–4, 26.

Newmann, F., & Wehlage, G. (1995). *Successful school restructuring.* Madison, WI: Center on Organization and Restructuring of Schools.

Nineteenth Annual Report to Congress on the Implementation of The Individuals with Disabilities Education Act. (1997). Washington, DC: Department of Education, U.S. Printing Office.

Norris, G., Haring, L., & Haring, T. (1994). *Exceptional children and youth* (6th ed.). New York: Macmillan.

Norton, P., & Drew, C. J. (1994). Autism and potential family stressors. *American Journal of Family Therapy, 22,* 68–77.

Oakes, J., Quartz, J. H., Ryan, S., & Lipton, M. (2000). *The struggle for civic virtue in education reform.* San Francisco: Jossey-Bass.

Odden, E., & Wohlstetter, P. (1995). Making school-based management work. *Educational Leadership, 52,* 32–36.

Ohlrich, K. B. (1996). Parent volunteers: An asset to your technology plan. *Learning and Leading with Technology, 24,* 51–52.

Okun, B. (1996). *Effective helping: Interviewing and counseling techniques* (5th ed.). Pacific Grove, CA: Brooks/Cole.

Olson, L. (1998b). Study: School-wide reform not easy. *Education Week, 22 (18),* p. 3.

Osborn, R. N., & Hunt, J. G. (1975). An adaptive-reactive theory of leadership: The role or macrovariables in leadership research. In J. G. Hunt and L. L. Larson, (Eds.), *Leadership Frontiers,* Kent: Ohio State University.

Oswald, D. P., & Sinah-Nirbay, N. (1992). Current research on social behavior. *Behavior Modification, 16,* 443–447.

Overton, T. (1992). *Assessment in special education: An applied approach.* New York: Macmillan.

Pallas, A. M., Natriello, G., & McDill, E. L. (1989). The changing nature of disadvantaged population: Current dimensions and future trends. *Educational Leadership*, pp. 16–22.

Parnes, S. J. (Ed.). (1992). *Sourcebook for creative problem-solving*. Buffalo, NY: Creative Education Foundation.

Pennsylvania Association for Retarded Children (PARC). Commonwealth of Pennsylvania, 343 F. Supp. 279. (E.D. Pa., 1972).

Peterson, J. V., & Nisenholz, B. (1998). *Orientation to counseling* (4th ed.). Newton, MA: Allyn & Bacon.

Pike, K., & Salend, S. (1995). An authentic assessment strategy. *Teaching Exceptional Children, 28*(1), 15–19.

Podemski, R. S., Marsh, G. E., Smith, D., Tom, E.C., & Price, J. B. (1995). *Comprehensive administration of special education*. Englewood Cliffs, NJ: Prentice Hall.

Podemski, R. S., & Steele, R. (1981). Avoid the pitfalls of citizen committees. *American School Board Journal, 168*(4), 440–442.

Popham, W. J. (1999). Why standardized tests don=t measure educational quality. *Educational Leadership, 56*(6), 8–15.

Potter, L. (1996). Making school parent-friendly. *Education Digest, 62,* 28–30.

Powell, D. R. (1998). Reweaving parents into early childhood education programs. *Education Digest, 64*(3), 22–25.

Powell, D. R., & Diamond, K. E. (1995). Approaches to parent-teacher relationship in use early childhood programs during the twentieth century. *Journal of Education, 77*(3), 71–94.

Putnam, M. L. (1992). Characteristics of questions on test administered by mainstream secondary classroom teachers. *Learning Disabilities Research and Practice, 7*(3), 29–36.

Rabe, B. G., & Peterson, P. E. (1988). The evolution of a new cooperative federalism. In N. J. Boyan (Ed.), *Handbook on research on education administration*. New York: Longman.

Rhodes, L. K., & Nathenson-Mejia, S. (1992). Anecdotal records: A powerful tool for on-going literacy assessment. *The Reading Teacher, 45*(7), 502–509.

Rich, D. (1998). What do parents want from teachers? *Educational Leadership, 55*(8), 37–39.

Riley, R. (1993). A conversation with the U.S. Secretary of Education. *National Forum, 73*(4), 5–7.

Roach, V. (1995). Beyond the rhetoric. *Phi Delta Kappan, 77,* 295–299.

Roberts, R., & Mather, N. (1995). The return of students with learning disabilities to regular classrooms: A sellout? *Learning Disabilities Research and Practice, 10*(16), 46–58.

Rogers, J. (1993). The inclusion revolution. *Research Bulletin, 1*(11), 106.

Ronker v. Walter, 700 F21058, 1063 (6th Cir., 1983).

Rosenholtz, S. J. (1991). *Teachers' workplace: The social organization of schools.* New York: Teachers College Press.

Roth, K. L. (1994). Second thoughts about interdisciplinary studies. *American Educator, 19*(1), 44–48.

Rowley v. Board of Education of Hendrick Hudson School District, 458 U.S. (1982).

Sack, J. L. (1997). Educational officials cite concerns about implementing IDEA rules. *Education Week,* 28, pp. 1–4.

Salinger, T. (1991). *Getting started with alternative assessment methods.* Workshop presented at the New York State Reading Association Conference, Lake Kiamesha, New York.

Salisbury, C. L., Evans, I. M., & Palombara, M. M. (1997). Collaborative problem-solving to promote the inclusion of young children with significant disabilities in primary grades. *Exceptional Children, 63,* 195–209.

Salvia, J., & Ysseldyke, J. E. (1991). *Assessment in special education and remedial education* (5th ed.). Boston: Houghton Mifflin.

Salvia, J., & Ysseldyke, J. E. (1998). *Assessment.* Boston: Houghton Mifflin.

Sarason, S. B. (1982). *The culture of the school and the problem of change* (2nd ed.). Boston: Allyn & Bacon.

Saxl, E., Miles, M., & Lieberman, A. (1990). *Assisting change in education.* Alexandria, VA: Association for Supervision and Curriculum Development.

Schaefer, C. M. (1995). Technology can extend your school's art program. *The Executive Educator, 22*(1), 37–38.

Schmelkin, L. P. (1981). Teachers' and non-teachers' attitudes toward mainstreaming. *Exceptional Children, 48,* 42–57.

Schmidt, W. H., McKnight, C. C., & Raizen, S. A. (1996). *Splintered vision: An investigation of U.S. science and mathematics education: Executive summary.* Lansing: U.S. National Research Center for the Third International Mathematics and Sciences Study, Michigan State University.

Schmoker, M., & Marzano, R. J. (1999). Realizing the promise of standard-based education. *Educational Leadership, 56*(6), 17–21.

Scruggs, T. E., & Mostropierei, M. A. (1996). Teachers' perceptions of mainstreaming/inclusion: A research synthesis. *Exceptional Children, 63*(1), 59–74.

Selby, D., & Murphy, S. (1992). Graded of degraded: Perceptions of letter grading for mainstreamed learning disabled students. *B.C. Journal of Special Education, 16*(1), 92–104.

Sergiovanni, T. J. (1995). *The principalship: A reflective practice perspective.* Boston: Allyn & Bacon.

Sergiovanni, T. J. (1996). *Leadership for the school house.* San Francisco: Jossey Bass.

Shanker, A. (1995). Full inclusion is neither force nor appropriate. *Educational Leadership, 50*(4), 18–21.

Sharpe, M. N., York, J. L., & Knight, J. C. (1994). Effects of inclusion on the academic performance of classmates with disabilities. *Remedial and Special Education, 15,* 281–287.

Shea, T. M., & Bauer, A. M. (1991). *Parents and teachers of children with exceptionalities: A handbook for collaboration* (2nd ed.). Boston: Allyn & Bacon.

Shirley, D. (1997). *Laboratories of democracy: Community organizing for school perform.* Austin, TX: University of Texas Press.

Shriner, J. G., & Thurlow, M. L. (1993). State special education results. (1992). Minneapolis: University of Minnesota, National Center on Educational Outcomes.

Silberman, R. K. (1996). Children with visual impairments. In E. L. Meyen (Ed.), *Exceptional Children in Today's Schools.* Denver, CO: Love.

Sixteenth Annual Report to Congress. (1995). U.S. Department of Education. Washington, DC: U.S. Government Printing Office.

Slavin, R. E. (1995). *Cooperative learning: Theory, research, and practice* (2nd ed.). Boston: Allyn & Bacon.

Smith, W. F., & Andrews, R. L. (1989). *Instructional leadership: How principals make a difference.* Alexandria, VA: Association for Supervision and Curriculum Development.

Sparks, D, & Hirsh, S. (1997). *A new vision for staff development.* Alexandria, VA: Association for Supervision and Curriculum Development.

Sparks, D., & Loucks-Horsley, S. (1999). Five models for staff development for teachers. *Journal of Staff Development, 10*(4), 40–57.

Sparks, D., & Richardson, J. (1997). A primer on professional development. *Journal of Staff Development, 18*(4), 1–8.

Staub, D., & Hunt, P. (1993). The effects of social interaction training on high school peer tutors of schoolmates with severe disabilities. *Exceptional Children, 60,* 41–47.

Staub, D., & Peck, C. (1995). What are the outcomes for non-disabled students? *Educational Leadership, 50*(4), 36–39.

Stoll, L., & Fink, D. (1996). *Changing our schools.* London: Open University Press.

Swanson, H. C., & Watson, B. L. (1989). *Educational and psychological assessment of exceptional children* (2nd ed.). Columbus, OH: Merrill.

Tampoe, M. (1998). *Liberating leadership.* London: The Industrial Society.

Taylor G. R. (1997). *Curriculum strategies: Social skills intervention for your African-American males.* Westport, CT: Praeger Press.

Taylor, G. R. (1998). *Curriculum strategies for teaching social skills to the disabled.* Springfield, IL: Charles C Thomas.

Taylor, G. R. (1999). *Curriculum models and strategies for educating individuals with disabilities in inclusive classrooms.* Springfield, IL: Charles C Thomas.

Taylor, G. R. (2000). *Parental involvement: A practical guide for collaboration and team work for students with disabilities.* Springfield, IL: Charles C Thomas

Taylor, G. R. (2001). *Interventions and services for children with exceptionalities: Strategies and perspectives.* Springfield, IL: Charles C Thomas.

Taylor, G. R. (in press). *Informal classroom assessment strategies for teachers.* Blue Ridge Summit, PA: Scarecrow Press.

The New IDEA Reauthorization Law. (1998). U.S. Department of Education.

Thompson, S. (1998). Moving from publicity to engagement. *Educational Leadership, 55*(8), 54–57.

Thorndike, R. L., Hagen, P., & Sattler, J. M. (1986b). *Guide for administering and scoring the fourth edition.* Chicago: Riverside.

Thorp, E. K. (1997). Increasing opportunities for partnership with culturally and linguistically diverse families. *Intervention in School and Clinic, 32,* 261–269.

Thousand, J. S., Villa, R., & Nevin, A. (1994). *Creativity and collaborative learning.* Baltimore, MD: Paul H. Brookes.

Thurlow, M. L., Scott, D. L., & Ysseldyke, J. E. (1995a). *Compilation of states' guidelines for accommodations in assessments for students with disabilities* (Synthesis Report 17). Minneapolis: University of Minnesota, National Center on Educational Opportunities.

Thurlow, M. L., Scott, D. L., & Ysseldyke, J. E. (1995b). *Compilation of states' guidelines for learning students with disabilities in assessments* (Synthesis Report 18). Minneapolis: University of Minnesota, National Center on Educational Opportunities.

Thurlow, M. L., Seyfarth, A., Scott, D., & Ysseldyke, J. E. (in press). *State assessment participation criteria and accommodations guidelines: 1996 analysis.*

Thurlow, M. L., Ysseldyke, J. E., & Silverstein, B. (1993). *Testing accommodations for students with disabilities: A review of the literature* (Synthesis Report 4). Minneapolis: University of Minnesota, National Center on Educational Outcomes.

Tiedt, P. L., & Tiedt, I. M. (1995). *Multicultural teaching: A handbook of activities, information, and resources* (4th ed.). Boston: Allyn & Bacon.

Turnbull, A. P., & Turnbull, H. R. (1990). Families, professionals, and exceptionality (2nd ed.). Columbus, OH: Merrill.

Turnbull, A. P., & Turnbull, H. R. (1993). *Participating research on cognitive coping: From concepts to research planning.* In A. P. Turnbull, J. M. Patterson, S. K. Behr, D. L.

Turnbull, H. R. (1993). *Free appropriate public education: The law and children with disabilities* (4th ed.). Reston, VA: Love.

Underwood, J., & Mead, J. (1985). *Legal aspects of special education and pupil services.* Needham Heights, MA: Allyn & Bacon.

U.S. Department of Education. (1995). *Sixteenth Annual Report to Congress on the Implementation of the Individuals with Disabilities Act.* Washington, DC: U. S. Government Printing Office.

U.S. Department of Education. (1997a). *Individuals with disabilities education act amendments of 1995.* Washington, DC: U.S. Government Printing Office.

U.S. Department of Education. (1997b). *Nineteenth Annual Report to Congress on the Implementation of the Individuals Disability Education Act.* Washington, DC: Author.

U.S. Department of Education. (1998). *Profiles of successful school-wide programs.* Washington, DC: Author.

Vann, A. S. (1995). Give us a say on school budgets. *The Executive Educator, 22*(1), 41.

Vargas, B. C., & Grose, K. (1998). A partnership for literacy. *Educational Leadership, 55*(8), 45–48.

Vars, G. (1991). Integrated curriculum in historical perspective. *Educational Leadership, 49*(2), 14–15.

Viadero, D. (June 1989). Who's in, who's out. *Education Week*, pp. 1–12.

Waldron, N. L., & McLeskey, J. (1998). The effects of an inclusive school program on students with mild and severe learning disabilities. *Exceptional Children, 64*(3), 395–405.

Wallace, G., Larsen, S. C., & Elksnin, L. K. (1992). *Educational assessment of learning problems: Testing for teaching.* Boston: Allyn & Bacon.

Wang, J., & Wildman, L. (1996). The relationship between parental influence and student achievement in seventh grade mathematics. *School Science and Mathematics, 96*, 395–399.

Waterman, B. (1994). Assessing children for the presence of a disability. *National Information Center for Children and Youth with Disabilities, 4*(1), 1–22.

Wayman, K. L., Lynch, E. W., & Hanson, M. J. (1990). Home-based early childhood services: Cultural sensitivity in a family system approach. *Topics in Early Childhood Special Education, 10*, 56–75.

Wechsler, D. (1958). *The measurement and appraisal of adult intelligence* (4th ed.). Baltimore, MD: Williams & Wilkins.

Wechsler, D. (1967). *Manual of the Wechsler preschool and primary scale of intelligence.* San Antonio, TX: The Psychological Corporation.

Wechsler, D. (1991). *Wechsler intelligence scale for children III.* San Antonio, TX: The Psychological Corporation.

West, J. F. (1990). Educational collaboration in restructuring of schools. *Journal of Educational and Psychological Consultation, 1*, 23–40.

Whiteford, T. (1998). Math for moms and dads. *Educational Leadership, 55*(3), 64–66.

Wiersman, W., & Jurs, S. (1990). *Educational measurement and testing.* Boston: Allyn & Bacon.

Wilczenski, F. L. (1992). Measuring attitudes toward inclusive education. *Psychology in the Schools, 29,* 306–312.

Witt, J. C., Elliott, S. N., Daly, E. J., Gresham, F. M., & Kramer, J. J. (1998). *Assessment of at-risk and special needs children.* Boston: McGraw-Hill.

Wohlsteter, P., & Mohrman, S. A. (1994). School-based management: Promise and process. *Consortium for Policy Research in Education,* pp. 1–8.

Wohlsteter, P. (1995). Getting school-based management right: What works and what doesn't. *Phi Delta Kappan, 77,* 22–26. ED379771.

Wolf, D. P. (1989). Portfolio assessment: Sampling student work. *Educational Leadership, 46*(7), 35–39.

Wolf, J. M. (1998). Just read. *Educational Leadership, 55*(8), 62–63.

Wood, M. (1998). Whose job is it anyway? Educational roles in inclusion. *Exceptional Children, 64,* 181–195.

Young, M. W. (1993). Countdown: The goals 2000 Educate American Act. *National Forum, 73*(4), 3–4.

Ysseldyke, J., & Alozzine, B. (1990). *Introduction to special education.* Boston: Houghton Mifflin.

Ysseldyke, J., Alozzine, B., & Thurlow, M. (1992). *Critical issues in special education.* Dallas, TX: Houghton Mifflin.

Ysseldyke, J. E., & Thurlow, M. L. (1994). *Guidelines for inclusion of students with disabilities outcomes in large-scale assessments* (Policy Directions 1). Minneapolis: University of Minnesota, National Center on Educational Outcomes.

Ysseldyke, J. E., Thurlow, M. L., McGrew, K.S., & Shriner, M. (1994). *Recommendations for making decisions about the participation of students with disabilities in statewide assessment programs* (Synthesis Report 15). Minneapolis: University of Minnesota, National Center on Education Outcomes.

Ysseldyke, J. E., Thurlow, M. L., McGrew, K.S., & Vanderwood, M. (1994a). *Making decisions about the inclusion of students with disabilities in statewide assessments* (Synthesis Report 13). Minneapolis: University of Minnesota, National Center on Education Outcomes.

Ysseldyke, J. E., Thurlow, M. L., McGrew, K.S., & Vanderwood, M. (1994b). *Making decisions about the inclusion of students with disabilities in large-scale assessments: A report on a working conference to develop guidelines on inclusion and accommodations.* Washington, DC: U.S. Department of Education (ERIC Document Reproduction Service No. ED 372 652).

Yukl, G. A. (1981). *Leadership in organizations.* Englewood Cliffs, NJ: Prentice Hall.

Zigmond, N., Jenkins, J., Fuchs, L., Fuchs, D., Baker, J., Jenkins, L., & Couthino, M. (1995). Special education in restricted schools: Finds from three multi-year students. *Phi Delta Kappan, 76,* 531–540.

Index

About the Authors

George R. Taylor, Ph.D., is professor of special education and chairperson, Department of Special Education at Coppin State College, Baltimore, Maryland, and CORE faculty, The Union Institute, Cincinnati, Ohio. Dr. Taylor has made significant contributions to the professional literature through publications. He has published more than eighteen professional articles and eight textbooks in the areas of special education and research techniques.

Frances T. Harrington, Ph.D., is a teacher of multicategorial special education students at the junior high level. She is also an adjunct professor of special education at Fayetteville State University, Fayetteville, North Carolina. Dr. Harrington has contributed to the professional literature in special education in several publications.